BELIEVING
SKEPTICS

Contributions in Political Science
SERIES EDITOR: *Bernard K. Johnpoll*

BELIEVING SKEPTICS

American Political Intellectuals, 1945-1964

ROBERT BOOTH FOWLER

CONTRIBUTIONS IN POLITICAL SCIENCE, NUMBER 5

 GREENWOOD PRESS
WESTPORT, CONNECTICUT • LONDON, ENGLAND

FOR EMILY

Library of Congress Cataloging in Publication Data

Fowler, Robert Booth, 1940-
  Believing skeptics.

  (Contributions in political science ; no. 5.
ISSN 0147-1066)
  Bibliography: p.
  Includes index.
  1. Political science—United States—History.
2. United States—Politics and government—1945-
I. Title. II. Series.
JA84.U5F68   320.5'0973   77-87967
ISBN 0-313-20026-2

Library of Congress Catalog Card Number: 77-87967
ISBN: 0-313-20026-2
ISSN: 0147-1066

First published in 1978

Greenwood Press, Inc.
51 Riverside Avenue, Westport, Connecticut 06880

Printed in the United States of America

10   9   8   7   6   5   4   3   2   1

Contents

Preface

This study began when I started teaching political science and the history of political thought at the University of Wisconsin-Madison in 1967. Turbulent conditions there forced me as a typical postwar "skeptical liberal" to examine my liberal American political thought, which I do in this book. I came to understand that I had accepted without examination many norms, attitudes, and assumptions and that my stance of skepticism hid from me the elements of certainty in my perspective.

It occurred to me that the same might be true for much of American intellectual life expressed in political thought from 1945 to the early 1960s. The immediate result was a test study of the heavily normative intellectual history of Peter Gay, Enlightenment historian and skeptical liberal. (See Robert Booth Fowler, "Peter Gay and the Politics of Skeptical Liberalism," *Politics and Society* [November 1970]. Other matters intervened before I returned to this interest. I knew I needed to understand much more about **intellectual thought relevant to politics after 1945. I also needed to** consider and develop perspective on the complex tangle of skepticism and belief contained in modern liberal thought. Only now, ten years after I first began to conceive this project, have I felt ready to argue a fuller analysis of political thinking in America from 1945 to the early 1960s.

My subject matter is the political thought of intellectuals in the United States spanning the two decades after World War II. My materials, of course, are their written works, particularly their books written for a broader public than are most articles for professional journals. Since my objective is thematic and interpretive, I include no survey data, content analyses, or depth studies on the intellectual figures I have considered. Some intellectuals emerge in the following pages as salient, but the study is not basically about them. Few of those considered will be unknown to informed readers of American political thought of the last three decades.

Particularly vexing was the problem of boundaries: who was to count as a political thinker for the purpose of this study? I took as my guide no hard and fast measure, but rather the notion that postwar political thinkers were mostly prominent intellectuals involved with issues concerning the nature and the ideal of America, its political order, and its political values. I have used the writings of selected sociologists, historians, political scientists, and literary intellectuals in particular, but the rule was their interest and their involvement and not their "field."

On occasion I have made use of certain non-American intellectuals who seemed to me to have had undoubted influence on political intellectuals in America in the postwar era. For example, I drew on the democratic theory of Giovanni Sartori, a visitor to America, because he was a favorite democratic theorist for many postwar social scientists. I used a few British thinkers like Stephen Toulmin, because of their influence in America. Yet for obvious reasons most of my illustrations are Americans.

Time posed a similar boundary problem. It is clear that many of the trends with which I deal began to fade in the early 1960s; I adhered to a termination date of 1964 because the Kennedy era was very much a part of the post-1945 era and not of ours, and certainly the 1964 election was a kind of culmination of what went before. Sometimes I drew on works by an author before or after my period in cases that were not in disagreement with his views from 1945 to 1964.

It is only fair to acknowledge that the question of boundaries is never easily solved. Strict time or geographic boundaries would have been as foolish as none at all would have been absurd. I did the best I could, but I make no pretense to having magically solved an insoluble dilemma.

My hope is that this work helps illuminate our recent intellectual past. Now that the sometimes facile skeptical confidence of the postwar era is gone along with the angry cliches of the New Left period, it is possible to understand better the complex dialectic of

skepticism and certainty that was interwoven in intellectual
thought about politics in the United States after World War II. In
truth, it is a fascinating subject.

I would like to thank Louis Hartz for the never-receding inspiration to me that his combination of teaching and scholarly energy
provided. I am very grateful to Charles Anderson, Steve Daniels,
Roy Hovey, Larry Joseph, Mark Kann, and Sandy Levinson for
reading an earlier version of this study in its entirety and having the
loving faith in me to help. I also want to thank my students in Political Science 506, Spring 1977. They were wonderful critics. There
is no easy way to thank them fully, but I can assure them that I
accept all responsibility for the weaknesses in the book, which
they probably pointed out and I didn't change! I also am indebted
to Judy Lerdahl, Marge Nimm, Dorothy Shaw, Anne Stutts, and
Diane Van Dehei. Again and again I depended on them and they
did not fail to help me get the various versions of my manuscript
typed, proofed, and xeroxed.

BELIEVING
SKEPTICS

1 Skepticism and Ideology

The mood that dominated American political thought in the years after World War II was *skepticism*. Political intellectuals in the United States from 1945 to the early 1960s tended to view political action and political perspectives with a certain, often suspicious, detachment. The age of commitment, of faiths, and of radical action appeared to have ended. World War II had put out the fires of enthusiasm for radicalism that still remained by 1941. The war's own passions seemed remote surprisingly quickly after 1945. A new generation of political intellectuals began to dominate American political thought. They looked back to the 1930s sometimes with personal embarrassment and sometimes with no recognition for an age in which they had not always participated. Their watchwords *skepticism* and *realism* represented a self-conscious desire to give America and its political order and values a new view, accepting little on faith.

Although skepticism was the dominant word of the age, this study seeks to explore the extent to which postwar intellectuals were, in fact, as skeptical as they often believed they were. Certainly we shall see that most postwar intellectuals in America were skeptical of approaches to politics and the justification of all values in politics based on absolute claims to certain truths. They were skeptical as well of any proposals for radical social change and earnest hopes that one or another utopia might be achieved. Finally, they were skeptical of the rational capacities of citizens in political life and what they considered to be the unfortunate tendency of many past intellectuals to worship the goal of ever-expanding democratic participation.

These attitudes were important in structuring the patterns of postwar political theory that are still powerfully alive today. But the broader issue raised by a study of post-1945 political thought is the limits of skepticism in that self-consciously skeptical age. The question is, were American political intellectuals nearly as skeptical politically as they often suggested in the years from 1945 to 1964? My argument is that to understand political thought in the United States in this crucial, and still recent, period, one must understand how sharply limited were the boundaries of skepticism. The crucial fact is that there was little skepticism of liberal values and less of American institutions. The mood of political intellectuals was more complex than it often appeared. It was skeptical but it was also believing; it was anti-ideological but it was also ideological; it was detached but it was also committed; it was liberal but it was also conservative.

The pride in skepticism so many postwar political intellectuals expressed makes the existence of the substantial limits to skepticism somewhat paradoxical. The question so many of these intellectuals raised about others is applicable to them. Were they skeptical enough or were they too often misled by their conviction that they were skeptical into an unskeptical conservatism at home and an unskeptical (and eventually disastrous) anti-Communism abroad?

THE HATRED OF IDEOLOGY

Central to this mood was skepticism of absolute answers in politics. Nothing, in fact, was as memorable or as distinct about the political thought of 1945–64. Part of that milieu was informed by a general existential aura that allowed many American intellectuals to agree with Arthur Schlesinger when he wrote that "Western man in the twentieth century is tense, uncertain, adrift . . . . The grounds of our . . . certitude are breaking up under our feet."[1] But as much if not more of the mood may be explained in quite a contrasting manner that better illuminates the fact that most thinkers welcomed the rise of skepticism with relief and even joy.

The postwar era in political thought began after a great world war, which, among other things, was a war of ideologies, and a war American thinkers almost unanimously believed was a just war to defeat "totalitarian" societies. Moreover, it was followed soon enough by the Cold War and the sense that Russia posed another deadly threat to America in the old totalitarian manner. Few political intellectuals disagreed with Sidney Hook's judgment that by "all odds the central political fact of our time is the existence of Soviet Communism" whose commitment to ideology and fanaticism was frightening.[2] Few political intellectuals disagreed with Leslie Fiedler's analysis that it required "no sophistication to understand Communism . . . . history has defined for anyone with a sense of political fact what Marxism-Leninism has become—namely, the rationalization and defense of that which Russia or its agents do for the sake of expansion or self-defense."[3] Few disagreed with Peter Viereck's observations that "Armed communism is obviously the greatest single threat to the world today" and that the "Soviet threat to the West is the most important political fact of our day."[4] The force of time and historical change would soften this perspective, so by the early 1960s many intellectuals' sense of threat would diminish and there would be increasing sympathy with Arthur Schlesinger's eventual recognition that "Communism is not a monolith; it is a spectrum."[5]

The memory of Nazism and the danger of Communism were decisive, determining realities that molded the thought of two decades. What American intellectuals most often suggested the Nazis and Communists had in common was ideology, faith in all-encompassing, action-oriented belief systems that were held to be absolutely true. Nazis and Communists were true believers who claimed to know the truth in politics and had a terrifying willingness to seek, through political and military action, to impose their truth around the world. They were the living manifestation of those who did not doubt, a manifestation of the danger of being too sure. They were not skeptical.

It was in this context that American thinkers observed with pride that there was a decline in ideology in the United States after 1945. Edward Shils first announced this event at the Congress of Cultural Freedom in 1954, but many others followed suit. Gabriel Almond claimed that ideological thinking was on the wane and he believed this fact was a sure sign of health, a sign that at last "ideological sales resistance" was high.[6] Clinton Rossiter was proud of the role the United States and its thinkers played in the intellectual defeat of ideology in the West.[7] Most famously, Daniel Bell enunciated his thesis that the age of ideology was over in the West, including the United States: "ideologies are exhausted . . . . Such calamities as the Moscow Trials, the Nazi-Soviet pact, the concentration camps, the suppression of the Hungarian workers" had taught bitter, yet profound lessons.[8]

Some writers concentrated on exploring and attacking Nazi totalitarianism and its ideology. Hannah Arendt focused on Nazism and the horrors of its ideology in a way that made her work classic. Peter Gay crusaded against Nazism and the lack of Enlightenment skepticism surrounding it.[9] Others concentrated more heavily on Stalinism or Russian totalitarianism. Reinhold Niebuhr diagnosed Communism as "a mania of absolutism, composed of Messianism and a lust for power." Almond explored the ideology and practice of Communism, convinced it was "the greatest evil of the twentieth century."[10] John Hallowell described it as a false religion, gripping in its hold on its true believers.[11] So went the broad assault on Communism in theory and practice.

No one can read the literature of those years and quite understand how Senator Joseph McCarthy and others of that era believed that Communist ideology was widely held by American intellectuals. Nothing could have been further from the truth. In 1962 Richard Rovere correctly observed that the American intellectuals had a clear record of anti-Communism in the postwar period all the way from their rejection of Alger Hiss to their enthusiastic support of N. A. T. O.[12] They made consistent and repeated attacks on Communism as the most dangerous form of ideological thinking.

Perhaps Arthur Schlesinger's *The Vital Center* best illustrates the sentiment, particularly in the first fifteen years after 1945. Schlesinger insisted that one could not understand modern conditions or modern political thought without a thorough grounding in the challenges posed by Soviet Communism. Not only was Russia at fault for the Cold War, but the domestic reality of the Russian state under Communism was truly horrifying. The lack of freedom, the work camps, the dictatorship, all revealed a totalitarian Russia that was ghastly by any measure or standard.[13]

Schlesinger believed its ideology was a principal explanation for what had happened. Indeed, it was a widespread assumption among intellectuals besides Schlesinger that the ideology of Communism was no mere form used by Moscow for the purposes of manipulation. Sidney Hook contended that ideology was vital to the operations of Russia's rulers, something he did not think Americans understood well because they were empirical and skeptical in their orientations.[14] C.J. Friedrich and Z. Brzezinski agreed in their sometimes judicious study of totalitarianism. They assured their readers that Russian, and to a lesser extent Nazi, elites were influenced by their respective ideologies.[15] For Schlesinger this meant that Leninism was a good guide to what took place under Stalin. Lenin's attitude about democracy, freedom, and power was the nourishing place for Stalin.[16] So was the radical hope of Marxism. "The degeneration of the Soviet Union taught us a useful lesson, however. It broke the bubble of false optimism of the nineteenth century."[17]

One might read many pages of Schlesinger's work, like that of others, and be puzzled how they saw themselves as skeptics in such total contrast to the ideological totalitarians they denounced so often and so fiercely. Virtually every page of Schlesinger's discussions of Russia and Communism bristles with words and phrases such as "aggressive," "totalitarian imperialism," "Soviet expansion," and "Communist crusaders" with what would appear to be hardly a hint of skeptical reservation.[18] Yet this reflection does not help us comprehend the enterprise of American political thought after World War II from the perspective of postwar intellectuals. For them, the rejection of Nazism and Stalinism was a rejection of the costs of totalitarianism and with it the fallacy of ideology. Schlesinger may not seem skeptical from a contemporary perspective, but his mission as he saw it was to show the consequences of political action that was not undertaken in a skeptical spirit. The attack on ideology was integral to his entire effort.

Schlesinger, in fact, concentrated more on Communism than Nazism, but he took it for granted that there was an "essential kinship among all totalitarians" and therefore among all ideologies.[19] Hook maintained a similar position. Although he could

appreciate that totalitarians were not the only ideologues, his inclination was to link all forms of totalitarianism, Nazism and Communism, together in a camp of dangerous ideologues.[20] This
linkage was important to many political intellectuals. It suggested
that history supported their belief that the politics practiced by
true believers was all too often dangerous when not utterly disastrous. This is not to say that all intellectuals could not make distinctions. For example, the social scientist Seymour Martin Lipset
did in his study of European Fascist movements–"Fascism–Left,
Right, and Center"–but there was a tendency to lump all ideology
and totalitarianism into one framework.[21] Even William F. Buckley,
not exactly a skeptic, insisted that he wanted nothing to do with
ideology, which inevitably invoked in his mind Communism and
Hitler.[22]

The skeptical reaction of postwar political intellectuals toward
absolutism of any sort may explain why many intellectuals reached
for the religious analogy when they analyzed Soviet society or
Communism. Schlesinger was fond of describing Russia as a "theological" society.[23] Lewis Coser and Irving Howe in *The American
Communist Party* (1957) suggested that to obtain insight into the
Communist mentality one had to comprehend the dynamics of the
will to believe.[24] For Clinton Rossiter religious belief was the best
point of comparison, even though he considered the doctrines of
Christianity and Communism radically opposed. Communism
was like a religion, only magnified, since "few men in all history
have surrendered so completely to the lure of the absolute as have
the Marxists."[25] Daniel Bell saw Communist commitment in similar
religious terms, and Murray Kempton thought it valuable to see
Lenin as a kind of "inverted" Christ.[26]

The mood of skepticism toward ideology was rooted in more
than an instinctive antipathy among many political intellectuals
toward any form of absolute value claim, including religion, and
in more than their reaction to historical experiences of the 1930s
and the 1940s. Moreover, it amounted to a good deal more than
merely a ritualistic stance and a dependable slogan. Postwar intellectuals made a set of well-articulated arguments explaining why
they wanted nothing to do with ideology and why they derived
so much of their skeptical mood from their hostility to ideology.

Three reasons in particular may be noticed in the writings after 1945.

The first and most basic reason was the writers' opposition to the fanaticism that political intellectuals believed was inevitably associated with ideological thinking. Practically every discussion of ideology contained an objection to what Edward Shils termed "the fanaticism which is associated with ideology."[27] Sidney Hook was indignant in his endless denunciations of ideological fanaticisms, "fanaticisms of political and social creeds emotionally based on Weltanschaungen." The lesson he wanted everyone to learn was that "we cannot make absolutes . . . without inviting the evils of fanaticism."[28] It was no surprise, Murray Kempton observed, that many overzealous American anti-Communists of the 1950s had been Communist zealots two decades or less earlier. The ideological temperament was inevitably associated with fanaticism no matter how much the substance of its ideology was altered over time.[29]

Clearly the fact that so many political intellectuals accused ideology of breeding fanaticism was a very important charge in their minds and might therefore tell us a great deal about the assumptions that underlay the political thought of the age. But aside from a few references like Shils's to the difference between American politics ("civil politics") and the politics of fanaticism, the attack on ideological fanaticism did not prove enlightening.[30] In many cases the association was made between ideology and fanaticism and more or less left at that. Readers were assumed to know that this was in itself enough to condemn ideology. The context of European totalitarianism was assumed, and few intellectuals felt more need be said about fanaticism and why it was bad. Much of Eric Hoffer's popular and stormy study The True Believer treated ideology and fanaticism in just this fashion. It took for granted that they were evil, and the problem was to isolate what it was that so deluded people.[31]

Sometimes, however, there was a definite argument made. It was rarely finely tuned to be sure, but it was there. It often concentrated on what postwar intellectuals insisted was the foolishness of fanaticism. Fanaticism suggested the impossible in a skeptical age. It implied that truth was known, but most political intellectuals denied that anyone could know the truth firmly enough to be fanatical about it. Fanaticism was an inappropriate response because it suggested an astounding absence of skepticism about the truth in the view of many American thinkers. It was this naive approach that Bernard Crick criticized for an admiring American audience. It was what he called "student politics," the smug assumption that the answers are existent and that what is needed is not more thought but more "affirmation."[32]

The second part of the attack on fanaticism was also crucial. Political intellectuals assailed fanaticism as a terrifying companion of ideology because it led to ill-considered and often disastrous action. Fanatics felt impelled to change the world to make it conform to the truth they "knew" to be true. The result was that fanatical ideologues were frequently victims of "messianic arrogance."[33] Since true believers were self-confident, even driven, utopians, critics insisted that their fanaticism was bound to be costly in human terms. Edward Shils contended that "a movement of perfectionists of any sort is dangerous," and Peter Viereck declared that "the impossibility of any very rapid social improvement leads [fanatics] to an ever more ruthless attempt to force it on human nature by terrorism."[34] Liberal political theorists such as Giovanni Sartori and Henry Mayo joined in the denunciation of fanatical ideologues for similar reasons. Sartori, for example, singled out ultra-Democrats for attack. Their rigid intellectual convictions about the worth of an equalitarian, participatory democracy could lead to political extremism and human suffering.[35] Mayo feared ideological political parties composed of fanatics. They were "intransigent, uncompromising, and of course not responsible."[36] It was not merely, as Sidney Hook put it, that "intellectual integrity thus becomes the first victim of political enthusiasm,"[37] but rather that there were likely to be far greater and more elemental victims. As Hannah Arendt wrote, the "tyranny of logicality" of true believers led to killing. Here was the real danger of fanatical ideology. It polarized societies, brought conflict, and ended in murder. The totalitarian experience taught this harsh lesson above all else.[38] Peter Viereck put it bluntly: "Communism and Nazism are alike in their main business; total and

permanent war upon mankind and the murder of millions of innocents."[39]

Michael Oakeshott, a British thinker much admired by many
American political philosophers, challenged anyone who thought
he had answers in politics, whether or not he held a recognized
ideological position. These rationalists in politics, of whom he, too,
had seen enough in his time, were under the sway of "a form of the
moral life which is dangerous in an individual and disastrous in a
society."[40] They would bring down an established order in a hail
of bullets as they chased after the will-o-the-wisp of perfection.
Oakeshott had in mind not only Nazis, Communists, and Socialists,
but also liberals very much like those who dominated postwar
political thought in America. Few liberal intellectuals reflected
on judgments like his in the 1940s or 1950s. They had in their minds
the Lenins of this world as their image of the dangerous and repugnant ideological fanatic. Indeed, Arthur Schlesinger contrasted
Lincoln with Lenin. One was a wise and gentle realist, the model
appropriate for a postwar mood of skeptical intellectuals; the other
was a political fanatic, spreading destruction in his wake.[41] It was
not surprising that an American political thinker like Henry David
Thoreau suffered a decline in reputation for reasons similar to the
attacks on Lenin. After all, he was "the fanatical Thoreau."[42] One
might as well dethrone fanatics at home as well as abroad. No one
was spared.

Richard Hofstadter, the leading American historian of the postwar decades, warned that the greatest threat from ideological
fanaticism did not come from the Lenins or the Thoreaus. They
were exceptional men, but Hofstadter believed there were a great
number of unexceptional citizens who possessed "the one-hundred
per cent mentality." These people were fixed in their parochial
beliefs in "the full range of the dominant popular fatuities and
determined that no one shall have the right to challenge them."
They were also zealous in spreading their fanaticisms. They gave
him a shock of recognition, since they reminded Hofstadter that
the fanatic could be a home-grown as well as a foreign product.
The fanatic was everywhere and everywhere dangerous.[43] Hofstadter's marked disdain for popular beliefs that bordered on ideol-

ogies and were often rooted in evangelistic religious sentiments
was not entirely shared by Hans J. Morgenthau in his classic
Politics Among Nations. But Morgenthau did agree that ideological
fanatics were always an unmitigated disaster for the conduct of
international affairs. The world situation was so often so volatile
because many nations acted as if their beliefs were utterly certain
and worthy of fanatical devotion. Nationalists and nationalism
were especially dangerous, although all tendency to lapse into
"ideological preferences" and action was unfortunate at best.[44] It
was all too easy for nations, like people, to slip into the dogma
of "universalistic principles" with consequences that soon enough
appeared as "utter depravity in action."[45]

Intellectuals' objection to ideology because it seemed to promote
fanaticism is revealing because it suggested that the reaction
against ideology after World War II cannot be understood merely
as an expression of the postwar mood of skepticism. There is no
doubt that this aspect was important. C. Wright Mills was quite
accurate when he observed of many postwar social scientists:
"Many, I should say most, social scientists in America today are
easily or uneasily liberal. They conform to the prevailing fears of
any passionate commitment. *This*, and not 'scientific objectivity,'
is what is really wanted by such men when they complain about
'making value judgments.'"[46] Yet we can see there is little question
that there was no skepticism about the evils of ideology and
fanaticism. They were simply unacceptable. There is no discussion
of their possible value, if any, in the era. Their evil is a "given" and
so was the ironic sentiment voiced quite candidly by the historian
Peter Gay that. of course, "we must hate some things, especially
fanaticism."[47]

It is hard to think when fanaticism might ever be of value, but
it is quite another thing to assume that ideology is always bad or
that fanaticism must always accompany ideology. But these beliefs
were rarely questioned in the two decades after World War II. Nor
was there much challenge to the implicit conservatism that underlay the attack on fanatical ideology. Daniel Bell's charge was
common: "The tendency to convert concrete issues into ideological
problems, to invest them with moral color and high emotional
charge, is to invite conflicts which can only damage a society."[48]

Consider this remarkable statement for a moment. It says that ideological conflicts, fanaticism in action, can "only" damage a society. They could never do good; they could never produce a long-run benefit. This is a strong claim indeed, but not at all an unusual one in America from 1945 to 1964. The almost unanimous rejection by leading political intellectuals of Barry Goldwater's candidacy for the presidency in 1964 closed the era on the same note on which it had begun. It was not surprising that few agreed with him when he said "extremism in the defense of liberty is no vice . . . moderation in pursuit of justice is no virtue."

To be so sure is not to be skeptical, obviously, but beyond that the point is that there was an implicit calculation here, present in all the outrage about fanatical ideologies. The calculation was that the present is better than the costs that would be entailed by the futures of any of the assorted ideologues. Translated into history, this confidence of postwar American intellectuals signified belief that the United States, whatever its flaws, was a satisfactory society. This was the deepest meaning of the revolt against ideology, although not its only meaning. This was the master premise of American political thinking from 1945 to 1964. We may not dare to compress all of its richness into this single theme, and we will not, but without this premise the remarkable period of American thought for two decades after World War II cannot be understood.

IDEOLOGY AS A DISTORTING AND/OR SIMPLIFYING LENS

Another objection to ideology frequently found among thoughtful political writers in the two decades after World War II was the argument that ideology did not accurately describe reality. Arthur Schlesinger, for example, complained that "dogmatists and monists" simply did not demonstrate they were genuinely empirical.[49] This was a natural and significant argument for an age in which "reality testing" was deeply respected and in which social science attained previously unknown levels of respect and achievement. At times the argument consisted of asserting that ideologies were superficial because they reduced the full complexity of the world to some simple model far short of reality. Daniel Bell evoked a general opinion when he stated: "The point is that ideologists are 'terrible simplifiers.'"[50] James Ward Smith, whose own sensitive and thoughtful considerations on values we will examine later, complained in *Theme for Reason* of what he called "Ism-thinking." It was indefensible in his view since it distorted any sophisticated appreciation of the world.[51] Gabriel Almond in his *Appeals of Communism* agreed. Communism *as* an ideology was sadly simpleminded.[52]

Some intellectuals located this problem with ideology among American ideologues in particular, suggesting that our "idealism" was often "of a peculiarly adolescent kind–unyielding, unrealistic, and unworldly–in a word, romantic."[53] Daniel Bell pointed to American Socialist ideologues as a clear historical example. The American Socialist party failed because its ideological blinders had not permitted it to deal with a complicated reality. It had made the fatal mistake of substituting ideological cliches for the rich magnificence of reality.[54] Richard Hofstadter in his *Anti-Intellectualism in American Life* (1963) saw these forces operating among American intellectuals at all times. The demon that most threatened the perspective of the American intellectual was the single idea, the single notion that gripped him and led him into a commitment that obscured rather than enlightened his consciousness.[55] Hofstadter's temper was quite close to Richard Rovere's of *The New Yorker*. For Rovere "the tragedy of political passion" was its speedy sacrifice of "a tempering" that bred the "sophistication" of genuine understanding.[56]

Even as ardent a defender of ideology as Henry David Aiken did not completely deny the common opinion. It was true that ideologies glossed over the rough hills and valleys of human life, but that did not mean they were necessarily false. He believed some simplification was quite important to achieve action, to inspire men and women with an outlook they could act upon. He suggested that the popular critique revealed how little his fellow American intellectuals were interested in change. He charged that instead of change, they sought the comfort of the status quo and "managed to fashion a kind of counter-ideology, or fetish, of complexity, difficulty, and uniqueness."[57] Aiken's description was by no means wrong, but that does not in any way refute the anti-ideologists' assertion that ideology was unacceptable because it simplified reality. Aiken's concession on this point is significant and, the anti-ideologists would have said, extremely damaging.

A related, but perhaps more serious, charge against ideology often heard in those years was that it fatally distorted events. It was not merely that ideology reduced complexity but that it twisted reality into demonstrably false images. Reinhold Niebuhr, for instance, asserted that all ideologies could only distort human nature either into something far too optimistic for the facts or something hopelessly and inaccurately pessimistic.[58] David Riesman charged that intellectuals influenced by ideological Marxism in particular trotted out "stereotypes" to explain events instead of earnestly seeking to understand them as they were.[59] Hannah Arendt claimed that ideological thinking inevitably took on a life of its own that "becomes independent of all experience from which it can learn anything new."[60] Hans Morgenthau surveyed much of international politics with an eye that saw similar baleful effects of ideology. He could only report with regret that "it is not the sensitive, flexible, versatile mind of the diplomat, but the rigid, relentless, and one-track mind of the crusader that guides the destiny of nations."[61]

THE ALTERNATIVE TO IDEOLOGY

Critics of the mainstream of postwar intellectual opinion have not been convinced that the attacks on ideology for simplifications and distortions represented much more than a sophisticated expression of a differing ideological viewpoint. This critique is one we will explore, but always with the understanding that, although it may be right, it does not address the framework in which postwar intellectuals made their objections to ideology. American political thinkers did not see themselves objecting to other ideologies in the name of their own, but rather objecting to all ideologies in the name of empirical science, which reported a complex and intricate social reality.

This, of course, did not mean there was no political alternative except that sanctioned by dangerous and simpleminded ideologies. Political intellectuals mainly agreed in the twenty years after World War II that America's liberal democracy was the alternative. We proved that societies did not need an ideology and that, in fact, genuine democracies dared not allow ideology a foothold or else democracy might give way to totalitarianism. It was a staple of social science argument that democracy could best be sustained by avoiding absolutes and ideologies of any sort.[62] Arthur Schlesinger made the same point many times.[63] Political intellectuals insisted that democracy was about openness not ideology. It was "a matter of proximate choices, not of ultimate goals."[64] It was, as Leslie Fiedler put it, "dominated less by aspiration toward a well defined future state than by identified social ills that seem to call for remedy."[65] This model of democracy as an open, problem-solving institution which served as a "standing reproof to dogmatism"[66] was attractive to political intellectuals like Clinton Rossiter who consequently argued in 1960 that "the ideas of Marx and his heirs are a fearful challenge to American democracy."[67]

Social scientists like Bell and Seymour Martin Lipset envisioned the democratic alternative as one where politics concerned interests rather than ideology. It was their analysis that people participated in politics to advance their own position in life–or to defend what they had. They did not care particularly about abstract principles, eternal truths, or utopian futures.[68] As we will see in chapter 7, most political intellectuals in the two decades after World War II agreed that *pluralist democracy*, democracy which was characterized by openness, compromise, practical problem solving, and the politics of interests, was the practice as well as the norm in America. In that world the evils of fanaticism and the distortions of ideology were banished, they believed, to the benefit of all Americans.

THE HUNT FOR OTHER IDEOLOGUES

So strong was the agreement that ideology was indefensible, dangerous, and in irreconcilable opposition to postwar liberal democratic values–which somehow were not an ideology–that American political intellectuals after 1945 devoted great effort to exposure of those who might be ideological and totalitarian. There was a great effort to hunt out the ideological wherever it was and to exorcise its threat wherever it appeared. The truth was that many American intellectuals were sure that Stalinism and Nazism were not the only manifestations of the ideological. Indeed, intellectuals assumed there were, or had been, many other manifestations over time. A large number of intellectuals were obviously fascinated as well as repelled by them, and eager to broaden the attack on ideology by object lesson after object lesson. It is hard in retrospect to make clear how much time and attention were devoted to this endeavor. It was a central project of postwar political thought. It showed how great the concern with ideology was and how great the fear of and distaste for ideology became.

THE AMERICAN IDEOLOGUES AND TOTALITARIANS

Samuel Stouffer found that besides the American public's great antagonism to international Communism in the heyday of anti-Communism in the 1950s, there was also a distinct perception that American Communists presented a real danger. Nineteen percent of the public thought they were a very great threat, and 24 percent, a great threat.[69] American political intellectuals shared this alarm. To be sure, their anxiety did not derive so much from immediate apprehensions as from the experience of the recent past projected into an open future. In many cases, of course, intellectuals were concerned with Communist influence in the past and those most concerned had often been American Communists or fellow travelers in the 1930s, but there was also interest based on the phenomenon of Henry Wallace's 1948 Communist-influenced campaign for the presidency. Books poured forth and they almost universally demonstrated the strong disapproval their authors had for anyone disposed toward Communist ideology. A great many of the books were issued in the series "Communism in American Life" under the general editorship of Clinton Rossiter and financed by the Fund for the Republic. Among these were Theodore Draper's *The Roots of American Communism* (1957), Nathan Glazer's *The Social Basis of American Communism* (1961), Daniel Aaron's *Writers on the Left* (1961), and Clinton Rossiter's study of Marxist ideology in comparison with the American tradition.[70] Other important books by intellectuals on the subject included Bell's *Marxian Socialism in the United States (1952)*, Coser and Howe's *The American Communist Party (1957)*, and Hook's *Political Power and Personal Freedom* (1959), but the list was virtually endless.[71] There is absolutely no doubt of the passionate interest of American intellectuals in the subject of Communism in America after 1945.

Not one of these books and not a single work by a major intellectual dealt with the Communists or their ideology with any sympathy. All attention was given, instead, to formulating an explanation for how America had ever had any Communists or fellow travelers. Arthur Schlesinger favored the psychological and social-psychological explanation. He pointed out that "even America has its quota of lonely and frustrated people, craving social, intellectual and even sexual fulfillment that they cannot find in existing society."[72] They were the breeding ground for Communists. Others agreed. Murray Kempton remarked on the alienation and loneliness of sailors as the key factor that contributed to the relative strength of Communism among sailors in the 1930s. Moreover, he tended to be especially patronizing in describing the psychological motivations that led women into the party.[73] Daniel Aaron stands out as an exception who knew the motivation of Communists or fellow travelers, at least among literary figures, was often complex and was not always a "desperate act" by the "maladjusted."[74] His opinion, however, was unusual. Much more typical was the intriguing analysis of Eric Hoffer in *The True Believer* and the stolid analysis of Gabriel Almond constructed from social scientific data. Both found social-psychological causes quite adequate explanations. Neither took seriously the idea that human values and hopes might have played a role.[75]

These attempts to analyze why Americans fell into the Communist delusion represented the more thoughtful approaches to Communist totalitarianism. Many political intellectuals simply chose to denounce American Communism for its ideological and other errors rather than do anything else. Denunciations of this sort appear to be almost obligatory in the writings of political intellectuals in the 1940s and 1950s. Edward Shils offered a characteristically firm, if understated, view: "The Communist Party of the United States is and has been malevolent in intent."[76] Peter Viereck's attacks were a good deal more heated, but they were not more controversial. For Viereck, "Membership in the Communist Party is morally an act comparable to murder. Mass-murder, in fact."[77] Perhaps the best writing by political intellectuals after the war on the evil of Communism in America came from ex-Communists who had worked in the party. Their observations–Granville Hick's *Where We Came Out* (1954) is a good illustration—often substituted thoughtful reflections on party and personal errors for fiery denunciations.[78] They often forged an intelligent critique, one still worth reading even today.

Although American intellectuals were careful to support free speech for all, Communism in America was not interpreted as just another political movement whose members should have all ordinary First Amendment rights. Many political intellectuals were convinced that Communists constituted a "conspiracy" of a "pernicious" nature that could not be tolerated.[79] They denied there could be any compromise with totalitarians when they went beyond words and ideas to actions. The examples are many. Most famous was Sidney Hooks' blistering attack on the conspiratorial aspects of the American Communist movement—"Conspiracy No"—and his insistence that Communist party members were too compromised by allegiance to totalitarianism to allow them to teach in American schools.[80] Arthur Schlesinger worried about Communist actions at home, too, and was by no means antagonistic to the attorney general's list of subversive organizations.[81] Daniel Bell, although judging the Communist threat in the United States to be virtually nonexistent, still approved completely of attacking every evidence of Communist conspiracy. He was delighted that by 1950 the "communist movement stood revealed before the American people not as a political party but as a conspiracy, and that conspiracy was being driven out of American life."[82] This was only a reasonable fate, since, Theodore Draper remarked, it was no more than "the American appendage of a Russian revolutionary power."[83]

The Wallace campaign for the presidency in 1948 was a crucial postwar event for many liberal intellectuals who rallied to the fight against Communism. Its degeneration into an ill-concealed Communist front was proof enough to them of the unwillingness of some American liberals to face the facts about Communism. There were still liberals who were not toughminded. Hook was always ready to criticize "ritualistic liberals" who apologized for Communists, the type who had often given support to Wallace. He frequently expressed his despair of liberals who sometimes were so astonishingly naive about politics.[84] Schlesinger found Wallace an especially sad case of a vulnerable liberal: "well-intentioned, woolly-minded . . . made to order for Communist exploitation."[85] Coser and Howe agreed completely as did Leslie Fiedler who dismissed Wallace's naivete as "the blindly 'idealist,' hands-across-the-sea approach to the Soviet Union made flesh."[86] Even Eric Goldman, whose *Rendezvous with Destiny* managed a spirited and sometimes lyrical celebration of all kinds of American reformers and radicals, disapproved of the Wallace campaign. Wallace had become a fellow traveler and had lost his way in the miasma of Communist propaganda.[87]

There was a fine line to be walked here, but most thinkers who addressed the problem walked it. They expressed their considerable hostility toward the Communists and their ideology. They denounced Communist dangers in every way. But at the same time they were unhappy about what they called "witch hunts" that hurt the innocent and people who had given up Communist beliefs. Hook argued that it was necessary to thread a way between those he called the "cultural vigilantes" who vastly exaggerated the Communist threat and consequently overreacted and the "ritualistic liberals" who blithely ignored the entire problem.[88] Some sought to make crucial distinctions they thought reflected well on American intellectuals. Murray Kempton and Daniel Aaron both contended that few really significant American novelists or intellectuals had ever been sucked into the Communist morass in the 1930s. Despite the cries of "cultural vigilantes," it was only second-rate figures who fell for the evil of Communism.[89]

Many thinkers sought to preserve an atmosphere that would protect the toleration of Communist *ideas* even as they denounced them in no uncertain terms. This was the position, for example, of Gabriel Almond.[90] It was the stance of the American historian Richard Hofstadter, although he expressed his fury at "totalitarian liberals" who "denied or granted special indulgences to the barbarities and tyrannies of Soviet politicals."[91] It was the viewpoint of Arthur Schlesinger. He disliked the witch hunters and he defended J. Robert Oppenheimer against them, while he repeatedly warned against "doughface" liberals, democratic men with "totalitarian principles" who naively played into the hands of anti-democratic forces at home.[92] He appreciated the wisdom of Whittaker Chambers' *Witness*, a book about a man who had learned the error of Communism and was not afraid to say so. He was not a "doughface" liberal who did not understand that in America and everywhere "the personal word of the Communist is worthless and cooperation with him is impossible."[93] Doughface liberals did not understand what Sidney Hook described as "the unremitting crusade of the Kremlin."[94]

The intensity and the longevity of this argument seem puzzling in the light of a post-World War II intellectual climate in which there were few "doughface" or "totalitarian" liberals to be found. To be sure, in the late 1940s both the bitter, final struggles against Communist control of a few unions and the events of the Wallace campaign provided a limited explanation, but the argument appeared to be more a quarrel with the long-gone 1930s and a defense against Senator McCarthy and his allies than anything else. It simply was not true after World War II that there was any radical left-wing "strike of the middle-class intellectuals" and no "reluctance to conserve the very heritage that protects from Russia their freedom and their security."[95] Even among literary intellectuals, the group most drawn to Communism in the 1930s, the appeal of Communism was over. The 1940s saw "the desertion of the Communist Party by virtually every talented author it had ever enlisted in this country."[96]

DANGER ON THE RIGHT

In the 1950s and early 1960s the main alarm among American political intellectuals was directed toward the American Right as an expression of the absolutist and ideological mood. These intellectuals thought the Right was composed of people who, even more than domestic Communists and fellow travelers, had not yet perceived the threat of ideology. They had to be watched with considerable vigilance, for they were as dangerous as Communists.

There is little doubt that sometimes distaste for the Right turned into hysteria. William Newman in *The Futilitarian Society* (1960) lashed out at American conservatism as the "enemy." Like some other intellectuals, but by no means at all, he could distinguish among types of conservatives, but he was so swept up in concern over "the menace that conservative ideas held for America" that he could scarcely resist viewing all conservatives as in a conspiracy against America.[97] Richard Hofstadter was similarly attracted to this position with regard to American conservatives, especially John Birchers.[98] This conspiracy interpretation, which had been so often applied to American Communists, proved irresistable for treating the Right, or its more "radical" forms, and was often carried over and applied to them. As with the linkage of foreign Communism and Nazism, so with the linkage of domestic Communism and the Radical Right, distinctions became blurred in the process. The point of the critique of political intellectuals, though, was that the distinctions were not as important as the bond of fanaticism and ideological politics.

Once again, this time with the Right, political intellectuals frequently chose to approach their subject by studying what they saw as a diseased phenomena of right-wing ideology and behavior, and by this means attack the Right. Seymour Martin Lipset, for instance, devoted considerable energy to the study of a wide variety of groups on the American Right. He continued this project well into the 1960s exploring the sociological bases and the ideological illusions of groups ranging from the Coughlinites of the 1930s to the Birchers of the 1960s. Lipset argued that the source of support for assorted factions of the Right varied. The Coughlinites, for example, were often lower class Roman Catholics and the Birchers usually were members of the upper economic levels and belonged to diverse branches of Christianity. Yet Lipset made no distinction in his attitude toward all the groups. He inevitably treated them in a clinical manner that scarcely hid his belief that they were confused and dangerous.[99]

Daniel Bell was fascinated with the same theme, and in 1963 he published a collection of essays by a variety of authors, including Lipset, entitled *The Radical Right*. He was less worried about the threat the ideological Right posed than were many of his contributers, but like them he had no respect for a Right that was motivated by "sour impotence" of the "dispossessed." It was a fundamentally unpleasant reality in America because its members substituted ideology for civility in public life. There was, however, no chance that they could win control of the American political system, for they were obviously out of touch with the American moods of skepticism and consensus.[100]

Yet a third example of the common fascination was Richard Hofstadter's virtual obsession with the Right. Hofstadter preferred to explain the Right in terms of psychological fallacies, specifically in terms of paranoia, but his conclusion was a standard liberal one. The Right was encircled in an ideology that failed to reflect reality. Moreover, it was necessarily dangerous, because it wanted to transform ordinary life "into a spiritual Armageddon."[101] Hofstadter linked Barry Goldwater, the Rightist presidential candidate of 1964, with this style of politics, pointing to Goldwater's exaggerated fears about American decay at home and abroad as a case of paranoid delusion in action.[102]

Hofstadter represented another tendency as well. He dipped into American history to discover antecedants of the radical Right, and he found a good many disturbing examples. He reported in *The Anti-Intellectual Tradition in American Life* (1963) that the problem was ultimately one of political fundamentalism—in our terms ideology—which had long bedeviled the American scene in the somewhat different form of religious fundamentalism. Hofstadter bitterly castigated the America's experience with Protestant evangelism. It was not so far from the absurdities of eighteenth and nineteenth-century evangelistic crusades to meetings of radical Rightists. He explicitly compared the Scopes Trial of the 1920s with the madness of McCarthy and what he described as "the Great Inquisition of the 1950s."[103]

But it was Senator Joseph McCarthy who drew the most fire as the very epitome of the Rightist enemy whose inchoate ideology and wild actions were labeled as the greatest danger from the Right. McCarthy, the tempestuous Senator from Wisconsin, 1947–57, was so often and so severely denounced by American intellectuals that the reaction to him requires special attention. What was it about McCarthy and "McCarthyism" that was so upsetting? What was it about McCarthy that made him so bitterly opposed, so bitterly hated? What was it about his memory that provided continued provocation throughout this entire period, even though he was dead by 1957 and destroyed politically well before then?

McCarthy was understood as a radical, above all, a man who wanted to change America in fundamental if usually unspecified ways, a man who did not care about liberal values, and a man who was an ideological fanatic. McCarthy was all that American intellectuals had come to fear as the result of European totalitarianism, and it was no surprise they hated him with a passion that belied any attitude of skepticism.

McCarthy's values and aspirations, or those of people who seemed to like and admire him, were never considered worth any consideration as a legitimate position in politics. They were dismissed, and intellectual effort was instead spent, as usual, in attempting to explain how such fanaticism had attracted so many supporters in America. Daniel Bell was inclined to the popular theory of status anxiety that Richard Hofstadter developed most thoroughly. It held that McCarthyism fed on the anxieties of those who were not secure in their status in society, either those who believed they were losing status or those who felt their newly attained status was not secure. Either way there were many in the restless, mobile, postwar American world who did not think their position was secure and these anxious people were McCarthy's natural constituency.[104] A similar social-psychological approach impressed Seymour Martin Lipset. Although he had his reservations, Lipset argued that the status-strain theory was plausible. No more than Bell did he seriously explore whether there was an intellectual framework in the McCarthyite universe and, if so, what it was about. He was too busy noting such "obvious" absurdities in McCarthy's speeches as his frequent theme that "the common man in America has been victimized by members of the upper classes, by the prosperous, by the wealthy, by the well-educated."[105] Yet Lipset was sensitive to the angry radicalism that existed side-by-side with the search for security in the McCarthy movement. He argued that McCarthyism was improperly understood as conservatism. Richard Hofstadter's label for McCarthyism and other radical Right positions was *pseudoconservatism*. Both thinkers heavily stressed their view that the Right, like all fanatical and ideological movements, was hardly oriented toward stability.

Lipset stood out, however, as one of the few political intellectuals who understood the significant implications of this analysis for American intellectual life. He recognized that the essence of his argument was that American intellectuals were increasingly conservative, wedded to postwar America. McCarthy was their enemy largely because he was a radical and was not committed to the status quo.[106]

There were other explanations for the rise of McCarthyism as well. Talcott Parsons, the most renowned American social theorist of the postwar decades, was inclined to blame McCarthyism on strains caused by the United States' increased domestic and foreign responsibilities. He maintained that Americans were unprepared to accept the fact that America after World War II was saddled with big government and an active role in international affairs. He felt this was an essentially irrational reaction, but it showed that many citizens were incapable of accepting reality. On the other hand, they proved very capable of taking refuge with McCarthy.[107] Or there was the authoritarian personality analysis, which contended that McCarthy appealed to those citizens who were in search of dominating authority figures. Proponents of this view had scant sympathy for the numerous Americans who followed McCarthy, since they assumed all rational people realized that authoritarianism in such a form was a type of sickness. It was a type of sickness many intellectuals obviously found intensely disturbing.[108]

The Populist interpretation of the McCarthy movement was another favorite of postwar political intellectuals. According to this analysis, McCarthy tended to activate masses of citizens who often lived in the geographical centers of late 19th-century populism and who demanded instant gratification of their every wish. McCarthyism brought such Populist sentiments to the fore with no concern about their consequences for the nation and for minority rights among a citizenry of widespread ignorance and frequent irrationality. Some fumed that the result was likely to be manipulation of the masses by McCarthy, if the Wisconsin Senator ever gained (or had gained) power. This analysis was the favorite of intellectuals as diverse as Edward Shils and Leslie Fiedler, and it was the most damning in its caustic image of the American citizen.

Even more than the other social-psychological interpretations, it appeared to explain McCarthy by condemning a large proportion of the American people.[109] It was an early sign of what became a second important ingredient of postwar skepticism, loss of confidence in the capacity of the ordinary citizen in politics.

Most of these social science theories purporting to explain McCarthy's appeal did not, of course, prove plausible in the long run. They usually operated at the highest levels of abstraction with the inevitable consequence that they did not provide much illumination on the occasions when social theorists attempted to consider any individual citizen's behavior rather than one grand social type or another. Sometimes the arguments proved to be wrong even as abstractions. This was the case with the Populist thesis when later studies demonstrated there was little connection between traditional bases of Populist sentiment and McCarthy's support, which tended to be composed of conservative Republicans and citizens who were particularly concerned about Communism rather than a mass movement of "irrational" ultra-Democrats.[110]

Another, frequent tack of American intellectuals in dealing with McCarthy was less an attempt to elucidate his bases of support than to go after McCarthy himself. Sometimes this approach got no further than blunt ad hominem as in Philip Rahv's dismissal of McCarthy as "a political bum employing 'vicious antics,'"[111] Hofstadter's repulsion from "the ugly image of McCarthy" and "the McCarthyist pack,"[112] or Newman's disgust for "McCarthy and his gang warfare."[113] Simply branding McCarthy a "demagogue" was common among intellectuals such as Edward Shils, although that was too mild for those who perceived McCarthy "as America's outstanding example of the unscrupulous demagogue."[114] Suggesting that McCarthy was a liar, as political intellectuals such as Arthur Schlesinger did, was also routine.[115] Sometimes the attack on McCarthy proceeded on a less vituperative plane. Sidney Hook, for instance, tried to avoid personal denunciation in favor of analysis of McCarthy's values. Hook believed that part of McCarthy's problem was his basic "distrust of freedom of thought," which made him a threat.[116] The best approach to the McCarthy phenomenon that emphasized McCarthy as a person was made by Richard Rovere in his *Senator Joseph McCarthy* (1959). Rovere, a respected and perspicacious intellectual and a political reporter for *The New Yorker*, treated McCarthy as a dangerous demagogue, defeated by the time he wrote his book, but an ugly memory nonetheless. Rovere's McCarthy was nothing but a cynic, out for his own advantage. What he said and did had more to do with his own compulsions than any ideas or political programs. It is significant that Rovere, much as he hated McCarthy, was relieved that the senator was a cynical rather than ideologically committed personality. Rovere adhered to the conventional horrors of anything ideological and consequently was convinced that even utter cynics were better than sincere fanatics.[117] Cynics at least knew the world and knew when to draw back before the limits of reality. The ideologue did not.

It was quite possible to look back at McCarthy with calm perspective once he and his movement were spent. When Max Lerner did this he remarked that after all America had survived McCarthy and he suspected the real lesson of the entire experience was the fact of survival.[118] But there was no doubt that for many thinkers McCarthy was as great a shock as could be. His impact on the political thinking of the twenty years after World War II was enduring. He seemed to warn that it could happen here. Fanaticism had not died with Hitler or Stalin.

William F. Buckley, in his *McCarthy and His Enemies* (1954), made the only serious attempt to defend McCarthy from within the broader intellectual community. Buckley had no use for totalitarians of either Right or Left, but his estimation of the Communist danger exceeded his fears about the fanatical Right. He did not see any basis for the "nonsense" that the United States was enmeshed in a Rightist "reign of terror" in the 1950s, but he did think that America was engaged in a "fight" with "international Communism" that we were losing since it "thrives increasingly with each passing year."[119] If we had a properly keen consciousness of "the immediacy of our peril," we would get busy "fighting the enemy in our midst."[120]

Buckley claimed that many, indeed most, of McCarthy's charges were on target and that his record overall was *"extremely good."*[121] Buckley did not simply indulge in sweeping charges that satisfied many critics of McCarthy but went through the tedious process of studying case by case what the record actually was. He was con-

fident that anyone who followed the examination would have to
agree that the State Department in particular was riddled with
security risks and that there was no will to get rid of them.[122]
Buckley went further, however, and demonstrated the depth of
his fears of Communism when he argued that the costs of failing
to stop the domestic Communist threat required that we relax
traditional protections for the innocent. He defended McCarthy's
actions in this light. Some innocent citizens would have to suffer
to root out Communists. There was no time any longer to allow
due process and a "quasi-legal adjudication" for everyone who was
to be fired. There was a need for action now.[123]

Yet Buckley's book was much less a total defense of McCarthy
than McCarthy or his allies could have wished. Buckley understood very well that McCarthy overdid things, often hurting his
cause. In this sense, and to this degree, Buckley shared the sentiments of the age. McCarthy's famous claims of specific numbers of
Communists in government, made in Wheeling, West Virginia, and
later, were labeled "excesses." Buckley acknowledged that more
than once McCarthy was "misinformed," that he "exaggerated,"
and that a few of his accusations had "no apparent foundation
whatsoever." He knew that McCarthy did not seem able to distinguish Communists from the much larger group of people who
did not agree with him, and he found McCarthy's famous attack
on General George Marshall appalling.[124]

On balance, though, Buckley justified McCarthy. He stood outside the conventional view, a fact that led him a little later to
observe that the reaction of most American intellectuals to Mc-
Carthy was puzzlingly inconsistent with their professed skepticism
and tolerance. To him the passion and pervasiveness of the assault
on McCarthy "reflected an obsession, and induced the kind of
behavior, intellectual and moral, that Liberals do not officially
approve of."[125] A few other intellectuals—Leslie Fiedler was one—
were also disturbed by some aspects of the intellectual response to
McCarthy. One view was that the reaction to McCarthy was
exaggerated and overblown, indicating "a remarkably adolescent
view of the world."[126] Another was that when it was true (in the
1950s) that "for intellectual respectability . . . it is required that
one consider McCarthyism a major threat to liberty," something

was seriously wrong about the standards of skeptical intellectuals.[127] Few intellectuals agreed and thus they left themselves
vulnerable to the suspicions of men like Buckley. These suspicions
about the existence of more than a trace of unskeptical dogmatism
among liberal intellectuals were surprising only to those who took
too seriously the mood of skepticism, who had specifically expected that postwar political intellectuals would be skeptical about
their rejection of ideology and fanaticism. This, it should be clear,
was not the case. Peter Gay's admonition to his fellows that they
should hate "fanaticism" was widely shared, and widely practiced,
never more so than when American political thinkers faced Senator
Joseph McCarthy.

RUMMAGING THROUGH HISTORY

European totalitarianism and McCarthyism were two contemporary phenomena that many intellectuals believed reflected the
dangers of ideology and its attendant fanaticism. But they were
not alone. All of history, including intellectual history, was reexamined in a search for ideologues or the totalitarians, reaching
the situation where serious scholars thought it worth their time to
argue the question of whether or not Plato was a totalitarian.[128]
American historians concentrated their search on the American
past. They often wrote history in the years from 1945 to 1964 to
alert their fellow citizens to the danger of ideology whose markings
they uncovered in many eras and many corners of our common
past. Their discussions of past political leaders in America were
often meant as thinly disguised messages to the present. For example, one historian of note denounced Thomas Jefferson as a
"true believer" and compared him in an unflattering manner with
"modern libertarians" who were alleged to be "skeptical."[129]
William Jennings Bryan was another famous American who
often criticized as a shameless and fanatical moralizer, who was
another bad memory lurking in the past.[130] The 1930s were frequently singled out as an embarrassing period in American life,
followed closely by the Populist Era. The postwar image by political intellectuals of the 1930s retained great respect for the New
Deal and for Franklin D. Roosevelt, but many intellectuals harshly

judged the faults they perceived among 1930s intellectuals. Some dwelt on the affinity of "literary Stalinoids" for ideology and totalitarianism.[131] Others went out of their way to show the similarity between McCarthy and quite a few left-wing intellectuals of the 1930s: both were doctrinnaire, distrusted politicians, displayed too much "impatience with the traditional legal and political institutions," and actually believed in "the moral superiority of the people."[132]

Daniel Boorstin crusaded against any hint of what he considered to be ideological thinking or action. Boorstin's historical work throughout the twenty years after war frequently included pointed arguments against ideology and regret that it had occasionally sullied even American experience. For example, Boorstin went out of his way to attack colonial Quakerism because it was, in his view, rigid and doctrinal. He delighted in the fact that it had failed to be practical and could not govern Pennsylvania, but he was not surprised. Ideology was no substitute for reality, only an escape into inevitable failure.[133] He contrasted the Quakers with the Puritans; the latter, despite their beginnings, eventually learned not to be rigid ideologues. They discovered that the "Big Lie could not help against a snowstorm; it would kill no wolves and grow no corn. Therefore, it was less important to make a grand plan, to make generalities glitter, than to know what was what and how to control the forces of nature."[134] Even better than Puritan society, though, was colonial Virginia. Its history offered no examples of the "cut-throat enthusiasms and fanatic fervor of the [early] Age of the Puritans."[135]

Boorstin's reflections on the Civil War were particularly interesting. At first Boorstin was inclined to interpret the Civil War as a conflict that had not involved opposing values so much as it had involved differing regional sociologies. He did not blame ideological fanaticism for the war. Later, though, he changed his mind. Then he saw significance in the Civil War as a sad example of ideological excess.[136] He became especially critical of pre-Civil War political thought, North and South. Southern thinkers fell into the error of "metaphysical politics," which made them fanatical like the Quakers. Boorstin acknowledged that the South produced some memorable political theory in the process, but to him this was of no particular benefit. In truth, it was a bad sign.[137] Similarly, Boorstin had little regard for the northern transcendentalists. Like many others in the postwar decades, he found their moralism and self-righteousness unattractive and described their reputation as vastly "inflated."[138]

It was Boorstin's impression that most of the history of American political theory was blessedly free from fanaticism and ideology. Indeed, the poor reputation America had for generating any creative political thought was well-deserved in his opinion, and it was the consequence of a healthy condition. It meant that we rarely became deluded by ideology. He was confident that in his own time this healthy tradition was still alive: "we should be inspired that in an era of idolatry, when so many nations have filled their sanctuaries with ideological idols, we have had the courage to refuse to do so."[139]

George Kennan did not evaluate the American record, at least in our attitude toward foreign policy, in nearly so "optimistic" a light. He agreed with Boorstin's analysis that ideology was something America must avoid, but he bewailed a historical record he found replete with American failures to avoid ideology. For instance, he was severely critical of American behavior during both the great wars because it showed that Americans had a tendency to slip into ideological frameworks. Our record before, during, and after World War I was terribly flawed. We had insisted on making it a crusading war, seeking to gain great moral aims and lapsing in the end into disappointed pacifism, another moral absolute.[140] The same alarming pattern was duplicated in World War II, above all in our insistence on "total" victory. We ought to have proceeded in quite another manner, using diplomacy as much as possible and seeking compromise and marginal gains. Kennan claimed that our failure to do so was another evidence of America's weakness for the absolute.[141]

The discoveries of ideological moments in the American past by Boorstin and Kennan were hardly unusual. Many others pointed up the evidence that the American experience had been far from flawless in this regard. The most famous and controversial of all efforts that followed the same path was Richard Hofstadter's remarkable and influential consideration of the Populists and Progressives in *The Age of Reform* (1955), a book whose relevance to McCarthyism was no secret nor was it intended to be a secret.[142] Hofstadter's argument was that both Populism and Progressivism were addicted to a "moral absolutism" that inevitably leads to "ruthlessness in political life."[143] Both, but especially the Populists, were unable to operate as pragmatic reformers and constantly had to invoke total enemies, rampant conspiracies, and great crusades, all hallmarks of ideological thinking. The Populists even seemed to be infected by anti-Semitism. In all, Hofstadter contended that they were at best ambiguous heroes for American liberalism. If anything, they were a warning against mass movements that had many attractive goals and yet ominously operated within a framework of true belief.[144]

The contrast he had in mind was embodied in the Franklin Roosevelt he described in *The American Political Tradition* (1949). Roosevelt had his failings in Hofstadter's eyes, for "good intentions and month-to-month improvisations" were not quite sufficient for dealing with the modern world. Yet Roosevelt was above all a pragmatist in politics, one not swept up in moral absolutes and ideologies. It was predictable that Roosevelt, more pragmatist than ideological humanitarian, had helped people in fact, but Herbert Hoover, rigid in his principled humanitarianism, failed so ignominiously to do so.[145]

THE LARGER QUESTION

The massive search in the American past for totalitarians and those who had had ideological inclinations cannot be ignored in the pattern of thought of postwar political intellectuals. They felt a deep commitment to wage war against the ideological menace at home as well as abroad, against the Communists, the McCarthys, the Populists, and even the Herbert Hoovers. But what happened only rarely was the moment of reflection that led intellectuals to ask whether American thinkers were too sure in the battle and whether American policy was itself a product of an ideology of its own. Intellectuals agreed that ideology existed in the American present and in the American past, but it was not normally associated with America itself in the period 1945–64. It did not represent the mainstream. It was the danger, but not the reality.

Yet there were two thinkers who wondered about this larger question, two thinkers who speculated that America itself was not skeptical. One of these was Louis Hartz to whose book *The Liberal Tradition in America* (1955) we will often refer. The other was Reinhold Niebuhr. Neither of them saw the tradition of American political thought, nor the present political attitudes of American thinkers, as particularly skeptical. Instead, what they saw was an enormous amount of confidence in liberal values, a confidence that in their minds was surely ideological and even utopian. As Niebuhr put it, from "the earliest days of its history to the present moment, there is a deep layer of Messianic consciousness in the mind of America."[146]

This was disturbing to both Hartz and Niebuhr. Niebuhr insisted that Americans, including American intellectuals, must learn to be "modest," must learn to appreciate the complexity of the world, and must learn to recognize what they were always urging on others, that there "are no simple congruities in life or history."[147] Americans had too great a self-assurance that the American way was the only way, that American perspectives were the only perspectives, that America was virtuous and innocent. These were illusions. They could not be overcome until American intellectuals took more seriously the skepticism they applied so often and so vigorously to others who dared to lapse into the ideological mood.[148] Their hope was that this goal could be reached as Americans became less insular and more acquainted with a larger world. Hartz, in particular, looked to America's expanding participation in the world as a potential learning experience that could teach the tolerance America so needed to practice.[149]

The dispute between thinkers such as Niebuhr and Hartz and many other political intellectuals was basically a matter of degree. There was disagreement over how skeptical America, or American intellectuals, were in the postwar years, but there was no disagreement on the value of being skeptical of ideology and ideological approaches to politics. On this, the fundamental question, Hartz and Niebuhr were characteristic intellectuals of their time. They belonged to the period in American political thought, from 1945 to 1964, when ideology had no attraction and skepticism was the dominant norm. What made them memorable was that they raised questions about the relationship between what they saw as a paradox: a rhetoric of skepticism and a reality of absolutism. They did not resolve this paradox in postwar American political thinking, but they pointed it out. They were pioneers.

NOTES*

1. Arthur Schlesinger, Jr., *The Vital Center* (London: Andre Deutsch, 1970–1949), p. 1.

2. Sidney Hook, *Political Power and Personal Freedom* (New York: Criterion, 1959), pp. 105 and 108.

3. Leslie Fiedler, *An End to Innocence* (Boston: Beacon Press, 1955), pp. 59–70.

4. Peter Viereck, *Shame and Glory of the Intellectuals* (New York: Capricorn, 1965–1953), pp. 132 and 168.

5. Arthur Schlesinger, Jr., "Varieties of Communist Experience" (1960) in *The Politics of Hope* (Boston: Houghton Mifflin, 1962), p. 265.

6. Gabriel Almond, *The Appeals of Communism* (Princeton: Princeton University Press, 1954), p. 397.

7. Clinton Rossiter, *Marxism: The View from America* (New York: Harcourt, Brace and World, 1960), p. 4.

8. Daniel Bell, *The End of Ideology* (New York: Collier's, 1962–1961), p. 402.

9. For example, Peter Gay, *Weimar Culture* (New York: Harper & Row, 1968), p. 85.

10. Reinhold Niebuhr, *The Irony of American History* (New York: Scribner's, 1952), p. 85.

11. John Hallowell, *Main Currents in Modern Political Thought* (New York: Holt, 1950).

12. Richard Rovere, *The American Establishment* (New York: Harcourt, Brace and World, 1962), pp. 285–94.

13. Schlesinger, *Vital Center*, pp. 93–94.

14. Hook, *Political Power*, pp. 109–10.

15. Carl J. Friedrich and Z. Brzezinski, *Totalitarian Dictatorship and Autocracy* (Cambridge: Harvard University Press, 1965–1956), ch. 9.

16. Schlesinger, *Vital Center*, ch. 5.

17. Ibid., p. xxii.

18. Ibid., p. 98.

19. Ibid., p. 59.

20. Hook, *Political Power*, pp. 17 ff. and 122 ff.

*Some books listed here have two dates: the first is the date of the edition referenced here; the second is the date the work was originally published.

21. Seymour Martin Lipset, *Political Man* (Garden City, N.Y.: Doubleday-Anchor, 1963-1960).

22. William F. Buckley, Jr., *Up from Liberalism* (New York: Hillman, 1961), p. 52.

23. Schlesinger, "Varieties," in *Hope*, pp. 279-80.

24. Lewis Coser and Irving Howe, *The American Communist Party* (Boston: Beacon, 1957), ch. 11.

25. Rossiter, *Marxism*, pp. 60-61, 195, and 200-201.

26. Daniel Bell, *Marxian Socialism in the United States* (Princeton: Princeton University Press, 1967-1952), p. 13; Murray Kempton, *Part of Our Time* (New York: Simon and Schuster, 1955), p. 67.

27. Edward Shils, *The Torment of Secrecy* (Glencoe, Ill.: Free Press, 1956), p. 16.

28. Hook, *Political Power*, pp. 6 and 16.

29. Kempton, *Part*, pp. 151-52.

30. Shils, *Torment*, pp. 232-34.

31. Eric Hoffer, *The True Believer*, (New York: Harpers, 1951), ch. 13.

32. Bernard Crick, *In Defense of Politics* (Chicago: University of Chicago Press, 1962), pp. 129-30.

33. Editors, "After the Apocalypse," *Encounter*, October 1953, p. 1.

34. Shils, *Torment*, p. 17; Viereck, *Shame*, p. 111.

35. Giovanni Sartori, *Democratic Theory* (New York: Praeger, 1967-1962), p. 237.

36. Henry Mayo, *An Introduction to Democratic Theory* (New York: Oxford University Press, 1960), p. 153.

37. Sidney Hook, *Heresy Yes, Conspiracy No* (New York: John Day, 1953), p. 246.

38. Hannah Arendt, *The Origins of Totalitarianism* (New York: Meridian, 1958-1951), pp. 472-73.

39. Viereck, *Shame*, p. 53.

40. Michael Oakeshott, "The Tower of Babel," in *Rationalism in Politics* (New York: Basic Books, 1962), p. 70.

41. Schlesinger, *Vital Center*, p. 88.

42. Mayo, *An Introduction*, p. 181.

43. Richard Hofstadter, *Anti-Intellectualism in American Life* (New York: Knopf, 1963), p. 118.

44. Hans J. Morgenthau, *Politics Among Nations* (New York: Knopf, 1960-1948), pp. 6 and 259.

45. Ibid., p. 259.

46. C. Wright Mills, *The Sociological Imagination* (New York: Oxford University Press, 1959), p. 79.

47. Peter Gay, *Voltaire's Politics* (New York: Vintage, 1965-1959), p. xiii.

48. Bell, *End*, p. 121.

49. Schlesinger, "Varieties," in *Hope*, p. 292.

50. Bell, *End*, p. 405.

51. J.W. Smith, *Theme for Reason* (Princeton: Princeton University Press, 1957), pp. 199–200.

52. Almond, *Appeals*, pp. 370–79.

53. Abraham Kaplan, "American Ethics and Public Philosophy," in *The American Style*, ed. Elting Morison (New York: Harper and Bros., 1958), p. 33.

54. Bell, *Marxian Socialism*, p. viii.

55. Hofstadter, *Anti-Intellectualism*, p. 29.

56. Rovere, *Establishment*, p. 305.

57. Henry David Aiken, "The Revolt Against Ideology" (1964), in *Ideology, Politics and Political Theory*, ed. Richard Cox (Belmont, Calif.: Wadsworth, 1969).

58. Reinhold Niebuhr, *The Children of Light and the Children of Darkness* (New York: Scribner's, 1944), p. 41.

59. David Riesman, *Partisan Review* 19 (May-June 1952): 311.

60. Arendt, *Origins*, p. 470.

61. Morgenthau, *Politics*, p. 551.

62. Edward Purcell, *The Crisis of Democratic Theory* (Lexington: University of Kentucky, 1973), p. 111.

63. Schlesinger, *Vital Center*, pp. 7–8 and 146.

64. Kaplan, "American Ethics," in Morison, ed., *American Style*, p. 103.

65. Fiedler, *Innocence*, p. 147.

66. Rossiter, *Marxism*, p. 206.

67. Ibid., p. 193.

68. This point is drawn from James P. Young, *The Politics of Affluence* (San Francisco: Chandler, 1968), p. 10.

69. Samuel Stouffer, *Communism, Conformity and Civil Liberties* (Gloucester, Mass.: Peter Smith, 1963-1955), p. 156.

70. Theodore Draper, *The Roots of American Communism* (New York,: Viking, 1963-1957); Nathan Glazer, *The Social Basis of American Communism* (New York: Harcourt, Brace and World, 1961); Daniel Aaron, *Writers on the Left* (New York: Avon, 1961); Rossiter, *Marxism*.

71. Bell, *Marxian Socialism*; Coser and Howe, *The American Communist Party* (Boston: Beacon, 1957); Hook, *Political Power*, part II.

72. Schlesinger, *Vital Center*, p. 104.

73. Kempton, *Part*, pp. 86–104, ch. 7, passim.

74. Aaron, *Writers*, p. 403.

75. Almond, *The Appeals*; and Hoffer, *Believer*.

76. Shils, *Torment*, p. 61.

77. Viereck, *Shame*, p. 298.

78. Granville Hicks, *Where We Came Out* (New York: Viking, 1954).

79. William E. Leuchtenberg, "Anti-Intellectualism in the United States," *The Journal of Social Issues* no. 3 (1955): 16.

80. Hook, *Heresy Yes*, pp. 21–22, 210, and ch. 9.

81. Schlesinger, *Vital Center*, pp. 126–28.

82. Bell, *Marxian Socialism*, p. 186; Daniel Bell, "Interpretations of American Politics" (1955), in *The Radical Right*, ed. Bell (Garden City, N.Y.: Doubleday-

Anchor, 1964-1963), pp. 72-73.

83. Draper, *The Roots*, p. 395.

84. Hook, *Heresy Yes*, pp. 251 and 260.

85. Schlesinger, *Vital Center*, pp. 115-116.

86. Coser and Howe, *Communist Party*, ch. 10; Fiedler, *Innocence*, p. 79.

87. Eric Goldman, *Rendezvous with Destiny* (New York: Vintage, 1956-1952), p. 323.

88. Hook, *Heresy Yes*, pp. 9-11.

89. Kempton, *Part*, ch. 4; Aaron, *Writers*, passim.

90. Almond, *Appeals*, pp. 383, 394, passim.

91. Richard Hofstadter, *The Age of Reform* (New York: Vintage, 1962-1955).

92. Schlesinger, *Vital Center*, pp. 205-7; ch. 3; Schlesinger, "The Oppenheimer Case" (1958), in *Hope*, p. 215.

93. Schlesinger, *Vital Center*, p. 123; Schlesinger, "Whittaker Chambers and His Witness" (1952), in *Hope*.

94. Hook, *Heresy Yes*, p. 105.

95. Viereck, *Shame*, p. 109.

96. Chester Eisinger, *Fiction of the Forties* (Chicago: University of Chicago Press, 1963), p. 88.

97. William Newman, *The Futilitarian Society* (New York: Braziller, 1960), pp. 24 and 48.

98. Richard Hofstadter, *The Paranoid Style in American Politics and Other Essays* (New York: Knopf, 1965), pp. 27-29.

99. Seymour Martin Lipset, "The Sources of the 'Radical Right'" (1955) and "Three Decades of the Radical Right: Coughlinites, McCarthyites, and Birchers" (1962), in Bell, ed., *Radical Right*.

100. Bell, *Radical Right*.

101. Richard Hofstadter, "The Pseudo-Conservative Revolt" (1955) and "Pseudo-Conservative Revisited: A Postscript" (1962), in Bell, ed., *Radical Right*, pp. 2 and 41-42.

102. Hofstadter, *The Paranoid Style*, pp. 93-141.

103. Hofstadter, *Anti-Intellectualism*, pp. 41, 129-30, 132, 134, and 135.

104. Bell, "Interpretations," in *Radical Right*.

105. Lipset, "Sources," in Bell, ed., *Radical Right*, p. 362.

106. Lipset, *Political Man*, pp. 369-70.

107. Talcott Parsons, "Social Strains in America," in Bell, ed., *Radical Right*.

108. Lipset, "Three Decades," in Bell, ed., *Radical Right*.

109. Shils, *Torment*, p. 103; Fiedler, *Innocence*, pp. 76-77.

110. Ronald Berman, *America in the Sixties: An Intellectual History* (New York: Free Press, 1968), p. 181; Michael Rogin, *The Intellectuals and McCarthy* (Cambridge: M.I.T. Press, 1967), pp. 247-48, 262, and 269.

111. Philip Rahv, "Our Country and Our Culture: A Symposium," *Partisan Review* (May-June 1952): 307.

112. Hofstadter, *Anti-Intellectualism*, p. 222.

113. Newman, *Futilitarian*, p. 25.

114. Shils, *Torment*, pp. 192–93; G.M. Gilbert, "Anti-Intellectualism in the United States," *The Journal of Social Issues*, no. 3 (1955): 52.

115. Schlesinger, "Bernard De Voto," in *Hope*, p. 175.

116. Hook, *Heresy Yes*, p. 260.

117. Richard Rovere, *Senator Joseph McCarthy* (Cleveland: Meridian Books, 1961–1959), pp. 254, 260, passim.

118. Max Lerner, *America as a Civilization* (New York: Simon and Schuster, 1957), pp. 458–59.

119. William F. Buckley, Jr., and L. Brent Bozell, *McCarthy and His Enemies* (Chicago: Regnery, 1954), pp. 246 and 310–11.

120. Buckley, *McCarthy*, p. 4.

121. Ibid., p. 277.

122. Ibid., part I, passim.

123. Ibid., pp. 4 and 246–47.

124. Ibid., pp. 57, 189–91, 277, 301, appendix F.

125. Buckley, *Liberalism*, p. 39.

126. Leuchtenberg, "Anti-Intellectualism," p. 15.

127. Fiedler, *Innocence*, pp. 54–55.

128. Thomas Thorson, ed., *Plato: Totalitarian or Democrat* (Englewood Cliffs, N.J.: Prentice-Hall, 1963).

129. Leonard Levy, *Jefferson and Civil Liberties* (Cambridge: Harvard University Press, 1963), p. 163.

130. Kaplan, "American Ethics," in Morison, ed., *American Style*, p. 57.

131. Viereck, *Shame*, p. 118.

132. Shils, *Torment*, p. 133.

133. Daniel Boorstin, *The Americans: The Colonial Experience* (New York: Random House, 1958), part 2.

134. Daniel Boorstin, *The Genius of American Politics* (Chicago: University of Chicago Press, 1953), pp. 64–65.

135. Boorstin, *The Colonial Experience*, p. 138.

136. See John Diggins, "The Perils of Nationalism: Some Reflections on Dan Boorstin's Approach to American History," *American Quarterly* 23 (May 1971).

137. Daniel Boorstin, *The Americans: The National Experience* (New York: Random House, 1965), pp. 212, 216, and 218.

138. Ibid., p. 44.

139. Boorstin, *Genius*, p. 170.

140. George Kennan, *American Diplomacy 1900–1950* (New York: Mentor, 1951), pp. 64 and 77–79.

141. Ibid., pp. 77–79, 87–89.

142. Hofstadter, *Reform*, p. 14.

143. Ibid., p. 16.

144. Ibid., passim.

145. Richard Hofstadter, *The American Political Tradition* (New York: Vintage, 1959–1948), ch. 12.

146. Reinhold Niebuhr, *The Irony of American History* (New York: Scribner's,

1952), p. 69.

147. Ibid., p. 62.

148. Ibid., pp. 2-5; Arthur Schlesinger, Jr., "Reinhold Niebuhr's Place in American Thought and Life," *Reinhold Niebuhr: His Religion, Social and Political Thought,* eds. Charles Kegley and Robert Bretall (New York: Macmillan, 1961), pp. 126-50.

149. Louis Hartz, *The Liberal Tradition in America* (New York: Harcourt, Brace and World, 1955).

2 Broader Bases of Skepticism

Much of the skeptical approach to politics that characterized American political thought from 1945 to 1964 took the form of a pervasive attack on ideology. But the skeptical mood that produced so much hostility toward absolute justifications in politics consisted of much more than the rejection of ideology. There were important philosophical arguments. There were frequent claims that absolutes were impractical. Finally, there was repeated recourse to the common statement of postwar confidence that underlay the age's alleged skepticism, the contention that Americans did not need an ideology or any other form of absolute. Together these arguments reflected a general consensus among American political intellectuals, who agreed in proclaiming skepticism of absolute claims in politics.

SKEPTICISM OF ABSOLUTES

The Philosophical Arguments against Ideology and Absolutes

If the assault on ideology was the most noticeable dimension along which absolutism was found wanting, it was not the only one. An important, yet contrasting, set of arguments might be called philosophical. These arguments were constructed in the shadow of totalitarianism at home and abroad, but they rarely took note of this fact. Instead, they raised problems for those who thought they could find secure footing in political theory, first, by undermining the possibility of using deduction and, second, by proposing that reason was too limited for the task of discovering absolute values.

The Turn from Deduction   Political philosophers echoed each other after the war in their assertions that deduction would not work as a basis for democracy or any other political value. Sometimes they thought this result was sad, and sometimes, most often, they rejoiced, but they usually agreed that what they saw was a fixed fact in the human universe. *Deduction* had certainly been the characteristic approach of most of the great political theorists of the Western tradition. It involved the assertion that there were certain true principles, natural laws, divine laws, or basic normative axioms of one sort or another, which people could discover by reason, and from which one could deduce the proper political values. The models were not merely Plato and Aristotle who believed in such ultimate principles, but also the entire natural rights tradition of liberalism based on the assumption that there were certain rights grounded in nature from which one could draw political norms. These laws or rights had been invariably considered fact as well as value. They might proclaim, for instance, that the human person was "free" by nature as well as assert that he ought to be free in daily life. Because one was naturally free, and one ought to be free, thinkers concluded that the best political community was one that promoted "freedom." The "fact" of natural freedom, to continue the example, and the value of freedom were so tightly linked that most traditional deductive thinkers held that if somehow they misunderstood the *facts* of nature or the *facts* of God's will, their basic *values* were without justification, since basic facts and basic values were the same thing.

The rise of social science in the first half of the twentieth century greatly influenced the reaction against deductive reasoning by political philosophers. It was not a phenomenon that had its beginnings after 1945.[1] Social science tended more and more to take as its standard of meaning the empirical world and to insist that one must produce empirical verification for assertions of fact. As applied to natural laws and other alleged first principles, this approach was bound to be fatal. Natural rights could not meet social science tests of verification, nor could other first axioms. These "facts" could not be verified empirically, and consequently intellectuals were less and less inclined to take their existence as given. Indeed, after 1945 their existence was more and more denied. The idea that no facts, however firmly established, could provide premises from which anyone could deduce a normative political philosophy also gained increasing popularity. Many social scientists insisted that questions of fact and matters of value were two distinct realms and no fact could justify a value or vice versa. The result was further skepticism about the possibility of providing any absolute justification for political norms.

The evidence for the growth and spread of skepticism of deduction abounds in postwar political theory. Robert Dahl in his landmark book *A Preface to Democratic Theory* (1956) made clear that he rejected any political theory that claimed to deduce its principles from natural rights. Dahl could not accept pluralist democracy based on such a position. He made the same objection to Populist democratic theory. Advocates of each wanted to ground themselves in absolute principles from which they thought they could somehow derive their version of democracy. Dahl saw no basis any longer for making such assertions that floundered in the face of the inadequacies of deductive reasoning.[2] His conclusion was shared by other social science theorists. They assailed deductive approaches to democracy. These approaches could never provide the absolute justifications they promised. It was widely concluded that political theory was at a dead end, unless postwar intellectuals realized the fallacy of the old approach. As one social scientist remarked, if "we take demonstration in its strict, rational sense, I would not know how to demonstrate democracy."[3] Sidney Hook's advice that intellectuals accept the fact that they were "in a world in which we cannot achieve final truth" received considerable assent.[4]

James W. Smith, in his essay *A Theme for Reason*, urged the same conclusion. Smith fearlessly attacked much of the great political philosophy of the past for employing "pretentious metaphysical doctrines" combined with much "irresponsible hocus-pocus" in an attempt to ensure itself a safe deductive framework. He thought that in the postwar era remnants of the Hegelians, Marxists, and Thomists were continuing this wrong path, unwilling to face the fact that political norms could not speak to the modern world in this manner any longer.[5] His position paralleled that of the widely read English thinker, T.D. Weldon, who produced the most savage polemic of the era on the fallacies of deduction in politics in his *The Vocabulary of Politics*. Weldon systematically attacked all the great political thinkers of the Western tradition, showing their dependence on deduction, and then dismissed them as hopelessly inadequate.[6] Thomas L. Thorson shared the same view. His special contribution was to make the case against deduction in political theory with a tone of respect for previous political thinking. He did not consider himself a self-conscious debunker as Weldon obviously did, but he was no less relentless in concluding that the path of deductive analysis had to end in modern political theory. Facts and values were not the same thing, nor could much empirical basis be found for the "facts" of the claims of traditional thinkers.[7]

Political intellectuals often reflected on the inadequacies of the deductive style of political theory in a perspective we know was self-consciously skeptical. The ultimate weakness of the traditional philosophical method of value justification was that it did not fit well into a doubting age. Yet, as always, the skeptical mood was severely qualified. It was not only the general agreement that deductive reasoning had outlived its usefulness that seemed a bit final, but also the conviction expressed by J.W. Smith that "the foundation of democratic political philosophy *consists in* the rejection of the concept of justification or proof" that seemed decidedly unskeptical.[8] Moreover, the widespread insistence that empirical verification was the only valid test of meaning or the growing belief that facts and values must be separated were themselves elements of a philosophy of social science of which there were few skeptics among influential American social scientists in the postwar years.

The Limits of Reason   Another philosophical theme that undermined confidence that political theory could have any absolute grounding was the widespread skepticism of *reason* as a mechanism for the discovery of ultimate truth. This was a point often made in postwar fiction,[9] but in more systematic forums, too, intellectuals repeatedly suggested that human reason was just not able to find any absolute truths. This did not necessarily mean there were not such norms somewhere, but it did mean that there was no point in worrying about them, because we could not learn about them. They might be real but they could not apply in a human situation governed by fallible reason. Charles Frankel in his optimistic *The Case for Modern Man* contended that this was the foundation on which liberal thought must build. It was clearly not possible "that men could ever say with certainty that they were in possession of any eternal truth."[10]

Judith Shklar in her polemic, *After Utopia*, insisted that it was time we recognized our limitations. Reason just could not take us by the hand and direct us to a comfortable place where we would discover ultimate ends. This is to give reason a task that "is next to impossible."[11] Thomas Thorson argued that everyone must understand that the human situation is one "of ignorance, of limited intellectual capacity. Socrates was right when he suggested that the essence of wisdom was the recognition of our intellectual limitations."[12]

Few intellectuals thought that it followed from the great emphasis on the epistemological limitations of reason that reason should be abandoned. There were few hints in the 1945 to 1964 period of any loss of trust in reason. What political intellectuals expressed, rather, was a chastened attitude, one that admired reason but did not expect it to find absolute values. They had no distrust of rational processes of thought and supported no diminution of efforts to illuminate "rational" behavior. Economic rationality became a subject of considerable study. So did voter rationality. So did policy rationality among management experts and defense department whiz kids. Some exponents of such forms of rationality may seem in retrospect to have been excessively optimistic about reason, but they rarely were optimistic about reason's capacity to discover ultimate values.[13] The degree of skepticism of the age toward reason was modest. It did not deny the central role reason had long played among American intellectuals, since this continued unabated. The problem was always a specific one, the error of rationalism.

The historian Peter Gay criticized *rationalists*, those who believed that through reason one could discover absolute principles, even in his beloved Enlightenment. He supported the post-World

War II consensus that was determined to curb exaggerated expectations of reason while preventing any rush to an anti-intellectual position. Some intellectuals, such as Richard Hofstadter, were alarmed at the status of intellectual values in an era in which reason's capacities were reexamined and, he believed, its worth profoundly dishonored by the ideologue and demogogue.[14] Reason remained an important value, but confidence in it had considerably diminished and it had certainly changed. Intellectuals viewed it more and more often as skeptical and empirical, not metaphysical and architectonic. The day of the "naive rationalist" was over.[15]

It was often difficult to tell how political intellectuals felt about this fact. Some clearly regretted the truth about reason's limitation, which they reported so often. But very frequently no regrets were expressed. On the contrary, it was clear that intellectuals such as Peter Gay were relieved to find further evidence that absolutist thinking in politics was worthless. They knew it was dangerous and they discovered it was rationally impossible. People might believe they had found political absolutes or ideologies, but they could not find them by reason. To be ideological was to ignore the epistemological boundaries of reason, another sign that true believers were irrational.

The Psychological Case against Absolutes

Another set of arguments many political intellectuals employed to assail absolutist political thinking was *psychological*. Intellectuals who liked this approach usually were concerned with the hold of myths and symbols on people. They consistently argued that absolutist political perspectives or ideologies were best understood as myths. They assumed that absolute justification had more to do with one's inner needs or the effectiveness of external manipulators than it did with the existence of truth. Thinkers such as Harold D. Lasswell and Murray Edelman continued the Freudian tradition of skepticism about absolutes. Like Freud, they believed that absolute value claims were best understood as rationalizations of human sentiment and behavior. They were acutely conscious of the human capacity for self-delusion and the human weakness for myths and illusions. But unlike Freud in his most optimistic view, they did not expect we would ever be free of rationalizations, although they hoped we would.[16] Their work and that of others took for granted that no rational person could seriously believe in any absolute ground of political value and certainly contributed to the widespread resistance to absolutes in America after the war.

Perhaps the two most prominent students of psychology who spoke to public concerns in the years after World War II were Erich Fromm and B.F. Skinner. Fromm maintained that people needed a set of values to operate in life, but he was openly scornful of any outlook that made absolute claims. Although he became increasingly interested in Marxism, Fromm consistently shied away from any version of Marxism that claimed absolute justification. He remained a Freudian in this regard, perceiving all claims to a higher truth as human rationalization. Skinner was even more unequivocal in dismissing ultimate truths. Although he was often characterized as a dogmatist, he viewed himself as a skeptical, rational scientist. He claimed that all beliefs about values were products of environmental determinism and had no connection whatsoever with alleged absolute truths. He was a last step in a process that began with Nietzsche and Freud, the psychological debunking of a realm of independent values and certain justifications.[17]

Amateur psychological analysis attracted other intellectuals. Richard Hofstadter, for example, frequently interpreted absolute claims and the political movements that accompanied them through a psychological lens. He did not find his observations reassuring and often complained of what he termed America's "periodical psychic sprees that purport to be moral crusades."[18] Judith Shklar was another intellectual who was fond of amateur psychological analysis, her particular interest being the myths she believed postwar political intellectuals had transcended.[19]

What Hofstadter and Shklar and many others rarely took into account were the findings of Adorno et al. in their monumental *The Authoritarian Personality* that psychological forces could work to make people view other systems or various absolutes as demons upon which they might vent deep-seated personal frustrations. Adorno and his associates noted in particular that many of his subjects tended to make Communists and Communism "a receptacle for all kinds of hostile projections, many of them on an infantile level somehow reminiscent of the presentation of evil forces in comic strips."[20] This suggests the problem with psychological explanations, their utility for those who sought to "explain" the error of absolutist thinking and their similar utility for those who might want to "explain" the campaign against absolutes.

Absolutes as Impractical

The taste for psychological analysis of absolutes was not nearly as popular, however, as the peculiarly American complaint that so filled the literature: the suggestion that true or not, absolutes simply were not practical and thus not worth anyone's time. Daniel Bell, ever the practical social scientist, was one of those most convinced of this weakness. The trouble with sweeping systems of absolute truth was that they did not help anyone engaged in practical politics. They simply failed on the empirical level, since they could not be specific about what to do, when to do it, and how to do it. They remained lost in abstractions. The history of socialism in America was a good illustration. According to Bell, American socialists had been dogmatic and absolutistic, so they naturally did not succeed in formulating any useful political program or in leaving themselves open to compromise. The inevitable result was that they failed to get anywhere: "Doctrine remained, but the movement failed."[21] David Riesman praised George Kennan and Reinhold Niebuhr because they were a very different breed. They were not trapped by absolutes and hence were not "unrealistic" thinkers. Instead they knew how to operate in the real world.[22] He might have cited Hans Morgenthau as another American thinker who advised that we should avoid impractical, ideological crusades and concentrate on the practical business of policy making in foreign affairs.[23]

The most complete marriage of philosophical and practical objections occurred in David Braybrooke and Charles Lindblom's *The Strategy of Decision*. They repeatedly criticized those who wanted to approach political decisions by using "rational deductive" models of values or objectives in day-to-day decision making. The reason they spurned these approaches had little to do with the usual postwar resistence to deduction, problems of verification, or the relationship between facts and values. They faulted them because they were simply "no help in the real world" of politics. To some people grand abstractions and affirmations might glitter in the sky, but meanwhile specific choices in the mundane world remained unmade. A better strategy was to recognize the hard decisions to be made and to concentrate on trying to obtain the practical information needed to illuminate decisions. This process was painfully costly enough. It was not aided by ringing enunciation of absolutes.[24]

The Absence of a Need for Absolute Justifications   One interesting feature of the broad intellectual revolt against absolutes in politics is the many routes by which so many political intellectuals proceeded to the same end. Some saw the problem as one of the futility of deduction, others the limits of reason, and still others the practical weaknesses of absolute values when one got down to concrete problems, but they all agreed on rejecting absolutes. This agreement suggests the pervasiveness of intellectuals' skepticism about absolute justifications in the two decades after World War II. A second feature, which is surely remarkable, is how rarely this skepticism about an ultimate ground for political values led to pessimism in the minds of postwar political intellectuals. The reason was the firm conviction of so many thinkers that there was no need for an absolute ground of justification. Absolutes could be and had to be abandoned, but this implied no crisis. Indeed, given the terrible evil that they had caused so often in human history, it was a finding made with very considerable enthusiasm and relief.

There were three explanations for the popular intellectual belief that absolutes were not needed. Two were practical and one was philosophical. They were that (a) the American consensus made absolutes unnecessary for the nation's political system, (b) America had met its problems without grand ideologies or "answers," and (c) no individual person really required any absolute, for there were other means to justify values without recourse to absolutes.

Consensus   The stress on the *consensus* supposed to exist among Americans on fundamental values was an important theme of political thought up to 1964. We will consider this theme in detail later. It is significant here because many political intellectuals drew the conclusion from the "fact" of consensus that there was no point to agonized worries about the absence of firm grounding for political values. Consensus provided a substitute for justification. This was not always the view of students of consensus such as Clinton Rossiter, Daniel Boorstin, Charles Frankel, Louis Hartz, and Richard Hofstadter, but it very often was.[25] Many of those who wrote most frequently of the American consensus and its role as a crucial and implicit substitute for formal justifications, were unclear who participated in the political consensus. Some thinkers included the general population of the United States; others, only intellectuals; still others, only political elites. There was little uniformity, only the constant invocation of "consensus" and the suggestion that it was a primary fact of American life for two decades after World War II. Who the exact groups in agreement were did need the careful formulation one so rarely got to test the truth of the multitude of consensus claims. This was especially true, because what fragmentary social science data appeared on the subject did not identify any sweeping patterns of consensus, at least among the population at large.[26] Moreover, definitions of the American consensus until the 1960s frequently ignored the voice of blacks, Chicanos, and the poor. They were rarely considered at all before 1960.

The main direction of postwar thought acknowledged and often applauded the use of consensus. Those who believed they were outsiders repeatedly confirmed the existence of a consensus and noted how it served many political intellectuals as a substitute for painful questions of justification of values. William F. Buckley, for instance, bitterly bemoaned the existence of a liberal ethos he claimed was totally in the saddle in the United States.[27] Herbert Marcuse's famous denunciation of the intellectual conformity and sterility of America in his *One Dimensional Man* (1964) was a classic expression of a similar analysis from the Left.[28]

Daniel Bell happily summed up the picture, which in his magisterial version went beyond American shores. "In the Western World, therefore, there is today a rough consensus among intellectuals on political issues; the acceptance of the Welfare State, the durability of decentralized power; a system of mixed economy

and of political pluralism. In this sense, too, the ideological age
has ended."[29]

Our Problems Were in Hand   We will devote the ninth chapter
to this central assumption of American political thought from 1945
to 1964 that our problems were in hand. But it is important to
remember here that the assumption of most American political
intellectuals was that change-oriented radicals, Nazis, Communists,
and McCarthyites propounded the ideologies and rigid, final
justifications in politics. They were not needed here in part because
there were no serious social, political, and economic difficulties
on which this radical disposition could feed. The major problems
in the United States were either solved or on the road to resolution.
This conviction is a most significant one for understanding postwar
American political thought. It was hardly universal. McCarthyism
and conformity worried some. Sputnik and the competitive quality
of American education worried others. The Bomb scared everyone.
After 1960 unease grew in the face of Martin Luther King's eloquent
appeals for blacks late in our period or Michael Harrington's
eventually influential book on poverty, *The Other America* (1962).
But generally there was a striking sense of happiness among intellectuals at the success of the American experiment after World
War II. Seymour Martin Lipset summed up the general view. There
was no need for ideology because "the fundamental problems of the
industrial revolution have been solved."[30]

   In retrospect, the period after World War II appears to have
been a relatively quiet time in American history. Certainly it was
quiet in terms of broad new governmental programs or popular
intellectual campaigns for action. It was an era between two
agendas, the past agenda of the New Deal and the agenda of the
middle and late 1960s, the War on Poverty and Lyndon Johnson's
other domestic programs. Although King and Harrington foreshadowed the new agenda, as did John Kenneth Galbraith earlier
in *The Affluent Society* (1958), they were not typical of their age,
nor even of the late 1950s and early 1960s. Kennedy liberalism
wanted to "get America moving again" but the actual agenda was
modest. It was logical that most political intellectuals approached
the 1964 election in that spirit as a fight between dangerous radicals

and a pragmatic liberalism that had our problems in hand.

As Individuals We Could Safely Avoid Absolutes Many intellectuals argued in a more philosophical vein, stressing the fact that none of us as individuals required absolute answers for politics nor any ideology to provide complete explanations. There were exceptions such as the natural-law school, which we will examine later. Much more typical were opinions such as Henry Mayo's Olympian disparagement of those who felt the need to engage in the "frenzied search" or Morton White's attack on Walter Lippmann because he "cannot bear the absence of a set of moral principles which are universally binding, certain, rationally established . . . ."[31]

Many liberals of the period prided themselves on being toughminded, an expression that had many meanings but certainly included a belief that one could go into politics without the crutch of absolute truth. Judith Shklar was an example. She had no respect for those who required "marketable ideologies for political movements and their leaders."[32] But she was moderate in her scorn compared with Daniel Boorstin. He affirmed what he felt was the American's special "genius," his toughminded ability to live without ideology and ultimate answers.[33]

Toughmindedness was not the only solution available to postwar intellectuals who believed people could escape ideology and absolutes. There was, in fact, considerable confidence that there were other satisfactory alternatives, such as rational discussion, existentialism, and pragmatism, which successfully skated between utter relativism and dreaded absolutism. We explore these alternatives in detail in chapters 4 and 5 because so much of postwar intellectual effort was expended on developing a middle way through the challenges posed by relativism and ideology. Many alternatives were found that encouraged the broad confidence that absolutes were not needed. They provided powerful support for intellectuals who felt they were able to declare their independence of ideology.

The overall impact of these forces was to create a bouyantly optimistic skepticism about absolutes. They were not a requisite for political thought in America. We did not need to worry. Con-

sequently, so many political intellectuals welcomed what they took
to be the "end of ideology" with the most expansive enthusiasm.
Daniel Bell's controversial essay on "the end of ideology" was
certainly the most famous expression of the mood. But to focus
exclusively on Bell is to miss how widely intellectuals shared the
sentiment that America, or the entire West, was entering into a
postideological era and then applauded this as a good development. Certainly Bell's vision was one of the most sanguine examples of a postwar mood that did not end until well into the
1960s. He maintained that the 1940s were a decisive moment, the
moment of "exhaustion of the nineteenth century ideologies,
particularly Marxism, as intellectual systems that could claim
truth for their views of the world."[34] With their demise came a
welcome "end to chiliastic hopes, to millenarianism, to apocalyptic
thinking . . . . For ideology, which was a road to action, has come
to a dead end."[35]

Henry David Aiken charged that what Bell and others had in
mind was a prophecy that was less general than it sounded. What
really delighted them was the decline of Marxism: "it is the end
of Marxism of which they mainly dream."[36] This was accurate for
Bell, who clearly showed that he was pleased about the "exhaustion
of socialist thought on the European continent and in England,"[37]
but it is too narrow a perspective for many others, who welcomed
the supposed end of all ideology in America and in the West.
Sidney Hook, for instance, went further. He was extremely pleased
that Marxism was no longer so attractive to American intellectuals,
but he believed that ideologies of all sorts were in decline and
looked to the day "when references to 'right,' 'left,' and 'center' will
vanish from common usage as meaningless."[38] Clinton Rossiter
applied the thesis to American conservatism. He claimed that
American conservatives were less and less likely to think in rigid
ideological terms.[39]

Sometimes political intellectuals were elated because they thought
a genuine dividing line had been crossed for all time. An example
was Lipset, who expected class conflicts to continue, but was
sure that the rise of the welfare state meant that ideologies were
a thing of the past. Lipset was careful to make clear that this applied
only in the West, since he recognized that the Third World would

continue to have "intense political controversy and ideology."[40] Other views, such as those of the social thinker Edward Shils, suggested less certainty that ideology in the West and America would remain absent for long. The decline of Marxism was the principal event of the current decline, and Shils welcomed it, but he had a prescient suspicion that the temptation to reach for absolute guides in politics would not go away so easily. He suspected that Americans should not "congratulate" themselves on the death of ideology just yet; it might be only a "subsidence."[41]

It was all very well for radicals in America to remark that all this enthusiasm for the death of absolute justifications and frameworks for politics worked, as Aiken put it, in "plain effect . . . to reinforce acceptance of our own institutional status quo," but such claims did not catch the disillusioned spirit of even those who opposed that status quo.[42] A good illustration may be found in C. Wright Mills, who acknowledged in *The Sociological Imagination* (1959) that the old frameworks were quite exhausted. They had failed as ways to understand change in the world.[43] Although Mills went too far in challenging the vitality of liberalism, intellectuals did agree in part; that is, many American political intellectuals did argue that parts of liberalism were in need of substantial revision, especially its democratic theory. Moreover, no matter how much one might bewail the effect of postwar reality, there was the question of whether one could go back to a more believing age. In the 1950s and the 1960s Judith Shklar reminded the Aikens of the liberal credo that there was no sense in "mourning the passing of the age of ideology." To do so was to ignore the reality of its passing, was to engage in "pure nostalgia."[44]

Conclusion

Our argument is that we must start on the road toward understanding American political thought from 1945 to 1964 by appreciating that the majority of intellectuals felt they were in a special situation. There were no longer any *Weltanshauungen* that had absolute justification in history or nature. Thinking people were now on their own. Ideologies and absolutes could be dissected by historical analysis; they could be dismissed as artifacts of psychological need; they could be vitiated by philosophical analysis. The procedure did not matter, and many theorists used more than one. But the conclusion was inevitable; the old nineteenth-century world of absolutes was gone, and it could not be resurrected. Intellectuals in America would have to proceed by other means, with other strategies. Political thinking would have to have other bases. This task was at the heart of political thought in America after the war.

But in what sense was the old certainty gone? This is in fact the crucial question, far more so than it seemed at the time. Was it gone in the sense that most intellectuals self-consciously considered themselves skeptical of absolute answers in politics? Was it gone in the sense that most intellectuals actually were as skeptical in their political thought and action as the skepticism they said they held should have led one to expect? Was it gone in the sense that American intellectual elites doubted America or even American liberal values to any noticeable extent? In general, political intellectuals in our two decades would have answered all these queries yes. Yet we cannot quite leave it at that. For we must come back to Louis Hartz and Reinhold Niebuhr. They were not exceptions in sharing the doubt that there were any adequate ideologies suitable for politics nor in sounding warnings about the dangers of true believers in political life, but they differed in their speculations about whether America and American thinkers were really so skeptical after all. American thinkers were skeptical of Marxism and a host of European ideologies, certainly, but were they skeptical of liberalism and liberal democratic values?

Why were American political thinkers so happy describing, but also promoting, the decline of absolutes? Why was the death of ideology such a blessed event? We know some of the reasons intellectuals of the period gave, from consensus to the availability of nonabsolutistic justifications for political values. But was there another reason they did not *always* perceive—were they really skeptical of their own ideal liberalism, or was it after all an ideology untroubled by skepticism? One step toward answering these questions proceeds along the track of postwar skepticism into another area inextricably linked to the loss of faith in ideology and ultimate justifications, the rejection of utopia.

THE CASE AGAINST UTOPIA

After 1945 utopian vision departed from American political thought on an irresistable wave of skepticism. The age was often identified by its leading intellectuals in terms that made this aspect of the skeptical mood the key one. Judith Shklar referred to the time as "After Utopia," Daniel Bell as "The Exhaustion of Utopia."[45] Such an analysis supported the general impression that the 1940s and 1950s in particular reflected what Philip Rahv called a "chastened mood" among American intellectuals. It was one Rahv felt was inevitably molded by the "exposure of the Soviet myth and the consequent resolve to be done with Utopian illusions and heady expectations."[46]

Perhaps the most obvious factor that influenced the resistance to radical change and utopian aspirations, of course, was the rejection of ideology. Its claims to certitude, its fanaticism, its murderous record in the hands of totalitarian European rulers produced few self-conscious ideologues and many self-conscious skeptics among American political intellectuals, as we know, with the result few thinkers claimed they had any utopian vision and few thought the costs of attempting to realize one worth it. In an age of value skepticism, utopian ideals are unlikely to flourish and clearly did not flourish after the war. It was generally taken for granted that Bell was right: "If the end of ideology has any meaning, it is to ask for the end of rhetoric, and rhetoricians of 'revolution.'"[47]

Although there was much consensus on the postutopian mood after 1945, there was nonetheless a good deal of nervous attention devoted to the subject of radical, utopian changes by political thinkers after 1945. Perhaps this was a matter of settling with the memories of the past in some cases, such as Bell's memories of his Marxism and its radical hopes. In other cases it reflected a sense that the world was hardly free of utopian impulses as yet. Some intellectuals suggested that "revolutionary millenarianism and mystical anarchism were with us still," and they did not expect that the search for utopia was likely to ever disappear as an aspect of the human condition.[48]

The appearance in the 1950s of the so-called *radical Right* in the United States, especially the controversial John Birch Society, as well as works by Ayn Rand, such as the dramatic and utopian *Atlas Shrugged*, suggested to many political intellectuals radical utopianism's staying powers in right-wing thought. This bothered many thinkers, as we know, and some of the most prominent intellectuals in America after 1945, including Daniel Bell, Seymour Lipset, and Richard Hofstadter, argued and wrote decrying the appearance of utopianism on the Right. The very term they coined for the movement, the "radical" Right, was an illustration of their inclination to treat intensely change-oriented groups, right or left, in a negative light. Radical came to denote something that was negative.[49]

Often the vision of utopia was a vision of antiutopia, of the possibilities of the emergence of profoundly evil societies. The enormous interest in the British antiutopias, Huxley's *Brave New World* and Orwell's *1984*, was evidence. So was the cold welcome given to B. F. Skinner's *Walden Two*. Irving Howe caught the spirit of the age when he wrote of *1984*: "In later generations *1984* may have little 'historic interest.' If the world of 1984 does not come to pass, people may well feel that the book was merely a symptom of private disturbance, a nightmare. But we know better: we know that the nightmare is ours."[50]

In any case arguments against utopian tendencies in politics abounded in American political thought from 1945 to 1964. They were part of the picture of skepticism and deserve our attention for this reason. Whether they also deserve our attention because they form part of a pattern that indicated a robust sense of identity or reconciliation, as Lionel Trilling described it, between American intellectuals and the world they knew at home is the controversial aspect of this issue. Was the attack on radical change and the utopian mood at its most basic level a statement of postwar American intellectuals' satisfaction with the status quo?

The Matter of Naivete'

The most frequent objection to utopian thinking about politics revolved around the naivete required to believe in utopias. Postwar intellectuals invariably made the point that to achieve an ideal society was far too demanding for any government, a criticism directed especially at utopias of the socialist Left. The realities of the modern world condemned governments to impotence if and when they sought to create social and political perfection. Reality doomed utopia, and it was only naive to think otherwise.

Liberal thinkers insisted that naivete must be set aside and reality embraced. There was no sense in people, as Arthur Schlesinger described them, who had the sad impression that "Dreams are better than facts."[51] The impressive feature of postwar liberalism to Schlesinger in 1956 was the fact that it "is realistic, even skeptical. Its objectives are limited. It is mistrustful of utopianism, perfectionism and maximalism."[52] He found these "facts" as convincing as ever in 1961: "The empiricism of the American party of Hope stands in sharp contrast to the millennialism which still inflames the ideologists," and he was proud that his political hero John F. Kennedy also had no patience with utopias.[53] Reinhold Niebuhr and David Truman had none either and they joined in the attack on the folly of chasing utopias. People had to learn that "visionary" proposals and dreaming impossible dreams did no good.[54] They were especially dangerous for democratic governmental systems, as Carl J. Friedrich warned, because they led people all too quickly to abandon democratic politics in a futile attempt to achieve perfection.[55] Absolute ideals were indeed "beyond the reach of democratic politics," as Henry Mayo characteristically warned, but they were also beyond any form of politics. Thus it was foolish to abandon the practical good of a democratic polity for the inevitable failure of radical hopes.[56]

The deeper question was: what was it that made so many intellectuals believe that it was beyond the powers of governments, or societies, to achieve one utopia or another? What were the bases of this "realistic" judgment? Political intellectuals offered a number of explanations, including the problems posed by modern social complexity, vast populations, and human diversity. But three explanations were most often cited: the lack of sufficient knowledge about processes of social change and how to direct them, the limitations of human nature-behavior, and the loss of confidence in human progress.

Many social scientists stressed how little information was available regarding the dynamics of social change and how little was ever likely to be available about the effects of changes until they had occurred. Robert Dahl was sensitive to these factors. Giovanni Sartori noted them. Braybrooke and Lindblom made a virtual fetish of them.[57] There was something more at work than the straightforward judgments of "practical" social scientists. There was a calculation of risk, to be sure, and an obvious antipathy to taking great chances. But there was also a reluctance to gamble for what sometimes seemed almost spiritual reasons. Daniel Bell ended one of his books with a quotation from Max Weber that seemed to sum up a common sentiment: "He who seeks the salvation of souls, his own as well as others should not seek it along the avenue of politics."[58] Postwar politics was to be a mundane affair, and American political intellectuals wanted it that way.

In the early 1960s, when many liberals were more eager for change than they had been since the Great Depression, there was no similar rise in support for radical change or ideal societies. Indeed, one of the lessons stressed by such political intellectuals as Arthur Schlesinger was the great difficulty in controlling government, managing bureaucracy, and directing even the most modest change. Necessary knowledge was often missing and too much policy went awry for unanticipated reasons. Social science skepticism about the problems of obtaining sufficient information to direct change seemed well-founded. The Bay of Pigs fiasco was not soon forgotten.[59]

The widespread skepticism between 1945 and 1964 regarding optimistic theories of human nature and human behavior provided another explanation for why intellectuals concluded that extensive changes, if possible at all, would not be easy. Thinker after thinker noted this impediment, and each invariably considered it decisive. Social scientists such as Hannah Arendt and Henry Mayo remarked on the bleak prospects for utopians posed by human nature. Arendt found the most remarkable aspect of the totalitarian movements to be their attempt to engineer a "transformation of human nature itself." It was something they could not, and did not, achieve, but the cost involved in seeking it stood for her as a permanent lesson in the dangers of trying.[60] Mayo's opinions reflected the commonplaces of social science thought of the age based on a vast literature on political psychology and voting behavior that foretold a tale of pessimism for the fate of utopian schemes.[61]

Schlesinger insisted that all utopias that were tried turned out to be "depressing," dreary failures caused by people who did not understand the difficulties human nature posed for realizing remarkable utopian visions.[62] Richard Hofstadter used his renowned analysis of the Populist reach for utopia in the 1880s and the 1890s in part for the same purpose. It was another effort within the historical mode to warn about the fallibilities of human nature and how much they stood in the way of utopians. Hofstadter found that the Populists were naive about themselves; they did not see that beneath their longing for a golden age lay the reality of a relentless pursuit of self-interest.[63] Irving Kristol was similarly concerned with the delusions of radicals of goodwill. He claimed to have learned from the shattering experiences of the 1930s and 1940s the pessimistic truth that the "horror that breathes into our faces is the realization that evil will come by doing good-not merely *intending* to do good, but *doing* it. That is the trap of social action that the movements of progress and enlightenment of the 19th and 20th centuries fell into."[64]

The general human-nature point was often made in theological and quasi-theological language. Glenn Tinder, for example, writing from an explicitly religious perspective concluded that politics simply could not create utopia, that given the weakness of human nature, above all human selfishness, utopia was not practically conceivable.[65] Of course, it was Reinhold Niebuhr who made the most famous argument of this cast. The "children of light," whether old-fashioned liberals or Marxists, simply did not have a "realistic" picture of the egoism of human nature. They did not perceive the glaring and permanent reality of sin which ordained that utopia was out of the question.[66]

This mode of criticism was a staple of conservative thinking after 1945 as it had been for centuries before. Conservatives insisted that modern liberals were in fact the main proponents of naive utopianism. William F. Buckley was particularly ascerbic in ridiculing liberal thinkers for their supposed belief that the "human being is perfectible . . . that the instrument . . . is reason; . . . that equality is desirable and attainable through the action of state power."[67] The complaints of Buckley and other conservatives about liberal utopianism were the counterpart of the establishment liberals' warning about the radical Right and its alleged utopian impulses. In truth, neither had much stomach for radical change and certainly not for leaps toward utopia. But that the intellectual atmosphere was filled with charges and countercharges of utopianism demonstrates very well the widespread mood that viewed utopianism as preposterous in the light of inflexible drawbacks imposed by human nature.

To chastened liberals such as Daniel Bell or Arthur Schlesinger the conservative suspicion of the dominant liberalism among postwar American intellectuals was puzzling, if not incredible. Certainly, this conservative reading of current intellectual opinion represented a serious confusion about reality. If many prewar liberals and radicals had ever believed in the radical perfectability of the individual, such opinions were rarely heard after 1945. Yet there was some insight in the conservative critique. There was none in their false attribution of absurd optimism about human nature to postwar liberal intellectuals, but conservative criticisms did serve as an important reminder that judgments about human nature and political change were very much a matter of degree. On the surface the theme of discouragement at human failure and sin appeared as often among the writings of Niebuhr and Schlesinger as it did in Buckley, but it is clear enough that Buckley was far more pessimistic, and his typically conservative resistance to any movement from the postwar situation in America was partly a statement of his pessimism. Skeptical liberals favored "realistic" change because they were not as pessimistic as conservatives like Russell Kirk and Buckley about human capacity for rationality and public concern. But both conservative and liberal intellectuals united in denouncing utopias for their alleged sin: they were formulated by thinkers sadly unrealistic about people.

Many intellectuals also assailed utopian thinking as naive because they thought it required confidence that inevitable moral progress lay ahead in the future. This frequent objection may seem strange in an era in which there was so much confidence in the United States and its future. How could one doubt the possibility that the human future might be enormously better and yet predict so much for America? The answer lay in the nature of intellectual expectations for America, which we explore in our ninth chapter. To a surprising degree, it is evident that many political intellectuals considered America to be in good shape, almost an example of utopia realized. Few thought any society would be likely to do better than America. Certainly hope in progress, however it was defined, was hardly gone in postwar political thought. The sun of progress hardly set, but there was no general assurance that progress would be automatic or even particularly likely in moral or political life.

Arthur Schlesinger was one of the most severe critics of the idea of automatic progress. This trust was no more than a "sentimental belief" that too many people had taken seriously. Such naivete had left people unready for the inexorable outbursts of evil in human history. He felt it had left many, including himself, quite unprepared in their own time for the appearance and impact of Nazism.[68] Many social scientists also insisted that it was far better to take a "realistic" attitude about progress. Over and over they suggested that there was no longer any point in expecting the ideal and that it made no sense for anyone to "long for some . . . future golden age of perfect harmony."[69] Hannah Arendt did not think that progress guaranteed utopia either. But she worried about her study of totalitarianism, which convinced her that "modern masses . . . are attracted by every effort which seems to promise a man-made fabrication of the paradise they had longed for."[70] Totalitarian elites had encouraged this belief in radical progress. Although these leaders did not actually believe all the propaganda they spewed forth, they did hold the incredibly dangerous notion that "human omnipotence" was a potential reality and thus "everything is possible."[71] Some detected the same fallacy in the approach to foreign affairs of many optimistic liberals. "The projected crusades of the liberals, as of . . . the Communists, must, if implemented, lead to unlimited war for unlimited ends. They may lead to perpetual war for perpetual peace."[72]

The problem was, Daniel Boorstin said, that too many thinkers had never understood the nature of America. They had wanted dramatic changes and an ideal society, but they had not realized the nature of social order, especially in the United States. Instead of manipulable units, there was the complexity of pluralist inter-actions. Instead of an unplowed field ready for utopians, there was a pattern of "seamlessness" that could not be easily altered or redirected. Although he knew that America had its share of utop-ians who wanted to prove him wrong, he took pride in the fact that so far the historical and social fabric of the United States had repulsed them and we had been spared the ravages of men with blueprints.[73] Clinton Rossiter was very much in accord with Boorstin. The American tradition was stronger than the lure of utopia. We had not been bewitched by any "will-o'-the wisp" like Marxism. We maintained a hard reality and forsook the sad "messianic complex" that so permeated Marxism.[74]

A Politician's Reality

Most intellectuals did continue to aspire to incremental progress; this was not, in their minds, naivete. Nor did their perspective on human nature and behavior lead them into the misanthropy that motivated the despotic haters of mankind whom Niebuhr called "the children of darkness." Nor, finally, did their reservations about the limits of human reason and the reality of unexpected consequences lead them away from the pursuit of greater under-standing and expanded control. What was in question was not the surrender of the radical hope of Marxism and classic liberalism to a philosophy of pessimism. There were aspects of the modern situation and the American scene that disturbed them, as we know, but the general mood was scarcely one of alienation. It has been argued that much postwar fiction suggests that literary intellectuals left "the frontiers of social revolution, or even social meliorism" and tended to be content with a rejection of "public experience," which indicated "the full face of the writer's alienation from his society."[75] Certainly there were some signs of alienation in literary circles such as a willingness to entertain the idea that society was always the enemy.[76] But there is no particular reason to link sig-nificant postwar writers such as Faulkner, Capote, or O'Hara with a mood of alienation, nor were most political intellectuals inclined in this direction. It does not follow that one is alienated if one is not devoted to social revolution. On the contrary, it seems more plausible to suggest that advocacy of revolution constitutes a much better test of alienation. The same applies to withdrawing from interest in social meliorism. It does not prove that one is alienated from society. It may as easily be considered a statement of confidence in the ongoing order. Certainly the "alienated" verses of the Beat poets and the "alienated" posturings of James Dean were part of the era. Yet the overwhelming fact remains that political intellectuals in America from 1945 to 1964 were neither pessimistic nor alienated. What they contended was at issue was the degree of hope and the need to tone down expectations that no longer accorded with human behavior and historical experience. They insisted that the answer was not cynicism, but neither was it naivete; it was not resignation to events, but neither was it a rush toward utopia.

Lionel Trilling perfectly expressed this balance in his sensitive *The Liberal Imagination.* Trilling argued that there was still room and there had to be room for creative imagination in politics as in all aspects of the human drama. He was, in fact, an eloquent spokesman for the view that America needed to encourage imagination. But Trilling also thought that he could understand the general disinclination of intellectuals to look away from present America toward some future utopia. He appreciated all that had taken place in the world in recent decades, terrors that had often been inflicted by a search for the perfect society, despite the sober fact that "all movements fail." He was a warm admirer of Sigmund Freud, for his belief in human possibility, but also for his acute sense of human weakness. He saluted Henry James for his perceptive early glimpse into the horrors that lay ahead for the human species in the midtwentieth century.[77]

Richard Hofstadter put it another way when he wrote of the Populists in a rare moment of identification with them: "We may well sympathize with the Populists and with those who have shared their need to believe that somewhere in the American past there was a golden age . . . . But actually to live in that world, actually to enjoy its cherished promise and its imagined innocence is no longer within our power."[78] Hofstadter, like Trilling, was not without his regrets, but did not see how anyone could find it reasonable to believe any longer in the realization of utopias past or present. His conclusion was only another expression of the determination Peter Gay described as Voltaire's, to avoid "a poet's Utopia" and select "a politician's reality."[79] For historian Gay as for most intellectuals after the war, there was no other possibility. In Gay's view, the contemporary West was like the Enlightenment. Both demanded "toughminded" intellectuals who knew that the times required not merely the rejection of utopia but even the pursuit of a "campaign against Utopianism."[80]

The Great Danger of Utopianism

Human behavior, history, the limits of human knowledge, the relative impotence of government—all of them stood inflexibly in the way of radical aspirations. This argument, in its multiple forms, was the characteristic approach for intellectuals in America after World War II. It was a rather curious argument, because it was an attempt to defeat the claims of utopians or radicals without ever facing the normative issues they inevitably raised. Because utopians held faulty conceptions of human behavior or the nature of progress, it was common to conclude that their normative ideas did not merit much examination. The advantages of this approach are obvious enough. Normative arguments in politics do not promise the consensus many think an empirical approach can produce. What is intriguing is not only the choice of a strategy of "realism," but also the evidence of political intellectuals' *affection* for it. This was no last-ditch strategy, but one employed with considerable confidence and comfort. Many intellectuals obviously felt it was natural, as if it were logical and obvious that the empirical world they experienced—America after World War II—was an appropriate perspective from which to judge the worlds of human aspiration.

It is true that the critique of utopia for its empirical naivete was not the sole basis for objections to radical visions by political intellectuals from 1945 to 1964. Yet it was the major part of the explicit argument, indeed by far the greatest part. This is suggested by the fact that few thinkers expressed any regret about the empirical inadequacy of one or another utopian hope. We may safely say that although American political intellectuals usually attacked utopianism for its naivete, their skepticism was complemented by a disinterest in radical change. The failure of most intellectuals to seek to evade their "realism" suggests that it was not their findings about man or progress that ultimately determined their reaction to proposals for major change. This may have been the grounds of argument, but it was not the whole story. There were other bases for opposition, and they were normative.

These grounds did not usually emerge clearly in argumentation over utopias or radical change and they were certainly more developed, as we will see, in other contexts. But there were at least a few hints, a few suggestions of the deeper level of resistance or, rather, disinterest. Some thinkers made a normative case against radical changes, albeit in an indirect manner. The ordinary argument stressed the dangers of utopianism. Sometimes these dangers referred to the costs of human life, with the totalitarian experiences as an immediate backdrop. More often it was much harder to find a specific discussion of exactly what these dangers were. A reading of Reinhold Niebuhr who frequently emphasized them when he reflected on Marxism or modern liberalism, or Seymour Martin Lipset who did as well, suggests the answer. What many political intellectuals had in mind were dangers to the present social and political order, to stability and the ongoing American equilibrium.[81] To comprehend the skepticism about radical change that dominated American political thinking after World War II, one has to understand the freedom American intellectuals had from any sense of desperation. The acceptability of America was the unmistakable assumption shaping their view of the world. It was the normative assumption on which all utopianism floundered.

Conclusion

These intimations of a quite different argument against radical change did not, we know, dominate the discussion of utopianism, because political thinking after 1945, and political events too, did not force it to the level of public debate. There were few theorists indeed who had utopias in mind. Erich Fromm and Herbert Marcuse and men like them were clearly and decisively isolated.

Occasionally there was an outburst from an angry intellectual like Dwight MacDonald who went on proclaiming anarchism.[82] There were those like Norman Mailer who did not appreciate what they took to be a slavish intellectual obescience to the "American Century."[83] There were those who uttered vague statements praising the ongoing necessity of the utopian mind. David Riesman was one and Daniel Bell was another, although Bell wanted his utopian ideas somehow kept free from ideology.[84] But to more committed radicals like Henry David Aiken, the protestations of Bell and others did not ring true. Bell was obviously not attracted to the utopian side of human experience and his conservatism made this painfully apparent. Occasionally a former radical like Bell might sound the old themes, but the vision and the energy were, in fact, gone.[85]

Aiken's analysis may well have been rather preemptory, but he was not fundamentally wrong, and virtually no one pretended that he was. But that was not the issue. What mattered finally was the conception of liberalism and the liberal politics that one held. Schlesinger spoke for his generation of intellectuals when he remarked that to him liberalism was "a practical program to be put into effect" not a field for "the sentimentalists, the utopians, the wailers."[86] His message to Americans was straightforward: "We must grow up now and forsake the millennial dream."[87] American intellectuals from 1945 to 1964 did not ignore his advice.

NOTES*

1. Edward Purcell, *The Crisis of Democratic Theory* (Lexington: University of Kentucky, 1973), p. 11.

2. Robert Dahl, *A Preface to Democratic Theory* (Chicago: University of Chicago Press, 1956), ch. 1 and p. 45.

3. Giovanni Sartori, *Democratic Theory* (New York: Praeger, 1967–1962), pp. 166 and 219.

* Some books listed here have two dates: the first is the date of the edition referenced here; the second is the date the work was originally published.

4. Sidney Hook, *Political Power and Personal Freedom* (New York: Criterion, 1959), p. 27.

5. James W. Smith, *Theme for Reason* (Princeton: Princeton University Press, 1957), p. 35.

6. T.D. Weldon, *The Vocabulary of Politics* (Baltimore: Penguin, 1953), pp. 30-33, passim.

7. Thomas L. Thorson, *The Logic of Democracy* (New York: Holt, Rinehart and Winston, 1962).

8. Smith, *Theme*, p. 110.

9. Chester Eisinger, *Fiction of the Forties* (Chicago: University of Chicago Press, 1963), p. 118.

10. Charles Frankel, *The Case For Modern Man* (New York: Harper, 1956-1955), p. 77.

11. Judith Shklar, *After Utopia* (Princeton: Princeton University Press, 1957), pp. viii and ix.

12. Thorson, *Logic*, pp. 133 and 138.

13. See, for example, Anthony Downs, *An Economic Theory of Democracy* (New York: Harper & Row, 1957); David Halberstam, *The Best and the Brightest* (New York: Random House, 1972).

14. See, for example, Richard Hofstadter, *Anti-Intellectualism in American Life* (New York: Knopf, 1963).

15. Peter Gay, *Voltaire's Politics* (New York: Vintage, 1965-1959), p. 26; Gay, *The Enlightenment*, vol. I (New York: Vintage, 1968-1966), pp. ix and 141; Gay, *Party of Humanity* (New York: Knopf, 1964), ch. 4.

16. Murray Edelman, *The Symoblic Uses of Politics* (Urbana: University of Illinois Press, 1964), p. 62; Harold Lasswell, *The Political Writings of Harold Lasswell* (New York: Free Press, 1951).

17. Erich Fromm, *The Sane Society* (New York: Fawcett, 1967-1955); also see his earlier *Escape From Freedom* (New York: Holt, Rinehart and Winston, 1941); B.F. Skinner, *Walden Two* (New York: Macmillan, 1962-1949).

18. Richard Hofstadter, *The Age of Reform* (New York: Vintage, 1962-1955), p. 17.

19. Judith Shklar, "Facing Up to Intellectual Pluralism," in *Political Theory and Social Change*, ed. David Spitz (New York: Atherton, 1967), pp. 275-78, 285-86, and 288; although this article best expresses her view and comes after 1964, her earlier works, such as *Legalism* (1964), agree.

20. Theodor Adorno et al., *The Authoritarian Personality* (New York: Harper & Row, 1950), p. 723.

21. Daniel Bell, *The End of Ideology* (New York: Collier's, 1962-1961), pp. 278-79 and 298.

22. David Riesman et al., *The Lonely Crowd* (New Haven: Yale University Press, 1961-1950), p. xxxiii.

23. Hans J. Morgenthau, *Politics Among Nations* (New York: Knopf, 1960-1948), pp. 561-63.

24. David Braybrooke and Charles Lindblom, *A Strategy of Decision* (New York:

Free Press, 1970–1963), chs. 3 and 16.

25. Frankel, *The Case for Modern Man*, ch. 4; Daniel Boorstin, *The Genius of American Politics* (Chicago: University of Chicago Press, 1953); Louis Hartz, *The Liberal Tradition in America* (New York: Harcourt, Brace and World, 1955); Richard Hofstadter, *The American Political Tradition* (New York: Vintage, 1959–1948); Reinhold Niebuhr, *The Irony of American History* (New York: Scribner's, 1952).

26. For example, Samuel Stouffer, *Communism, Conformity, and Civil Liberties* (Gloucester, Mass.: Peter Smith, 1963–1955); Herbert McCloskey et al., "Issue Conflict and Consensus Among Party Leaders and Followers," *American Political Science Review* 54 (1960).

27. William F. Buckley, Jr., *Up from Liberalism* (New York: Hillman, 1961), p. 16.

28. Herbert Marcuse, *One-Dimensional Man* (Boston: Beacon, 1964).

29. Bell, *Ideology*, p. 402.

30. Seymour Martin Lipset, *Political Man* (Garden City, N.Y.: Doubleday-Anchor, 1963–1960), p. 442.

31. Henry Mayo, *An Introduction to Democratic Theory* (New York: Oxford University Press, 1960), p. 309; Morton White, *Social Thought in America* (Boston: Beacon, 1957–1947), p. 265.

32. Shklar, "Facing Up," pp. 273, 285, and 288.

33. Boorstin, *The Genius*.

34. Bell, *Ideology*, p. 16.

35. Ibid., p. 393.

36. Henry David Aiken, "The Revolt Against Ideology" ')1964), in *Ideology, Politics, and Political Theory*, ed. Richard Cox, (Belmont, Calif.: Wadsworth, 1969), p. 140.

37. Bell, *Ideology*, p. 259.

38. Sidney Hook, quoted in Christopher Lasch, *The Agony of the American Left* (New York: Vintage, 1969), p. 64; Hook, *Political Power*, part III.

39. Clinton Rossiter, *Conservatism in America* (New York: Vintage, 1962–1955), p. 208.

40. Lipset, *Political Man*, pp. 443–45.

41. Edward Shils, "Ideology and Civility" (1958), in Cox, ed., *Ideology*, pp. 220 and 235–36.

42. Aiken, "The Revolt," in Cox, ed., *Ideology*, p. 148.

43. C. Wright Mills, *The Sociological Imagination* (New York: Oxford University Press, 1959), p. 166.

44. Shklar, "Facing Up," p. 293.

45. Shklar, *After Utopia*; Bell, *Ideology*, p. 273.

46. Philip Rahv, *Partisan Review* 19 (May–June 1952): 304.

47. Bell, *Ideology*, p. 406.

48. See, for example, the widely read, Norman Cohen, *The Pursuit of the Millenium* (London: Temple Smith, 1970–1957), p. 286.

49. Daniel Bell, ed., *The Radical Right* (Garden City, N.Y.: Doubleday-Anchor, 1964–1963), passim.

50. Irving Howe, *Politics and the Novel* (New York: Meridian, 1957), p. 251.

51. Arthur Schlesinger, Jr., *The Vital Center* (London: Andre Deutsch, 1970–1949), p. 45.

52. Arthur Schlesinger, Jr., "Liberalism in America: A Note for Europeans" (1956), in *The Politics of Hope* (Boston: Houghton Mifflin, 1962), p. 70.

53. Schlesinger, *Hope*, p. xi.

54. David Truman, *The Governmental Process* (New York: Knopf, 1960–1950), p. 530; Reinhold Niebuhr, *The Children of Light and the Children of Darkness* (New York: Scribner's, 1944), ch. 1.

55. Carl J. Friedrich, *The New Image of the Common Man* (Boston: Beacon, 1950).

56. Mayo, *An Introduction*, p. 229.

57. Giovanni Sartori, *Democratic Theory* (New York: Praeger, 1967–1962); Robert Dahl and Charles Lindblom, *Politics, Economics, and Welfare* (New York: Harper & Row, 1963–1953); Braybrooke and Lindblom, *Strategy*, pp. 66–67.

58. Daniel Bell, *Marxian Socialism in the United States* (Princeton: Princeton University Press, 1967–1952), p. 193.

59. Arthur Schlesinger, Jr. *A Thousand Days* (New York: Fawcett, 1967–1965).

60. Hannah Arendt, *The Origins of Totalitarianism* (New York: Meridian, 1958–1951), p. 458.

61. Mayo, *An Introduction*, p. 123.

62. Schlesinger, "The New Mood in Politics" (1960), in *Hope*, p. 356.

63. Richard Hofstadter, *The Age of Reform* (New York: Vintage, 1962–1955).

64. Irving Kristol, "How Basic is Basic Judaism?" *Commentary*, January 1948, p. 33.

65. Glenn Tinder, *The Crisis of Political Imagination* (New York: Scribner's, 1964–1950), ch. 16.

66. Niebuhr, *Children of Light*, ch. 1 and p. 118.

67. Buckley, *Liberalism*, p. 23.

68. Schlesinger, *Vital Center*, pp. 38–40.

69. David Spitz, *Democracy and the Challenge of Power* (New York: Columbia University Press, 1958), p. 9; Truman, *Governmental Process*, p. 503.

70. Arendt, *Origins*, p. 446.

71. Ibid., p. 387.

72. Kenneth Waltz, *Man, the State and War* (New York: Columbia University Press, 1965–1954), p. 113.

73. Boorstin, *The Genius*, pp. 6, 7, and 3.

74. Clinton Rossiter, *Marxism: The View from America* (New York: Harcourt Brace and World, 1960), pp. 7 and 231.

75. Eisinger, *Fiction*, p. 19.

76. Ronald Berman, *America in the Sixties: An Intellectual History* (New York: Free Press, 1968), pp. 228–45.

77. Lionel Trilling, *The Liberal Imagination* (New York: Viking, 1950), pp. 60 and 193; Lionel Trilling, *Partisan Review*, May–June 1952, p. 318.

78. Hofstadter, *Reform*, p. 328.

79. Gay, *Voltaire's Politics*, p. 42.

80. Gay, *Enlightenment*, pp. 28 and 69.

81. Niebuhr, *Children of Light*, ch. 1; Seymour Martin Lipset, "Some Social Requisites of Democracy: Economic Development and Political Legitimacy," *American Political Science Review* 53 (March 1959).

82. Dwight MacDonald, *Partisan Review*, May–June 1950, p. 479.

83. Norman Mailer, *Partisan Review* 19 (May–June 1952): 298–99.

84. Riesman, *Lonely Crowd*, ch. 16; Bell, *Ideology*, p. 405.

85. Aiken, "The Revolt," p. 147.

86. Schlesinger, *Vital Center*, p. 159.

87. Ibid., p. 254.

3 The Revival of Natural Law

Although most American political intellectuals found themselves facing the problem of how to find a justification in politics within the new skeptical world, this was not the only path they followed. Relativism, "good reasons," and the "logic of democracy" were characteristic rather than exclusive solutions. There was a distinct undertone of sympathy with quite another path, the *revival of the absolutes of natural law.* Its proponents contended that the crisis of political justification could be resolved by recognizing that there was, in fact, no crisis, that all along there continued to exist natural standards for life and politics rooted in the eternities of the universe. If there seemed to be a crisis, this was only because so many intellectuals were so obviously lost, but the truth was not.

In the years after 1945 advocates of natural law made a determined fight to restimulate interest in natural law, arguing that never before did American intellectuals so need to appreciate the absolute ground of values. In the end as at the beginning of our period from 1945 to 1964, they were a distinct minority, but it would be a partial interpretation of postwar intellectual thought that did not acknowledge the vigorous role this convinced minority played. They were the alternative.

Walter Lippmann is a good illustration of a natural-law advocate. His intellectual contributions stretched over many decades and took many forms, but after World War II he adopted a natural-law stance. He presented it most coherently in his book *Essays in the Public Philosophy,* but his newspaper columns sometimes were a vehicle for similar views and the serenity that flowed from his natural-law principles. Lippmann maintained American society had to have—and fortunately did have—higher standards to follow than any that could be swayed by the winds of change and corrupted by the undependable and irrational masses. He did not often elucidate what he took to be the content of natural law beyond brief references to reason, tradition, and civility, but this was not Lippmann's purpose. He was determined to resuscitate the natural-law perspective. He appeared to be less interested in articulating a particular substantive content of natural law. He was optimistic about the chances that intelligent men would understand natural law's importance for an enduring America, but only if natural law rather than the foolish and faddish masses ruled.[1]

By the late 1930s a number of American intellectuals had begun a campaign to gain support for the view that American liberal democracy required natural law to sustain itself in a world increasingly filled with absolutes and ideologues. There is no doubt that this disposition had a good many advocates during World War II.[2] It might seem strange that this movement went on after the war, given the general revulsion against ideology, but it is not so peculiar once it is understood that the enthusiasts of natural law were always at pains to draw a hard distinction between natural law and the ideology they hated. They saw no connection between the two. Ideology focused on vulgar "truths" that were false. It pandered to the confusions of the mass culture and mass taste. It renounced reason in fact and often in theory. It lusted after action, frequently any action. Natural law, on the other hand, concerned the evocation of timeless principles. It did not respect popular whims, emotional fads, the temporary exigencies of "action" or anything else but eternal truths.[3]

This dichotomy was, to say the least, suspicious to more skeptical intellectuals. No matter how much Arthur Schlesinger, for example, admired Walter Lippmann he could not swallow Lippmann's leap to natural law. It was another version of the discredited affection for absolutes.[4] Others denied the dichotomy, too, and contended that from a sociology of knowledge perspective natural law was no more than a "covertly" constructed reification of personal needs and idealized traditions. Some asserted that as a justification it was unneeded as well as "trivial, for the 'basis' can be nothing other than a statement of the values themselves transposed into a metaphysical key."[5] More hostile critics recalled recent European history, suggesting that "the appeal to natural law . . . may involve both an invitation to mutual slaughter and a denial of democracy."[6]

The attempt to revive natural law was closely connected with the oft-discussed religious revival among intellectuals in the 1950s. During this time some thinkers were frankly religious in their orientation toward politics. Reinhold Niebuhr was one of the greatest political theorists of the age. Paul Tillich spoke to intellectuals in the language of Christian existentialism, of the "courage to be." Jacques Maritain, the French Catholic, had many admirers who agreed with him that much that was disappointing or discouraging in the world could be explained by human abandonment of divine transcendence. "After having put God aside in order to become self-sufficient man loses his soul; he seeks himself in vain. . . . He finds only masks, and behind those masks, only death. And then there follows the spectacle we are now witnessing, the *irrationalist* tidal wave."[7] There was even renewed interest in America's most famous religious people, the Puritans, who in the minds of historians such as Perry Miller and Samuel Eliot Morison suggested how attractive life was to those who were able to combine religious faith and intellectual commitment. There even appeared a survey or two of American political thought that at last acknowledged the enormous role religious ideas had played in American intellectual history.[8]

The emergence in the 1950s and 1960s of the movement for black civil rights was the most obvious evidence of currents of religiously based natural law entering into mainstream American intellectual life. There is little doubt that until the middle 1960s the black expression of the civil rights cause spoke in a Christian idiom. It was firm in its adherence to the authority of Christian natural law and deeply attached to charismatic Christian leaders who spoke confidently in terms of natural law. Of course, Martin Luther King was the central activist and the central intellectual figure. In his many writings and statements, perhaps especially his "Letter from a Birmingham Jail," he enunciated the view that God's sovereign laws must rule us and he declared that they utterly condemned racial segregation and discrimination just as they commanded nonviolent action and passive disobedience as the fitting means of change. King's significance in our context lay not only in his free use of natural-law argument, but also in his unself-conscious use of it. It was a medium that was second nature to him and to many other blacks who joined the cause.[9]

This fact about King and the black movement until the mid-1960s was always somewhat anomalous in the postwar, largely white, intellectual world. King probably had as much impact on American life as any man of his age, but his natural-law doctrines were uncomfortably Christian and absolutistic to many of his white (and, eventually, black) intellectual allies. There was something decidedly unskeptical and old-fashioned about King's approach for many of his intellectual supporters, which may have inspired respect, but not assent.[10] He tested and showed the sharp limits, which were evident even in the 1950s, of intellectual interest in religion and natural law as a basis for approaching politics.

Although in the 1950s figures poured in proving that church attendance was rising in the United States, and although some thinkers who spoke in the religious metaphor were quite fashionable, it is clear that most political intellectuals did not become interested in the revival of natural law. For every William Barrett, who was willing to admit that he had worked his way to a private religion, there were several Irving Howes and Dwight MacDonalds who, however much they were disgusted at the alternatives existent in the "horrors of Soviet Communism or the dull mediocrity of the Attlee and Truman governments," did not wish to make any leap to the reassurance of transcendent natural law or divine law.[11] Nor was there much indication that the majority of social science-oriented intellectuals found the revival of religion of any value to them in their work. The same story could be found in literature. There were novelists like William Faulkner who perceived the contemporary condition of acute spiritual impoverishment, but the fiction of the era revealed no major return to religion or religious-based natural law.[12]

Paul Kecskemeti got closest to the truth when he observed of the early postwar period that there was much "longing" for religion among intellectuals.[13] Certainly there was evidence of troubled minds among American thinkers as they thrashed their way to a personal and political stance in those uncertain days. We know that well, but it was quite another thing to choose the road to religion and natural law. Only a minority made that choice. When Arthur Schlesinger said, "The current American religious revival has everything except religion," he was right for most political intellectuals.[14]

SOME REPRESENTATIVE VOICES

Examining some representative expressions may be helpful for understanding the revival of natural law. Some views were frankly religious in origin. Consider political scientist John Hallowell of Duke, who was significantly isolated from most trends of modern social science in the United States. Hallowell demanded that social science devote itself to a search for eternal Christian principles for politics. Social science should not proceed in bewildered relativism, nor hold tightly to the new gospel of empirical theory. It must concern itself with "the eternal good and the ultimate truth."[15] It was a terrible error to believe that good government and the proper guidance for a polity were a matter open for every individual whim. There were eternal norms and only fools would not grasp onto them.[16]

Hallowell did not wrap his message in existential terms. He was frankly Christian in spirit and terminology. The task was obviously too urgent for him to try to speak in terms congenial to the age, and consequently he did not bother.

> Only if we are concerned about salvation of our souls shall we be of much use in saving the world, only if our eyes are focused on the Kingdom of God shall we see with clear vision what needs to be done here and now, only if we surrender our wills, as completely as men can, will we be enabled by the power of God to make the self-sacrifices which the salvation of the world demands—in short only by aiming above the world shall we succeed in mastering the world.[17]

Compared to Hallowell, Reinhold Niebuhr and Jacques Maritain were almost timid in their Christian language, at least in the sense that they made an effort to speak to the "realistic" and "skeptical" mood of the postwar United States. Yet they employed religiously grounded natural law to the same end. They wanted Christian democracy, to be sure, and they did not pretend it flowered in all its perfection in the United States, but they were convinced like Hallowell that American liberal democracy, on balance, had generous justification in natural law. Maritain was sure that the "more the body politic [is] imbued with Christian convictions and aware of the religious faith which inspires it, the more deeply it would adhere to the secular faith" of democracy.[18] Christian democracy for Maritain looked very much like the American political ethos. It was replete with the old faith in natural rights. Maritain even uncovered a natural right to welfare liberalism without a hint about where Western consciousness had been for the centuries when it did not include either democracy or welfare liberalism as part of God's will.[19]

Perhaps the most formidable of all the political thinkers who employed Christian language in defending natural law was Eric Voegelin. His intellectual difficulty and forbiddingly dense style did not, however, prevent him from reaching the audience that was disposed to respond to his argument. Although his terms were often unfamiliar to the modern ear and Voegelin's classical and Christian learning was intimidating, his message was one many postwar natural lawyers respected.

As Voegelin saw it, the world was sadly corrupted by "gnosticism" and it could not escape from this condition. The contemporary world, indeed, seemed to be more and more overwhelmed by "gnosticism." *Gnosticism* was a word with considerable resonance for Voegelin but not one easily defined. The reference was specifically drawn from religious impulses in the early Christian period that appeared both among Christians and in self-conscious opposition to them. Gnostics then and now might be best described, Voegelin thought, as people who believed in "self-salvation." In the post-World War II world this meant people who no longer acknowledged their dependance on God and the higher law, but instead sought to discover principles of politics and justifications for them from within themselves or from their immediate environment. Looking at American political intellectuals from the perspective of Voegelin, there was no doubt whatsoever of their "gnosticism." A limited natural-law revival did not alter the mainstream.[20]

Voegelin agreed with most of those intellectuals attracted to natural law in denying the claims to skepticism made by most American intellectuals. These pretensions were no more than a mask by which intellectuals hid from themselves their ideological loyalty to idealistic liberalism. Liberal intellectuals were gnostics and true believers at the same time. This position was possible because of the special nature of liberal values. These liberal intellectuals made the major truth the importance of the individual and his capacity to self-direct and self-govern. They made an absolute out of "self-salvation." The fallacy here, Voegelin asserted, was that this was a false faith and, ominously, one that could end in "destructions." Voegelin like other natural-law thinkers was firmly convinced that the outbreak of European totalitarianism was a sign of the results of gnosticism. He also insisted on what was perhaps the most controversial dogma of the natural-law revival and certainly the one most infuriating to many liberal intellectuals, that liberalism and totalitarianism were hardly the diametrically opposed opposites that skeptical liberals thought they were. On the contrary, Voegelin thought the true opposition lay between those committed to religious natural law and gnostics like liberals and totalitarians, who shared in common the heresy of belief that human action could make or remake truth and the world.[21]

Although historians were a significant part of the intellectual environment in America in the two decades after World War II and they contributed to the emphasis on American history and recent European history, which was one factor in molding the general intellectual milieu, the postwar era was perhaps more an age of social science than history. Certainly it was not a time when there was much sign of a historical consciousness that went back more than a few hundred years at best. Here again natural-law theorists like Voegelin were exceptions. This could be observed in Voegelin's time frame for explaining how modern gnosticism had emerged. He did not propose that it was an artifact of the years after 1945 or even 1918. He suggested that we could go all the way back to the ninth century to uncover the first elements of gnosticism as they began to creep into Western intellectual life. The modern-day fall had long been in preparation. Voegelin's points of historical contrast were two. Like so many natural lawyers of the years after World War II, he looked fondly to both the classical world of Plato and Aristotle and early Christianity. Here were ages in human experience in which divine and natural truths were discovered and then believed, ages in which gnosticism was recognized for the heresy he felt it was.[22]

Voegelin repudiated modern social science as a sorry contrast, a study in gnostic failure. Modern social science had lost touch with the ancient scientific mission: discovering the first principles of natural law for social and political life. It had enshrined fact gathering and empiricism instead of a decent regard for higher law. It had lost respect for ethical concerns and cared little about genuinely theoretical enterprises. Its adherence to a fact-value dichotomy and commitment to creating a value-free social science were its ultimate confessions of lost direction and purposeless gnosticism. What did the attraction of most modern intellectuals for social science rather than natural law have to show for itself? At best, the fashion had produced a massive "accumulation of irrelevant facts" and "trivialities," and at worst it promised totalitarianism. Voegelin did not grant that there was any particular basis for hope in the short run. Like other natural lawyers he viewed the Anglo-American world as the least destroyed so far by "Gnostic corruptions," but he was hardly sanguine about its immediate future: its "fate is in the balance."

In the long run, though, Voegelin was far more hopeful. He remained confident that truth could not be defeated forever. The follies of modern intellectuals would be overcome. "Human nature does not change" and the truths of classical philosophy and the Christian religion would break free of their current repression.[23]

This hidden hope as well as Voegelin's guarded support for the Anglo-American political and social order may seem surprising in light of his historical perspective and absolutist outlook. But they were quite common among natural lawyers of the period and formed a crucial link between their natural-law perspectives and the "skeptical" liberals in "the American Century." Voegelin may not have liked, trusted, or respected American liberals, but he did not really dissent from their conviction that America was special and very much worth defending.[24]

THE STRAUSSIANS

Another principal expression of the natural-law movement grew up around Leo Strauss, a political philosopher at the University of

Chicago. More than any other single political thinker, Strauss symbolized the case for the revival of natural law and he gathered a good many disciples around him. Although the so-called *Straussians* by no means mechanically followed Strauss, they were undoubtedly and often proudly his pupils. Like Strauss, they did not succeed in overcoming the prevalent hostility toward natural law, especially in their primary field of battle, social science, but they did raise the issue and they did stand for an alternative to social science relativism.

Strauss and those influenced by him argued their case in a multitude of forums, but the classic forum was Strauss's *Natural Right and History* (1953), a book of immense learning and trenchant argument. Strauss objected to two versions of modern thinking about politics and values, historicism and positivism. He charged that both were responsible for the failure of intellectuals in the United States to uncover any satisfying base for values. Modern history had more and more turned toward relativism, toward the recognition of plural universes and plural truths. It no longer believed in the possibility of locating any general patterns in human experience and chose to make a fetish of the particular or the changing. It had discovered flux and sacrificed truth. The result was only too predictable: it "culminated in nihilism."[25]

Social science was at least as bad, if not worse in its error. Strauss singled out Max Weber, the leading German social scientist of the late nineteenth and early twentieth centuries, as the chief exponent of the fallacies he felt so ruined contemporary social science. Like Voegelin, he resented the fact that modern social scientists simply would not acknowledge that there could be no escape from values, that values were profoundly interwoven in whatever they did.[26] He regretted the sad truth that social science had given up the search for a higher reality without giving good reason for that abdication.[27] He complained that liberals were wrong to believe that somehow tolerance would substitute for the existence of truth. But all these points were prolegomena to his essential message. Everything led to Strauss's deep disappointment at the unwillingness of contemporary social scientists and intellectuals to affirm the existence of the higher, natural truths Strauss was certain existed.[28]

Strauss described these truths as "natural right" and insisted that philosophy and reason were worthwhile because we could discover "natural right" through them. "Natural right" was, in fact, natural law and for Strauss the model lay in classical Athens. His Athens was one of moderation, of temperance, of duty, of aristocracy, of informed leadership, and of community. In Strauss's mind the world of the mid-twentieth century had departed far indeed from these natural principles Athens had embodied at its best and of which Aristotle and Plato were the great exemplars in thought.[29]

Misled by historicism and positivism, the world Strauss confronted did not appreciate natural truth, so it had only skepticism, atheism, hedonism, and inadequate government to show for its blindness.[30] Of course, one might protest that Strauss and the Straussian movement missed something essential in their own analysis. How could they explain why it was that the postwar era had departed so far from the principles of "natural right," if indeed these norms were open to human reason? This is surely an important question, and it was one that Strauss did not duck. In his often creative ruminations on the history of political thought he labored hard to craft his answer.

Strauss blamed the development of modern liberalism for the degeneration of the modern world and for leading thoughtful men away from the natural truths of reason. In particular he attacked Thomas Hobbes, the seventeenth-century English political theorist, who more than anyone promoted the terrible collapse of respect for "natural right." Hobbes may have appeared to talk of natural rights, as did many other liberal thinkers, but this apparent appeal to natural standards was actually a decisive step away from genuine "natural right." Strauss found Hobbes guilty of not caring about higher values or a virtuous society under natural law. Beneath the rhetoric of natural law lay the reality of slavish concern for peacefulness, order, and the individual, driving out from its vision the worth of duty to higher law and the value of the community.[31]

One might have expected that Strauss would respect Rousseau, since Rousseau also favored the classical ideal and stressed the importance of virtue. But Strauss believed that Rousseau was not really an exception to the noxious drift of modern liberal thought. What really mattered to Rousseau, according to Strauss, was not virtue nor community nor the Greek ideal as Strauss understood it, but freedom. To be sure, Rousseau's freedom was not the liberty envisaged by liberals such as Locke or Hobbes, but it was freedom nonetheless, and nothing, Strauss contended, could come before virtue in a polity under the rubric of "natural right."[32]

Part of Strauss's work concentrated on showing that the differences among thinkers who set the basis for twentieth-century liberalism, including Hobbes and Locke, were neither especially important nor especially real. Indeed, what Strauss wanted his readers to understand was their fundamental similarity. They were part of a disastrous flight from "natural right" that left people defenseless in a world of the most frightening dangers.[33]

In the light of the Straussian critique it is puzzling how he came to be identified with status quo conservatism. It is certainly true that Strauss and many of his associates did not view with favor every scheme liberals proposed in the postwar era. It is equally true that they had no use for Nazism and Stalinism, which they interpreted as hideous attempts to escape the commands of natural law. Yet they did not rush to embrace conservatism, for reasons Strauss explained in his discussion of Edmund Burke, undoubtedly the most eloquent spokesman for the conservative idea that whatever exists ought to be defended. Burke was not acceptable precisely because he confused what exists with what ought to be. Strauss believed the function of political theory was to identify and realize the principles of natural right that might or might not be identical with what existed at any given moment.[34] Moreover, Burke had a tendency Strauss found especially repugnant, whether it appeared in radicals or conservatives. Burke allowed his antipathy for radicalism to lead him to dismiss reason itself as the ultimate instrument in politics and ethics. For Strauss, on the other hand, ideas, even critical ideas, were to be treasured by the wise man, especially when they led to an appreciation of the wisdom of "natural right."[35] The conservative Burke had lost sight of this fact.

AMERICAN CONSERVATIVES

American conservative intellectuals united in defining the new conservatism, in Peter Viereck's terms, "as the rediscovery of values." This rediscovery in practice meant a determination to gain respect for values rooted in natural law and to distinguish conservatism from the intellectual confusion of the modern liberalism they felt was painfully lacking in any authority for its norms. Like the other proponents of a return to natural law, American conservatives thought about Hitler. He was somewhat like the typical liberal intellectual. Both lacked any firm basis for their faiths. Liberals might link totalitarianism with an absolutist approach to politics, but the truth was different. Relativism produced Hitler as well as modern liberalism.[36]

Although Clinton Rossiter, whose book *Conservatism in America* was a reflection of the renewed interest in conservatism in the United States in the 1950s, suggested that American conservatives were less committed to absolutely justified values after World War II than they once had been, this was not the case.[37] For example, William F. Buckley and Russell Kirk, who established themselves as the leading theoreticians of American conservatism after 1945, did not provide evidence for what was really Rossiter's personal desire. Buckley's angry *God and Man at Yale* expressed his personal despair at the ostensible intellectual skepticism he encountered at Yale after World War II. Although he assured his readers he had little but contempt for mindless ideologues, he remarked later in *Up from Liberalism* that he saw no purpose to "a dissolute disregard for principle," a disease he felt infected modern liberalism to its rotten core.[38] As far as he was concerned, there was scant room or respectability in his America for those like him who professed divine or natural-law norms. "Truth? Error? These are strange words, atavistic words" in the liberal lexicon Buckley thought ruled his time.[39] This was a bitter realization for him as for Russell Kirk. Both were completely committed to a world, and a politics, that was resolutely God centered. After all, as Kirk remarked, the entire "object of human existence is to know God and enjoy Him forever."[40]

Kirk and Buckley also agreed that human custom was another absolute ground for values. In their view tradition illuminated present experience by the lamp of divinely guided human effort in the past. Although Buckley scorned American liberal indifference toward tradition, Kirk endeavored to unearth a conservative tradition from within American political history and thought. His *The Conservative Mind* (1953) was a landmark study of the conservative intellectual life within the United States (and Britain). It was an effort in part to suggest that God-inspired roads lay near to home.[41]

Kirk, like Buckley, had no trouble in distinguishing adherence to natural law and tradition from ideology and utopia mongering, both of which he intensely detested. On the one hand, he saw no connection between ideology because ideologies were false while the conservative version of natural law tapped the truth. On the other hand, Kirk dismissed utopian visions as hopelessly out of touch with "established" realities.[42]

It is not without significance and it is hardly surprising that among professional political theorists neither Buckley nor Kirk obtained the hearing that was increasingly accorded to their English compatriot Michael Oakeshott. Oakeshott's writings, published in *Rationalism and Politics* (1962), obtained considerable popularity, so by the 1960s it was Oakeshott who was taken seriously among professionals as a political philosopher of conservatism. This was a status neither Buckley nor Kirk obtained among this largely liberal group of intellectuals.

Oakeshott's popularity was not based merely on his beautiful writing style, although it is likely this gave him an enormous advantage. The heart of his appeal was his proclamation of a new conservatism that was "not a creed or a doctrine, but a disposition."[43] He carried this theme so far as to break with the usual conservative reliance on natural law, while simultaneously denying that one could understand the world or the realm of value through independent a priori reasoning. He openly classed himself as a "skeptic" and insisted that one was left with "intimations" of truth and traditions of behavior that were not to be confused with the old absolutes.[44]

Oakeshott produced complex arguments in support of his point of view, but the activity he undertook may be described as another defense of tradition. He did not see it as an absolute, but as all we had in a situation in which even the possibility of rational, final answers was quite beyond our comprehension. His skepticism and implicit relativism undoubtedly accounted for a good deal of his popularity with many professional political theorists and was a sign of the age. It was, however, exactly the reason why few American conservative intellectuals could fully agree with him. Along with Voegelin, Strauss, and others, they represented the active minority in American intellectual thought from 1945 to 1964. They did not propose to hunt somewhat uncertainly for new justifications for old values, since they believed the old, absolute justifications would continue to serve very well. They did not triumph by any means, but they did not give up either, and they are a reminder that there were more options than may be supposed in the thought of political intellectuals in those days.

LEGALISM

Legalism was another approach to values in America in the postwar decades that was popular and that had more than a slight relation to natural-law thinking. The central thesis of legalism was that justice was closely bound up in the virtues of law following, equal application of the laws to all, and due process rights in the law and the courts. The last, the emphasis on due process rights, was its special feature and its proudest norm. For the legalist, a law-abiding society that respected each individual and accorded everyone protection of his rights was the ideal polity. In the 1950s and 1960s Earl Warren's Supreme Court was the most obvious arena in which the legalist struggle to expand due process rights went on. The effort was frequently admired and occasionally criticized by intellectuals in postwar America.

Some legalists clearly believed that legalism could resolve the problem of justification for liberal politics and many contended that what they sought had no obvious connection with natural-law analysis. Legalism, indeed, appeared to more than a few intellectuals to be a safe haven from absolute ends, a substitution of legalist procedures for substantive versions of justice.

A good illustration of a thinker who approached the law in this manner was Herbert Wechsler. He propounded the view that law ought to be interpreted according to "neutral principles" that avoided both natural-law dicta of Supreme Court judges who claimed to possess higher truth and the orientation of those who looked on legal interpretation as a matter of exercising "naked power" and nothing more. Between the absolutists and the pragmatists, Wechsler tried to formulate a legalist procedural path. Supreme Court justices, at the apex of the legal system, had a special responsibility to judge the constitutionality of laws by a "principled appraisal, in respect of values that can reasonably be asserted to have constitutional dimension." They were to make decisions that showed evidence of a commitment to "legal quality," to "generality" (as opposed to the immediate truths and results that might move them), and they were to demonstrate a faithful allegiance to reason at all times. Wechsler regretted that this kind of legalist practice, influenced by a serene aloofness from temporary passions, politics, and truth and a devotion to legal norms, generality, and reason too rarely appeared. The Supreme Court he observed in the 1950s seemed to him to ignore legalist procedures and he cited cases ranging from the ad hoc decisions on movie censorship to the sociological treatment of the segregation cases.[45]

An approach related to Wechsler's was Alexander Bickel's. Bickel was a liberal political intellectual of impeccable liberal credentials. He was a Yale law professor and a regular writer for *The New Republic*. Bickel contended, along with Wechsler, that legal decisions had to be reasoned and principled decisions when great issues of constitutionality were in question. He attacked the judicial "realists" or pragmatists. They saw the court as merely another legislature, a view that was as wrong in fact as it was sad in principle. The court was too important to be merely a political agency.[46] Bickel did not think, though, that the principles upon which the Court decided could be some rigid or "neutral" list of norms. This was quite impossible, and he obviously recognized the implicit natural-law character of such a stand for the Court. He was consistently critical of those like Justice Hugo Black who wanted to substitute other candidates, in effect, for Wechsler's neutral principles. Black's image of the Constitution as the expression of many doctrinal absolutes was only an invitation to unreason and dogmatism.[47] Bickel proposed that instead of one form of absolute or another, principled Supreme Court decisions ought to rely on "the evolving morality of our tradition."[48]

This judgment did not mean that Bickel thought tradition legitimized all political action and was an absolute. There is no doubt that there was at least as profound a respect for tradition within Bickel as could be found within any American conservative, but he stressed a notion of tradition as a growing and changing reality, not a fixed set of dogmas. Yet Bickel's focus on tradition was not as essential to his view as was his belief that law could not provide the answer that natural lawyers from Wechsler to Black hoped to invest in it. His argument was that much less attention should be devoted to "neutral" principles or absolute First Amendment freedoms than to avoiding making major decisions at all. The law and the Supreme Court, he insisted, should not be a font of all truth. This font did not exist. The function of the Court was mostly to bow to the people and their other institutions of government. This was the doctrine of judicial restraint so celebrated by Justices Holmes and Frankfurter. Bickel did not endorse either's perspective exactly. He did not share Holmes' usually genial contempt for the American masses nor did he share Frankfurter's enthusiasm for them either. He appeared to accept that in the absence of any absolutes in the modern world, it was hardly up to the Supreme Court to take over. Hence Bickel praised the "passive virtues" of the Supreme Court. These were the whole panoply of devices open to the Supreme Court to allow it to avoid classic decisions of principles. They included strategies that (1) avoided basic judgments by concentrating on problems of statute "vagueness," (2) held that in explicitly political areas ("political questions") the court should not intervene, and (3) insisted that decisions should be made only at the right moment ("ripeness")—which was usually a later time for Bickel.[49]

What Bickel sought was a Court that was "not doing".[50] To be sure, Bickel did defend the 1954 Supreme Court ruling on segregation. He believed it was a rare illustration of the propriety of principled judgments. It had been slowly developed and was properly ripe. It clearly accorded with the evolving American moral tradition. It was cautiously developed with maximum flexibility—"all deliberate speed"—at the level of implementation, avoiding dogmatism. On the other hand, Bickel rejected the arguments of those who claimed the Supreme Court was justified in its reapportionment decisions that affected legislative redistricting. Were this a matter of principle, Bickel said, he would have supported the ruling. But, like most else, it was not a matter of principle, only a political question. The Court should have stayed out. It could not substitute for missing absolutes in politics.[51]

Judith Shklar agreed with Bickel that law or the Supreme Court was not a fitting substitute for God. That was why she undertook in *Legalism* (1964) to expose legalists like Wechsler who she believed were offering legalism as an unintentional but nonetheless obvious form of natural-law absolutism. She suspected, in fact, that legalism had become a new ideology for many Americans, a mindless reification of proceduralism into an absolute as a substitute for serious political thinking about the objectives of public life, the good state, and the proper relations among citizens.[52] She deplored proceduralism also because it suggested to her how thin postwar intellectual skepticism could be. Legalism said the correct "skeptical" words while actually retreating back to natural law.

Only at the end of our period in the articles and eventually the book, *The Morality of Law*, of Lon Fuller did legalism receive a genuinely sophisticated exposition. Fuller was a legalist who had long since passed through the stage of naive legalism that so irritated Shklar. He understood that his belief in the proceduralist ethic was a type of natural-law argument, was "procedural natural law," but he did not agree that he was a close kin to those who campaigned for a natural-law revival. To his mind, the rights of due process were like the laws of carpentry, technical laws basic to any human activity. They were not analogous to any divine or natural laws of the universe. Fuller was predictably faithful to this understanding in denouncing judges who bent laws to accomplish substantive policy objectives. There were no great policy aims, nor any natural laws that concerned him as a legalist. The problem, then, with most intellectual anxiety about justification and politics, at least as it affected law, was that it was in search of will-o'-the-wisp ends and certainties that were not available. All we had were ourselves and the "inner morality" of due process.[53]

Fuller was unusual, however, in his own uneasiness with this resolution and his uncertainty about the need for some greater rationale to justify rating due process procedures so highly. Fuller did not have any solution. He said that if he had one, it would have based the several laws of due process on a natural law of human respect. But he had no solution that did this, so he fell back on some vaguely worded passages praising the utility of procedures to facilitate human communication.[54]

Shklar assailed Fuller and, even more tellingly, other legalists at just this point. She contended that they tended to be satisfied with legalism without much explanation, if any, of how they had acquired their enthusiasm for proceduralism. Over and over she insisted that legalists could not get away from value questions and justifications no matter how hard they tried.[55] Her deeper insight, however, was her suggestion that legalists attempted to escape because they did not like conflict. They hoped to create a "neutral" law and the ethic of rule following and rest there. Legalism became, like all ideology, a substitute for the give and take of politics, legalist democracy a substitute for the stresses of political choice, and legalism as an ideology an alternative to a world where answers were not vouchsafed.[56]

Of course, this meant, as Shklar did not fail to note, that legalism was committed to the status quo. It was in practice a persuasion that worked to uphold existing liberal values. Given its devotion to rule following and correct procedures, it could hardly be anything else in liberal America. Shklar did not mind that, but she did object to its ideological overtones. Her view remained in the early 1960s the same as it had been earlier. She was steadfastly convinced that skeptical liberal pluralism was the only viable option. Her criticisms originated from a perspective that interpreted legalists as thinkers who thought they were capable of tricking themselves out of insoluble boxes. They were misled in believing there could be any escape from the awesome burden of hard choices. Shklar maintained there was no path but the toughminded and realistic one she chose.[57]

CONCLUSION

Shklar's dissent from the natural-law aura that often lay just beneath the surface of legalist arguments was not characteristic of many liberal intellectuals who unknowingly accepted proceduralism without perceiving its absolutist dimension. Yet her dissent was characteristic of the reaction of most political intellectuals to any form of natural-law argument they recognized. Natural law and thinkers who participated in the revival of natural law in the post-World War II era simply could not pass the skeptical test most of their fellow political intellectuals administered. It remains true, however, that the open revival of natural law in the work of men such as Voegelin and Strauss and the covert natural law of the legalists demonstrated that not all political intellectuals were comfortable with the new mood of skepticism. They were not always comfortable either with the kind of alternatives, from relativism to the "logic" of democracy to pragmatic "realism," that thinkers proposed as alternatives.

NOTES*

1. Walter Lippmann, *Essays in the Public Philosophy* (Boston: Little, Brown, 1955); also see William Newman, *The Futilitarian Society* (New York: Braziller, 1960), pp. 217 and 272–73.

2. Edward Purcell, *The Crisis of Democratic Theory* (Lexington: University of Kentucky Press, 1973), p. 138.

3. Dante Germino, "The Revival of Political Theory," *Journal of Politics* 25 (1963): 437–60.

4. Arthur Schlesinger, Jr., "Walter Lippmann: The Intellectual vs. Politics" (1959), in *The Politics of Hope* (Boston: Houghton-Mifflin, 1962), pp. 151–52.

5. Abraham Kaplan, "American Ethics and Public Philosophy," in *The American Style*, ed. Elting Morison (New York: Harper and Bros., 1958), pp. 10 and 16.

6. David Spitz, *Democracy and the Challenge of Power* (New York: Columbia University Press, 1958), p. 127.

7. Jacques Maritain, *The Twilight of Civilization* (New York: Sheed and Ward, 1944), pp. 6–7.

8. Perry Miller, *Jonathan Edwards* (New York: Meridian, 1959–1949); Samuel Eliot Morison, *The Intellectual Life of Colonial New England* (Ithaca: Cornell University Press Reprint, 1960–1956; earlier version first issued 1936). Robert Skotheim, *Intellectual Histories and Historians* (Princeton: Princeton University Press, 1969), pp. 247–50.

*Some books listed here have two dates: the first is the date of the edition referenced here; the second is the date the work was originally published.

9. Martin Luther King, Jr., *Why We Can't Wait* (New York: Signet, 1964); Lenore Bennett, Jr., *What Manner of Man* (New York: Pocket Books, 1968–1965).

10. Ronald Berman, *America in the Sixties: An Intellectual History* (New York: Free Press, 1968), p. 93.

11. See William Barrett, Irving Howe, and Dwight MacDonald in *Partisan Review*, May–June 1950, pp. 456–61, 471–72, and 478.

12. Chester Eisinger, *Fiction of the Forties* (Chicago: University of Chicago Press, 1963), pp. 149 and 184–85.

13. Paul Kesckemeti, *Partisan Review*, May–June 1950, p. 475.

14. Schlesinger, "Probing the American Experience" (1958), in *Hope*, p. 48.

15. John Hallowell, "Politics and Ethics: A Symposium," *American Political Science Review*, 40 (April 1946): 310.

16. Ibid., p. 312.

17. John Hallowell, *Main Currents in Modern Political Thought* (New York: Holt, 1950), p. 695.

18. Jacques Maritain, *Man and the State* (Chicago: University of Chicago Press, 1961–1951), p. 113.

19. Ibid., p. 85 and 90; Jacques Maritain, *The Rights of Man and Natural Law* (New York: Scribner's, 1943), pp. 79–80, 87–88, 94–96, and 112–13.

20. Eric Voegelin, *The New Science of Politics* (Chicago: University of Chicago Press, 1952), ch. 6.

21. Ibid., pp. 173 and 174.

22. Ibid., pp. 133, passim.

23. Ibid., pp. 2–3, 4, 6, 9, and 11.

24. Ibid., pp. 165 and 187–89.

25. Leo Strauss, *Natural Right and History* (Chicago, University of Chicago Press, 1953), p. 18, passim.

26. Ibid., p. 52.

27. Ibid., p. 70.

28. Ibid., "Introduction."

29. Ibid., passim, especially "Introduction" and p. 30.

30. Ibid., p. 169.

31. Ibid., ch. 5 and p. 187.

32. Ibid., pp. 183 and 323.

33. Ibid.; see his remarkable Hobbes and Locke chs.

34. Ibid., p. 319.

35. Ibid., pp. 312–13.

36. Peter Viereck, *Shame and Glory of the Intellectuals* (New York: Capricorn, 1965–1953), pp. 195 and 245.

37. Clinton Rossiter, *Conservatism in America* (New York: Vintage, 1962–1955), p. 194.

38. William F. Buckley, Jr., *God and Man at Yale* (Chicago: Regnery, 1951); William F. Buckley, Jr., *Up from Liberalism* (New York: Hillman, 1961), p. 15.

39. Ibid., p. 128.

40. Russell Kirk, *The Conservative Mind* (Chicago: Regnery, 1953), p. 424.

41. Ibid.

42. Russell Kirk, *The Intelligent Woman's Guide to Conservatism* (New York: Devin-Adair, 1957), p. 14; Kirk, *A Program for Conservatives* (Chicago: Regnery, 1962–1954), p. 80; Kirk, *Beyond the Dreams of Avarice* (Chicago: Regnery, 1956), p. 22.

43. Michael Oakeshott, "On Being Conservative" (1956), in *Rationalism in Politics* (New York: Basic Books, 1962), p. 168.

44. Michael Oakeshott, "Political Education," in *Rationalism*, p. 111; and passim in *Rationalism*.

45. Herbert Wechsler, "Toward Neutral Principles of Constitutional Law," *Principles, Politics, and Fundamental Law* (Cambridge: Harvard University Press, 1961), pp. 16–21, 22, 27, and 28–47.

46. Alexander Bickel, *The Least Dangerous Branch* (Indianapolis: Bobbs-Merrill, 1962), pp. 58, 84, and 237.

47. Ibid., pp. 98 and 128–27.

48. Ibid., p. 236.

49. Ibid., pp. 68–70, 125, 143, 147, and 205–6.

50. Ibid., p. 125.

51. Ibid., pp. 192 ff. and 237–38.

52. Judith Shklar, *Legalism* (Cambridge: Harvard University Press, 1964).

53. Lon Fuller, *The Morality of Law* (New Haven: Yale University Press, 1965), note 4, part 2, pp. 19–96.

54. Ibid., ch. 4.

55. Shklar, *Legalism*, pp. 7 and 108.

56. Ibid., pp. 8, 54, and 122.

57. Ibid., pp. 10, 12, 17, and 71–72.

4 New Justifications

Although John Berryman greatly exaggerated when he suggested that the "chief cultural phenomenon of the decade has been the intellectuals' desertion of Marxism,"[1] the shift away from Marxism by some political intellectuals was certainly one element in an age in which most political intellectuals, despite the limited vogue of natural law, self-consciously turned away from all absolute justifications for Marxism and, much more often, for liberal democracy. Their skepticism, however, presented them with a dilemma that many thinkers did not believe they could escape: how could they find and justify any political values?

Many political intellectuals at first were clearly lost. Freed from the old absolutes and from shattered metaphysics, they often could not find a satisfactory direction in which to proceed. Berryman noted that, as a result, "nihilism is more articulate and impressive than in any other period of which I have knowledge."[2] His perception was widely shared, as Arthur Schlesinger demonstrated when he remarked that there was much evidence that the contemporary situation was "empty of belief."[3] Nor did this feeling end in the 1940s. More than a decade later a common view was that "the contemporary democrat has been puzzled at the level of his ethics . . . . Answers of earlier periods . . . are no longer completely satisfying, and no substitute has been found."[4]

Despite the natural-law revival, most agreed that justifications in the new era could not take old forms: "democratic politics has no place . . . for Platonic guardians, for 'ends' and policies beyond partisanship and beyond relaxation. Democracy . . . has no all-consuming purpose, no Form of Good, no final ultimate to serve."[5]

Liberal thinking in America increasingly absorbed its own critique of ideology in politics, an assault we know took many forms. It did not result in a deep change by American intellectuals, who increasingly affirmed skepticism about all absolutes and minimized the extent to which they were ideologically committed to liberal values. What took place was a search for new ways to justify old values.

RELATIVISM

One resolution that proved to be popular for a time was *ethical* and *political relativism*, the notion that all political positions were equally adequate, or inadequate, at least insofar as one sought to prove or disprove them. This was a declaration that there was no possibility any longer of genuine justifications for values in politics. Such a view was rarely a final stance for political intellectuals, but especially in the late 1940s it was attractive as a resting spot on the road from "ideology" to a more acceptable rationale for liberal norms.

Relativism gained great impetus from (and strength in) American social science after 1945. In fact, value relativism had made major inroads in social science before the war. As early as the 1920s and 1930s it had gained a surprising sway.[6] Yet its triumph was not complete until after the war, for only then was it taken for granted and only then did it expand outside its parochial social science home and enter the general intellectual mainstream. One reason for the delay was the attraction of various forms of Marxism for many intellectuals in the 1930s who were not social scientists. That attraction was largely gone after 1945 and relativism had a clear field.

Social science contributed to the relativist mood principally by its intense focus on empirical reality. On the one hand, dedicated empiricists simply could not find values in their study of the world as they saw it; they could find behavior; they could find attitudes; and they could find people who believed ideologies, but they could not find independent values. Natural laws or infallible ends in history did not seem to exist. Even if they did, social science taught that one could not confuse what existed with what ought to be.

Nothing that existed could be said to be morally true or false. Matters of fact and matters of value were two different realms and that they could not meaningfully be combined came to be part of the very fiber of American social science.

On the other hand, the aspirations of social science tended to push thinkers toward relativism. Social science in America after the war more and more described its task to be the creation of science, of empirical laws of human behavior in society and in politics. This was a task they held could be accomplished and one that would help people understand their world. But it was certainly not to be confused with the search after values. Social science gave up on values and the social scientist was left with relativism.

Perhaps the most able expositor of the ethos of social science was Arnold Brecht. In his remarkable book *Political Theory*, Brecht masterfully laid out the general position. He termed *value relativism* the "Seamy Side of Scientific Method," but he did not fear to accept the message.[7] He argued that there was no chance that science could free us from the problems of justification. We were left to our own, relative judgments. Science simply could not supply us any ultimate goals since it was concerned with empirical facts and theories. The enterprise of goal formation was beyond, or perhaps beneath, the realm of science, and it would always be so. Brecht thought social science could make only limited contributions. It could illuminate the consequences of various value choices; it could tell us what would happen in empirical terms, if we picked *x* or *y*, but it could not tell us whether or not we should make one choice or another. Perhaps it could help as well by clarifying concepts and noting the universal elements in all political outlooks, but nothing more.[8]

Meanwhile, Brecht argued that we must make our own way. Exactly how we should proceed, however, was usually left vague. Even in later years in many cases intellectuals devoted much more energy to establishing their credentials as skeptics than to suggesting how to deal with the consequences of skepticism. Somehow there was much more force to declarations that "Any fool or fanatic can embrace a doctrine . . . a *dogma*"[9] or to statements that one had no "social ideals or set of comprehensive principles"[10] than there was to what followed from them. Even from thinkers who were not relativists, often little more was offered than vague admonitions that every position should be "evaluated in the light of its alternatives and the relevant evidence"[11] or that we should engage in "a never-ending reconsideration of values";[12] or that "in the affairs of this world faith can never be a substitute for intelligence."[13] What distinguished later from earlier statements tended to be evidence of an effort to offer more systematic reflections *in addition to* vague affirmations that suggested (sometimes falsely) their authors were relativists.

One social science in particular contributed a great deal to the ambiance of relativism, and this was anthropology. Although the rise of anthropology into a place of respectability in American social science in the 1920s and 1930s added to the growing relativism in American social science before the war,[14] its greatest impact came afterwards. It was then that the Ruth Benedicts and Margaret Meads and the works of the less famous reached the wider intellectual public. They taught value relativism. They found that "primitive" society after "primitive" society had its own way of life, its own values looked more and more like cultural artifacts, expressions of one time and place only, quite dwarfed by the immense diversity of human values and life-styles. What we needed to do was to accept realistically the fact of diversity, to adopt an attitude of open-ended tolerance, and to avoid the temptation of imposing conformity at home or abroad.[15]

There is little doubt that there were some distinctions that disappeared in the considerable enthusiasm for relativism. For example, sometimes anthropological ideas were inappropriately applied, even by anthropologists, to suggest conclusions that did not follow. Cultural relativism, for instance, need not necessarily imply ethical relativism. It is one thing to recognize human diversity and quite another to accept the legitimacy of ethical pluralism. Similarly, there is no necessary relationship between devotion to empiricism and scientific value neutrality and belief in ethical relativism. The former may support a stance of ethical relativism or it may not. Empirical tests of meaning and commitment to value neutrality, after all, are not really indicators of a relativist attitude, but rather suggest quite firm decisions about the nature of meaning and science.

Nonetheless the relativist pressure grew. Another force for relativism was the rise of the sociology (and psychology) of knowledge. We can see now that much of the greatest of Western social thought in the twentieth century challenged the notion that people's ideas might have some independent validity. The pervasiveness of rationalization was the secret message of much, if not all, great twentieth-century political thought. Karl Mannheim and Sigmund Freud were significant examples. Although it took time for their analyses to enter American political thought, after World War II they had arrived with a vengeance. As their critics knew so well, they undermined the whole enterprise of seeking answers to value questions in politics.[16]

Mannheim, deeply influenced by Karl Marx, was a German social thinker who in the 1920s had proposed that we look at all political thought as the expression of either interests supporting the status quo (what he called "ideology") or change (what he called "utopia"). He went well beyond Marx in arguing that political theories could be used for the rationalization of interests not only by classes but by all kinds of groups large and small, but he agreed with Marx that a stance of marked skepticism was the best position to hold regarding all ordinary values.[17] Although Mannheim later sought means to develop rationales for political values, within a context of skepticism, it was not this Mannheim who proved especially attractive after World War II. He was admired for his sociology of knowledge, not for his efforts to escape its harsh conclusions.

Sociology and to a lesser extent political science took the sociology of knowledge for granted in the postwar era when considering political values and ideologies, although it is significant of the limits of skepticism in social science of the period that sociology of knowledge was rarely applied to the empirical findings of social science or to its empirical epistemology. It became almost axiomatic that ideologies and political theories were to be studied not for their truth but in terms of the social forces that had, of course, created them. One example of the method in action was displayed in the social science response to McCarthyism in the 1950s. Study after study sought to explain McCarthy. Each tried to do so either in terms of the groups whose interests McCarthy represented or in terms of the psychological frustrations he personified. None of them took his ideas *or the ideas of his defenders* seriously. They were only a phenomenon to be explained in terms of social-psychological origins. The same treatment was accorded various conservative or reactionary movements of the era, including the John Birch Society. Again, these ideas were not taken seriously in terms of what their advocates believed, but rather explained in the language of the sociology of knowledge.[18]

One of the most famous of the theories was Richard Hofstadter's *status politics theory*. American radicals, he argued, including "pseudoconservatives" of the 1950s, could be basically understood as people who constructed their political ideologies as a rationalization of their sense of displacement by new forces in America. Their thought did not merit attention, but the status anxieties that produced it did. Hofstadter was unusual in later confessing that he had been guilty of failing to examine their complaints and their aspirations. He admitted that the appearance of the "pseudoconservatives" represented an authentic cultural or normative disagreement he had ignored. He realized what too few of his colleagues did: that the sociology of knowledge was not necessarily wrong in what it told us of the origins of human thought, but it was certainly wrong in its tendency to ignore the substance of thought and its refusal to consider its plausibility.[19]

As time went on, sociology of knowledge became more sophisticated in that it discovered other phenomena besides group interest as the basis for human thought. Following George Herbert Mead, many social scientists adopted *role theory*. For example, Murray Edelman insisted that to explain people's ideas one had to look beyond class or group memberships and examine what roles individuals played. Edelman contended that the convincing lesson of role theory was that the roles people have in society created and determined their values or norms. In this sense our political values were a reflection of our roles . . . and usually nothing more.

> If the normative political philosopher asks whether the choice of one role rather than another does not depend upon a value hierarchy, we can answer . . . with the many empirical studies . . . as our evidence, that it is role-taking that creates the symbols in terms of which we rank values. Or, to put it another way, the ranking of values is the rationalization of our behavior: An aftermath and not a cause.[20]

Psychology of knowledge, the argument that human thought was best comprehended in terms of the inner human emotions and passions, was less popular than its sociological alternative, but it was not neglected. Harold Lasswell and others, whose work we will see had a good deal to do with the development of liberal skepticism about human capabilities in politics, contributed the most important argument. They set a tone for all social science, a tendency to assume that psychic needs generated all norms. It seeped into social science discourse in many forms to become a part of the accepted language. For example, Gabriel Almond took it for granted that values grow "out of the needs and aspirations of men" in a psychological sense.[21] Hans J. Morgenthau shifted the psychological analysis from individuals to nations: "the power drives of nations take hold of ideal principles and transform them into ideologies in order to disguise, rationalize, and justify themselves."[22] So it went.

The effect of these modern descendants of Freud and Mannheim was encouragement of relativism, since their work suggested that normative ideas had less connection with "truth" than they did with varying environments and personality traits. A faithful reader of their studies almost had to conclude that values were subjective and necessarily arbitrary. The consequences in terms of political thought after 1945 were reflected in several perspectives. One was a kind of fatalism, a view that involved a passive feeling there was no way out of the relativistic box. Its proponents were usually inclined to accept the world of politics largely as it was in America, hoping that no illusory ideologies could capture it, but admittedly helpless to do more than recommend a toughminded acceptance of an answerless world. John Berryman noted early that "your modern intellectual is astonishingly fatalistic" and "reconciled."[23] Although this was probably a disposition that declined over the years, there were intellectuals like Richard Rovere who retained much affection for this essentially stoical view even into the Kennedy-action 1960s when detachment and irony were not entirely in fashion.[24] The most prominent and skillful exposition of this persuasion was by Judith Shklar. Her *After Utopia* (1957) was written in the spirit of the wisdom produced by an intellectual hangover. Western political thought after World War II had a hangover from all the ideologies of great faith and illusions of grand hopes of the past 200 years. Since the hangover hurt, the objective now was to abstain from ideology and utopia in the future. We needed to admit our inability to find philosophical or practical schemes that would banish our dilemmas and we needed to recognize that pluralism and tolerance were the only possible resolutions. We also needed to revise the activist Western view of politics and recognize the cold fact that politics "have become futile."[25] About all we could do was to adopt "resignation and tolerance"—in that order.[26]

Shklar did not think her view was so much pessimistic as it was realistic. But her judgment did not attract as many supporters as did quite another form of liberal relativism. It was too pessimistic and fatalistic to fit the bouyant, if skeptical, mood of postwar political thinking in America. Max Lerner was typical of many thinkers who refused to regard a skepticism that merged into relativism as a doctrine of pessimism. He was full of hope, because he did not believe that skepticism need conflict with a social humanism and liberalism, which he took to be the most appropriate political outlook. Like so many others, Lerner was attracted by what the historian Peter Gay called the "humane relativism" stance.[27] As Lerner put it, the modern era called not only for the skepticism of Oliver Wendell Holmes, but also the "social humanism" of reform-minded Louis D. Brandeis.[28] Lerner wanted optimistic liberalism, too. Holmes, like Shklar, was a bit too stark, a bit too straightforwardly bleak.

Gay made an even sharper analysis of the postwar situation than Lerner, one seemingly similar to Shklar's. But Gay could describe the same situation and yet turn it, as so many did, into another reality, one of hope and opportunity. Of course, he said, one has to live with "uncertainty, with . . . no complete explanations"; he granted that "God is silent" and we "live in a disenchanted world." Yet this was not a cause for regret or even alarm. It was an exciting prospect. Now "man is his own master"; now man can "make his own way."[29] Now human reason was at last unshackled and could proceed critically: "holding nothing sacred, it moves freely through every subject and asks questions of all."[30]

The relation between optimistic relativism and democracy was almost always thought to be a positive one. By World War II, in fact, many political intellectuals assumed that intellectual relativism provided the best grounding for democracy, for the contrast was always the Nazis and the Stalinists, true believers, fanatical in their self-assurance and unwilling to tolerate those with opposing positions. They had to be "totalitarians" because they could not stand multiple inputs from varying subjective opinions. In contrast, there was relativism, an easygoing acceptance of many voices, a kind of democracy in thought.[31]

EXISTENTIALISM

The postwar era in Western Europe was, of course, the high point of the existential approach to politics. Jean Paul Sartre and Albert Camus developed and promoted the idea of existential politics. Although there were many other European predecessors and contemporaries who were also part of the fractious movement, if it could be described as a movement, clearly Sartre and Camus had the greatest impact. They abjured the label *existentialist*, but not the disposition. It held that although there were no answers "vouchsafed" in this world, one must and will choose anyway. Existentialists also insisted that although no choices could be defended in an absolute fashion, nonetheless some choices were better than others. The world might be a place of anguish, suffering, and estrangement, but it could be made better, if not perfect. One could not overcome the pain, but one could and should meliorate it. Their programs differed in many respects, but both French thinkers did agree that the ultimate objective was the expansion of human freedom and both were committed Socialists, if in rather different senses.

Existentialism was not nearly as popular a position among American political intellectuals as was its cousin relativism. For one thing, it seemed to be a gloomy outlook, which was hardly appropriate for a group of intellectuals who claimed to be skeptics but were not pessimists. Second, existentialism in the hands of its French enthusiasts was linked with a Socialist philosophy that did not excite many American intellectuals in the two decades after 1945. Sartre's existential-Marxism and his flirtation with assorted Communist movements certainly were not appealing. On the other hand, relativism seemed in practice to be more open, more tolerant, more truly an appropriately skeptical disposition.

Yet there were those who were existentialists in America, confident of its promise for the relief of human suffering and for the resolution of the problem of justification. The most prominent existential spokesman on the postwar American intellectual landscape was, of course, Paul Tillich, the theologian, whose *The Courage to Be* (1952) was a landmark work of existential theology and ethics. Yet despite the energy of Tillich, he was less than helpful when matters focused specifically on politics and justification or, it sometimes seemed, whenever precision was requisite. His words were often sensitive and noble, but they were vague and unfocused.[32] It was left to others like William Barrett to propound the existentialist theme of human "alienation," the need for courage in confronting the unpleasant realities of loneliness, death, and other "furies" of human existence. They did not often find a widespread recognition of these facts. There seemed to them to be too much naive optimism in the United States, too much sanguine belief that people could escape from the awful loneliness of personal choice and human suffering. There was, Barrett remarked, still the tempermental American resistance: "what the American has not yet become aware of is the shadow that surrounds the Enlightenment."[33]

Yet proponents of existentialism were convinced that it was the wave of the American intellectual future and that only it could provide a basis for intellectuals choosing and acting in politics. This was not to be the case, but it was fair to claim that "Existentialism is not a passing fad . . . but a major stream of modern history."[34] This observation is supported by the pervasive presence in the postwar era of what may be called the existential attitude among intellectuals. Everywhere the existential situation was acknowledged. Postwar fiction was dominated by a search for the individual, his roots, his needs, and his directions in a world without certain goals.[35] Reinhold Niebuhr contended that modern intellectual life was necessarily "existential" because we had supposedly all learned that we could not perceive any resolution to most fundamental human queries, including those in politics.

Neither Marxism nor scientism had been able to overcome the limits of the human situation and its inflexible boundaries on knowledge.[36] David Riesman spoke of the reality of "existential dilemmas" that trapped everyone in his time and that could not be wished away by any special magic.[37] Max Lerner called on Americans to respect the "tragic human experience."[38] Murray Kempton claimed that like so many ex-radicals he had now grown up and was ready to acknowledge what were existential facts. In the 1930s "We were, most of us, fleeing from the reality that man is alone upon this earth. We ran from the fact of solitude to a myth of community."[39]

These views and many more did not produce a sophisticated system of value justification nor did anyone pretend they were equivalent to a polished political outlook. In this sense existentialism in America after the war was no solution to the problems of justification and of politics within liberal democracy. Yet such views were part of the intellectual mood of worry about the absence of satisfactory answers, an expression of the relativism of the age, and for some a crucial starting point for later attempts to formulate firm grounding for political principles.

The widespread existential ambience forcefully pushed thinkers toward reconciliation with the American liberal order. In the hands of many American intellectuals the existential attitude was a statement of the limits of human possibility, a statement of restrictions on what individuals could know and do in life and in politics, a message that emphasized the necessities of the present, the roadblocks that stood in the path of change, and the wisdom of reconciliation. The effect lingered in the background and it constituted a kind of justification for conservative politics, for the omnipotence of the given. Henry David Aiken commented on this phenomenon when he observed that those who talked so often of human alienation (as existentialists did) as a fixture of human existence were in fact not so skeptical after all. Their judgment, he said, was "precisely one of those metaphysical and historical 'necessities' against which the ideologists rail when they find them in the writings of other ideologists."[40]

Perhaps Aiken was right, but his observation did not weaken the period's typical sense of existential anxiety. It was "authentic" wherever it led and whatever justifications it provided. What is most curious is why existentialism led in America toward acceptance of the status quo while in France it proceeded in quite different directions.[41] Does this imply that the essential point about existentialism in the West was that it was ethically vacuous, in the end scarcely more than an epiphenomenon of style? This assessment does not quite tell the entire story, for this does not mean it did not have great influence on those attracted to it and that it was not for them a solution to problems of justification. What for some was its ethical and political emptiness was for existentialists the great attraction. It required the individual, aware that there were no absolutes, to choose for himself or herself. What was chosen was properly a commentary on the choser, not on existentialism.

THE NEW PHILOSOPHY AND ITS CONTRIBUTION

If developments in European existentialism not only stimulated American intellectual doubts but also helped direct them, developments in Anglo-American philosophy were part of a similar process. Professional philosophers dealt yet another devastating blow to the hopes of those seeking secure justifications for political action, but they too produced results that helped to overcome the damage they had caused.

This is not the place to recount the growth of logical positivism as a doctrine of philosophy in the 1920s in Vienna; nor is it the arena to discuss the role of the philosophical genius of the early Wittgenstein, the ambivalent hero of the movement.[42] It is sufficient to observe that *logical positivism* was a philosophy that maintained meaning was properly established only when propositions could be empirically verified. Words, concepts, and, above all, propositions that were not empirically verifiable simply had no meaning.

There were many different versions of logical positivism and there was much argument regarding what test best determined meaningfulness. Exactly how clearly did language have to represent the empirical world? This was and is a fascinating as well as complex dispute, but it is outside our purview here. The point for us is that the logical positivists inevitably became fervent believers in the empirical approach to reality and the scientific method. They regarded all metaphysical and universalistic ethical statements with great disdain. As the influential British logical positivist A. J. Ayer wrote before the war, how could one find an empirical referent for assertions of God and morality? God and morality had none, and thus were not meaningful.[43]

Ayer and other logical positivists demanded attention for this teaching of logical positivism. If values no longer could receive any justification and no longer had meaning, we had to relegate value statements to the realm of psychology. Consequently, logical positivists formulated what they called the *emotive theory of value*. Values were to be understood as statements of personal feeling and nothing more. They were emotive assertions that we liked or did not like something, hence the description of this view as the "Boo-Hurrah theory of ethics." Many logical positivists insisted that this fact was always true and that it applied no matter how great the facade of any ethical system was, nor how illustrious the reputation of the philosopher who had propounded it. Kant, Plato, Hegel, or Marx—and liberal philosophers, too—all merely presented elaborate schemes to express their subjective feelings. Their work was a study in their personal psychologies rather than genuine philosophy, a statement of emotion rather than reason.[44]

Over time the emotive theory underwent various modifications. For example, there was the *imperative theory*, which suggested that ethical statements expressed moral commands as well as individual sentiments. There were other versions. They always came back to the same starting line, however—the claim that ethical assertions had no meaning in scientific terms.

Although American intellectuals were not leaders in the logical positivist movement before or after World War II, there is little doubt that logical positivism affected American philosophy. This was true not only as it spread from the great philosophical centers of Oxford and Cambridge to the United States, but also as it was brought over to America by several of the most creative European logical positivists, including Rudolph Carnap, who were fleeing the Nazis.

The discipline of philosophy was never compressed into a

logical positivist mold in the United States and even in its strongest postwar days logical positivism faced a host of critics. For a time, the battle raged fiercely, but it is little remembered because the logical positivists have long since moved off the center stage of the discipline. Often the arguments were technical, but the heart of the problem for philosophers and certainly for the broader intellectual community lay elsewhere. Logical positivism just did not offer any help to political or ethical thinkers because it could not provide any justifications for values. Logical positivism proved to be "morally irrelevant."[45] This objection was also posed by existentialists. They noted that logical positivists might proclaim their truths, but the flow of human experience did not stop. "Positivist man" was "a curious creature who dwells in the tiny island of light composed of what he finds scientifically 'meaningful,' while the whole surrounding area in which ordinary men live—is consigned to the outer darkness of the 'meaningless.'" It all seemed artificial and silly.[46]

Logical positivism could and did apply to political theory. The most famous and influential illustration on both sides of the Atlantic was T.D. Weldon's *The Vocabulary of Politics* (1953). Weldon, although a British philosopher, was quickly respected by political theorists in America as a powerful representative of logical positivism. Weldon dismissed every kind of traditional political philosophy, no matter how august its lineage. He exposed each in turn as grounded in one type of meaningless metaphysics or another. He meant everyone to be clear that logical positivism when applied to traditional political thought had to be another factor encouraging skepticism.[47]

Weldon is important, however, for another reason as well: for his attempt to reconcile his logical positivism with meaningful value assertions in politics. In the process he drafted one of the most intriguing intellectual efforts to escape from relativism while avoiding absolutism. His formulation was contained in his system of *appraisals*. According to this scheme, one could choose between political regimes and consequently alternative sets of political norms by comparing regimes in terms of empirical data, finding out with the aid of social science how various political systems functioned. To such empirical information one would add individual experience and judgment, of course, but Weldon did not at all believe that this need put him back in the realm of relativism or emotivism. His model was the assessment of art. There are no absolute standards for what constitutes great or poor art; yet we do not find ourselves in a situation of utter relativism in the fine arts. We depend on those who have studied art, who know its inner secrets, people who invariably add to their objective knowledge their own informed judgment to delineate distinctions. We ought, Weldon proposed, do the same thing with political systems and political values.[48]

Weldon's idea had obvious merit and it obtained a good deal of attention on this side of the Atlantic. It described quite accurately the method pursued by some political scientists, including Robert Dahl, when they set out to define what democracy was and ought to be. Dahl was not following Weldon's notion self-consciously, but he argued as other social scientists did, that we should depend on what expert political scientists found the nature of democracy to be through their empirical investigations mediated by their judgment and experience.[49]

Yet in the end neither Weldon's nor Dahl's related method resolved the central problem, because in comparing political systems, as in works of art, one has to begin with prior decisions about what one wants to compare. If one thinks, as Weldon did, that comparing the degree of liberty is crucial, then it is immediately necessary to ask where one got this prior normative stance.[50] It is not an answer to reply that experience teaches that this is a good place to start. The appraisal system was doomed because it could not establish any basis for the standards of appraisal other than individual preference. It was no solution, either, for Dahl to claim that experts who studied political life were best able to create appropriate standards. Normative judgment was involved and there was no reason to assume that Weldon's appraisers or Dahl's political scientists were somehow specially annointed.

By the early 1960s logical positivism had lost whatever popularity it had ever attained among American intellectuals. Its influence lingered on among some social scientists who believed they should mention their values in their prefaces, while acknowledging that they could offer no defense of them and carefully trying to keep them out of their work. Within political theory as a discipline there were few voices raised on behalf of logical positivism any more and certainly none who thought it might provide a way out of value uncertainty. Felix Oppenheim, an American logical positivist, felt there was a role he could play in political theory, but it could involve nothing more than clearing up linguistic confusions, striving "to arrive at a valuationally neutral system of definitions" wherein the words of political discourse could be tested by the sovereign world of emprical reality.[51] For instance, Oppenheim thought the concept of freedom was bandied about to no one's benefit, but if statements about freedom were carefully organized into testable scientific propositions, their truth or falsity could be assessed. Of course, Oppenheim had nothing persuasive to say about whether freedom in one sense or another was desirable. Clearly he thought so, but he could not really address this question—it was best left to relative judgments of individual people.[52]

ANALYTIC PHILOSOPHY AND "GOOD REASONS"

On balance, postwar philosophy in America did not belong to logical positivism, a fortunate result for those American intellectuals who wanted to justify political values. Instead, American philosophy fell under the influence of the latter Wittgenstein, whose posthumous *Philosophical Investigations* exercised an even greater influence, stimulating the development and present dominance of analytic philosophy. *Analytic philosophy* has gone in many different directions, and hardly constitutes a tidy unified world of its own, but the thrust of the movement was reasonably clear and coherent. Analytic philosophers contended that language could not be understood in terms of the pictures of the world it might form. They asserted that words and propositions varied in meaning according to their usage in *complex* sets of language rules and "games" we employed in "ordinary" language without a second thought. To give a simplified example, consider the variations in meaning the word *book* could have: it could be something we read, a verb referring to obtaining a reservation, or something to denote placing a bet as in "to make book." The word did not depend on empirical referents for each meaning, but rather on the complex linguistic contexts or usage in which the word was variously embedded.

The effect of this view was to continue philosophy's mission along the lines logical positivists had sketched for it. Linguistic analysis and clarification were its tasks, often starting, as Wittgenstein did, with "ordinary language." Some very good work was done by political philosophers who followed the prescribed method. Among the most useful, for example, was Gerald McCallum's study of the numerous linguistic uses of freedom. He was able to show that much of the confusion about the nature of the word *freedom* had to do with linguistic muddles.[53] In succeeding years up to the present more and more thinkers have applied the insights of analytic philosophy to political theory, notably Richard Flathman in *The Public Interest* (1966) and *Political Obligation* (1972) and culminating in Hannah Pitkin's *Wittgenstein and Justice* (1972).

Language analysts in our period rarely ventured beyond the task of clarification because they did not think they could go further. Words such as good, right, liberty, and the state did reenter the philosophical vocabulary as words with meaning, but their meaning did not derive from the mysterious essence in each word, but simply from the fact that they were often used by people in conventional ways. This was no basis for selecting one normative outlook or another, and it certainly could not justify liberalism or democracy.

At the same time, though, these limitations dissolved a little as it began to occur to some philosophers that analytic philosophy might after all be able to offer criteria by which rational minds could distinguish among values. By far the most famous illustration of this hope was the so-called *good-reasons argument* of the British scholar Stephen Toulmin. *His Reason in Ethics* (1950) has received great attention in America in the lengthening years since its appearance, especially among philosophically inclined social scientists and intellectuals professionally concerned with political and ethical theory. Here was yet another case of the influence of British thinking on the American search for new bases for justification. Toulmin started out with a straightforward acceptance of the logical positivist view that ethical statements and political norms did involve an element of command, of verbal urging that one agree. He also started out with the linguistic analysts' belief that many value conflicts could be resolved if disputants would work together to get clear what they were talking about; many conflicts were linguistic rather than normative in origin. Although Toulmin could agree with aspects of both the logical positivists and early language analysts, he did not think that either of them went far enough in appreciating one crucial element in understanding values and in permitting value construction. This element was human reason.[54]

It was Toulmin's belief that the trouble with the traditional moral reasoning in politics and elsewhere was the common assumption that rightness was somehow a property, what we have called an absolute. Toulmin was perfectly in agreement with many postwar American political intellectuals in insisting that this approach was no longer viable. "When I asked . . . two people which course of action was the right one, I was not asking them about a property—what I wanted to know was whether there was any reason for choosing one course of action rather than another."[55] His view was that although values were not justifiable in absolute terms, they could be defended as more than mere emotive expressions. He insisted, indeed, that they must be defended by a rational assessment on the basis of reasons presented for or against them. Reason and reasons legitimized normative argument and justification in politics. Toulmin insisted that we had to alter our entire conception of ethics from the search for absolutes to the provision of reasons: "In giving an ethical view, you are insisting . . . that his argument really is an invalid argument, that his reason is a bad reason and one which no one should accept."[56]

Toulmin declared that normative arguments deserved serious consideration only when they did in fact contain a rational element, when they demonstrated concern for producing a rational defense of the question at issue. Toulmin understood that there were a good many reasons that could ensure an argument was serious, but he was disposed to advance the case for one type of rational argument in particular, what he called "good reasons."

The standard Toulmin used to define good reasons often leaned heavily on traditional criteria for rational discourse, a view that was likely to have a wide appeal to intellectuals who rejected the "irrational" and emotional mass movements of recent memory. These criteria included evidence of a genuine attempt to reason with opponents; to present one's own argument clearly; to listen to differing points of view; to undertake to meet opposing arguments rationally. It included a commitment to logic, to thoroughness, and to openness; it involved rejecting any leaps from reason to absolute, or dogmatic, rationalities for one's positions. Above all, it meant making a judgment and taking into thoughtful account the complexities and consequences of many other perspectives.

This affection for rational normative argument and for offering reasons that might be considered "good" is now commonplace among many political theorists and intellectuals, as well as social scientists, but it made only partial headway before the middle 1960s. Yet it is not difficult to note many statements by other thinkers of the era that show not so much their awareness of Toulmin as their participation with him in the general affinity for what Toulmin labeled the good-reasons approach. Sidney Hook approved of this approach, which incorporated his basic principle for "good sense in the quest for the good life." He maintained that the crucial question was not "*what* ideals are held as on *how* they are held."[57] On the one hand, Hook insisted that no norms could be supported by subjective preference. This was an irrational position he firmly rejected.[58]

On the other hand, one could not ask too much of the human mind. This was the lesson of the modern era. Absolutes lay beyond our ken. "By justification . . . I do not mean 'proof' but the offering of the valid reasons."[59] Giovanni Sartori also strongly approved of this style of normative argument. He rejected any approach that rested on "illusory" claims about "objective truth," certain that democracy could receive support only by showing that it was "rationally warranted." His book *Democratic Theory* (1957) was a massive undertaking in this spirit, an effort to produce good reasons for his brand of democratic theory.[60] Social theorist Edward Shils wrote a good deal about what he called *civil politics* in these years, another ideal close to the model of political discourse Toulmin favored. Shils suggested that political disputes

ought to be resolved on a basis that avoided passion, that acknowledged the complexity of the social world and moral decisions, and
that employed reason to judge points of view on the basis of the
practical and moral merits of issues.[61]

These intellectuals appreciated that one obvious criticism of
the good-reasons method was that it did not guarantee any resolution to political value problems. It provided for no independent
absolute standard to settle normative dilemmas in politics. But
it was a good deal more than nothing, much more than relativism
and emotivism and, after all, there seemed to them to be no other
answer. Toulmin summed up the view: "All that two people need
(and all that they have) to contradict one another about in the case
of ethical predicates are the *reasons* for doing this rather than that
or the other."[62]

Unlike many others who self-consciously or not adopted the
good-reasons approach, Toulmin knew that the problems of what
constituted a good reason remained very much alive even after
there was general agreement on traditional Western values as
defining characteristics of good reasons. Two thoughtful and
quite rational souls might not be able to have much of a meeting
of minds if all they could agree on as the appropriate standard
of discourse was the offering of reasons in a fittingly rational or
civil manner. Toulmin wanted to go further. He proposed an
additional standard for a good reason, one that was derived
from a crucial and controversial assumption: he defined a good
reason in cultural terms. He declared that we should consider
a good reason as no more or less than what a given culture or society
understood to be a good reason. Toulmin claimed that a good
reason might be considered in relation "to an established maxim
of conduct." This formulation may not seem to have had any
provincial connotation, since established maxims of conduct
could cover a lot of ground.[63] It was clear, however, that Toulmin
had something much more specific in mind. He made this perfectly
obvious when he suggested that about all we could do when we
"reason about social practices" is to discuss alternatives *"within
one society."* "Pretended arguments about the merits of rival
systems are of value only as rhetoric."[64]

Even if it was not always self-evident at first how much "good reasons" depended on liberal consensus in America to function and even if it was not self-evident at first how many first-order conflicts "good reasons" could not address as a result, it became so later. Yet this did not vitiate Toulmin's contributions. In one sense they made them more impressive, since Toulmin was more aware than some who followed in his stead that all the good reasons in the world would neither resolve conflicts nor promote much communication among people with fundamentally contrasting value frameworks. Moreover, Toulmin's recognition that value disputes in ethics, and thus politics, take place at several levels of abstraction was a valuable contribution. He could not suggest a path out of ultimate value disagreements, but he did remind his fellow intellectuals that many disputes take place within one society, within one set of "established maxims," within a reasonably consensual society, and these were likely to be amenable to a good-reasons resolution. In that context, a context many postwar American intellectuals believed described America, there was a way out.

Yet because the good-reasons approach could not justify one political cultural order or one elaborate set of norms as opposed to others, it still might seem that it was of limited utility to postwar political intellectuals. After all, they often were looking for a basis to defend liberalism against outside ideologies, especially Communist ideology. This was not the case, however, because reasoned discourse had always been a central, if often unarticulated, liberal commitment. At the least, good reasons provided a basis for liberals to contrast their agreed devotion to an open and rational pluralist order with their image of the closed world prescribed by alien Communist ideology. Good reasons assumed a consensus to operate and within that liberal consensus it could work well. The nature of that consensus, in this case, the stress on openness and skeptical rationality, provided a reassuring picture of support, if not exactly justification, for liberal America in contrast to Russia. As skeptical attitudes dominated intellectual discourse, political intellectuals believed it was to America's credit that it was the home of skepticism, a home that contrasted sharply with Russia in this matter. Good reasons invoked both sides of postwar political thinking in America. It invoked both the conservative side in the stress on consensus and the skeptical side in the stress on skeptical openness without ever suggesting that it required commitment to an American ideology to make it all plausible.

Toulmin did not receive a particularly open hearing among American philosophers, since they were relatively unconcerned with ethical and political questions in the two decades after World War II. Although some political theorists and social scientists gave Toulmin an enthusiastic reception, philosophy became increasingly preoccupied with post-Wittgensteinian tasks of analysis, seeking to clarify meaning and usage. Other voices of dissent besides that represented by the good-reasons approach were heard within philosophy but it is important to understand that they always knew they were dissenters and that they had left the main road. Moreover, dissent did not come in a manner that reached a wider intellectual public until the end of our period, most savagely from Herbert Marcuse in *One-Dimensional Man* (1964). Marcuse blasted modern analytic philosophy as a surrender to the liberal status quo in America. Its obsession with analysis involved a choice to devote itself to second-order matters of clarification rather than ethical and political problems. Such a decision implied a second choice, no matter how many analytic philosophers denied it, the choice to support the existent liberal order in the United States. To abandon ethics and political theory for word and concept clarification was to leave the present order, and its values, free from criticism and basking in the assumption that they were acceptable.[65] All the fashionable talk among philosophers about the philosophic role as therapy, assisting people to get straight what they meant, had the necessary effect of urging intellectuals to get inside the confines of the circumscribed world of American language usage and accept both usage and the values that went with it. Marcuse protested that this was the last thing we needed. What we required was criticism from philosophy pursuing its ancient and honorable role as an enterprise that stood apart from the world and subjected it to searching judgment. The failure to fulfill this role, Marcuse claimed, was a statement of the collapse of philosophy in America after 1945 into conservatism.[66]

To be sure, Marcuse ignored all distinctions among American

philosophers in a rather brutal and certainly inaccurate manner. He did not catch the tensions and the cross-currents and did not appear to want to do so. He did not see the minority who continued to have ethical and political interests nor did he see those who were trying to work out a satisfactory perspective that went beyond analysis alone. Yet Marcuse was surely correct insofar as he perceived that leading American philosophers were not interested in playing a critical role in any political sense and did indirectly approve of America by this choice.

It is surely significant that Marcuse was one of only a few political intellectuals whose primary allegiance lay in an European world where conflict rather than consensus had long been considered the appropriate intellectual atmosphere. Many other prominent American intellectuals after 1945 were also refugees from Europe, but Marcuse was far less at home than they proved to be in a milieu where consensus dominated and philosophical concerns were consequently likely to be technical rather than normative. The advantages British thinkers from Weldon to Toulmin had in influencing American thought was that they too worked in a society with far more value consensus than the prewar Germany from which Marcuse had come. Marcuse's insight into the conservative disposition of American philosophers, however, depended on his contrasting experience even as it guaranteed him little influence in our era. It helped him offer an illuminating perspective even as it set him outside the consensus.

THE LOGIC OF DEMOCRACY

Another sophisticated attempt to deal with the problems of justifications of *liberal democracy* developed concurrently in the hands of political intellectuals such as James W. Smith and Thomas Thorson. Both began by agreeing that there was no chance of finding an ultimate justification, but that this situation was in itself the most powerful imaginable justification for liberal democracy. To them, in an age of skepticism liberal democracy emerged as the only defensible political persuasion.

Smith was hardly the first to propound this theory when he wrote *Theme for Reason*, but its publication in 1957 was the first full-scale enunciation of the idea. This date is significant in that the development of more self-confident defenses of liberal democracy came well after the war, representing a kind of recovery from the most relativistic and existential moods of earlier, more confused days. Men like Smith appeared who were sure they now had a plausible solution that would allow liberal Democrats to tread confidently in a rather hostile world. Smith contended that although there were no answers to ultimate value dilemmas, there was a basis for liberal democracy in a method: "the justification of democracy is methodological."[67] This method he called *fallibilism*, the acknowledgment that since we were not Promethean creatures able to transcend ourselves and reach into the heavens for absolutes, democracy was the best alternative. Only democracy did not try to replace the reality of our fallible perceptions with some dogmatic truth. Only democracy was an affirmation of the open universe, of the world as it was, a world in which if there was certain truth, we could not uncover it.[68]

Smith's position may appear synonymous with relativism, but such a conclusion would not really be accurate. Of course, both views stayed away from absolute value claims, but Smith believed one could go beyond relativism to a definite and defensible political position. His case for democracy was intended to be a strong normative bulwark for liberal democracy in a skeptical age, and not uncertain relativism at all.

Thomas Thorson shared this argument in his *The Logic of Democracy* (1962), but he made it a much tighter and more convincing one. Thorson claimed that democracy could be defended as a matter of basic logic—*the logic of democracy*. No grander justifications were possible, but at least democracy (majority rule and minority rights) had logic on its side. The "logic" in this case flowed out of the relationship among democracy, change, and a universe without absolutes. Since there were no guides to truth, one should keep all options open and maintain a flexible, change-oriented attitude. This would guarantee a sensible flexibility as one went about the process of living and governing. It followed, Thorson thought, that democracy was a logical political deduction from these premises, since of all political systems only democracy had an inherent commitment to openness and change.[69]

There was some elegance to Thorson's analysis, since he had constructed an argument that was clear and took account of the existent situation as he and so many others interpreted it. But certainly Thorson's uniqueness came only in his relatively detailed effort to explicate the theory. The idea itself was so often invoked in various dress by others that it became a popular rationale for liberal democracy in the 1945–64 era. For instance, Henry Mayo, who used every "skeptical" justification he could find for liberal democracy, employed this one too: "In the absence of knowledge from any source, the great virtue of democracy is that while giving the people what they want for the time being, it keeps the future open."[70] "Lacking the certainties of a closed system, democracy provides the greater challenges, the wider opportunities."[71]

In perspective we can see that the logic of democracy did not have any secure logic to it, for it is not necessarily logical to assert that if there are no absolutes, one should have a pluralistic and open political system. One might as well decide on a closed political universe and get on to other things in life. There is no logic here either way, although this may offend our prejudices, since we live in a culture where the belief that it is somehow logical to keep all options clear is nearly sacred. Nor is there any particular logic to the claim that if we want an open order, majority rule and minority rights are the appropriate political principles to adopt. Most modern political theories assert they, too, are open to change and seek to build change into their dogmas. Marxist humanists, for example, make a great deal of their flexibility, and even Mao Tse-tung emphasized the necessity of ongoing revolution, the value of nonantagonistic contradictions in ensuring openness, and the utility of continual struggle. What is at issue here is an empirical matter: do Western democracies, does the United States, offer the pluralism and flexibility Thorson, Smith and others took for granted in the postwar decades? They did not seriously address this question even though any answer could hardly be assumed to be obviously true.

It *is* true enough, however, that if one shared their unskeptical assumptions about liberal democracy (read: the United States), their attempt to construct a footing for liberal democracy was a quite innovative undertaking. It suffered, as did the good-reasons approach, from its liberal and Anglo-American insularity, but it demonstrated rather more convincingly than did American existentialism or the sheer relativistic wanderings what efforts American political intellectuals were capable of as they sought to devise a new justification for American beliefs.

CONCLUSION

None of these attempts to formulate a resolution to the problem of the justification of political values in a skeptical era swept all intellectuals before them. The intellectual response that relativism, "good reasons," and arguments from "logic" represented was diverse, agreeing only in firmly rejecting any approach that appeared to sustain ideology. No single current was overwhelmingly popular because the problem was difficult and no answers were self-evidently wise. Our examples are not inclusive either. There were a number of other recognizable proposals offered, but those we have discussed were significant and illuminate the existence of a wide search.

In the next chapter we will examine one final approach to the dilemma of constructing an adequate justification for political norms that so vexed many postwar political intellectuals: the unphilosophical tastes for pragmatism and "realism" that became, in fact, the most common and the most popular 'justification' for postwar political intellectuals.

NOTES*

1. John Berryman, "The State of American Writing, 1948: A Symposium," *Partisan Review* 15 (August 1948): 857.

2. Ibid.

3. Arthur Schlesinger, Jr., *The Vital Center* (London: Andre Deutsch, 1970–1949), p. 244.

4. C.W. Cassinelli, *The Politics of Freedom* (Seattle: University of Washington Press, 1969), p. 156.

*Some books listed here have two dates: the first is the date of the edition referenced here; the second is the date the work was originally published.

5. Henry Mayo, *An Introduction to Democratic Theory* (New York: Oxford University Press, 1960), pp. 266–67.

6. Edward Purcell, *The Crisis of Democratic Theory* (Lexington: University of Kentucky Press, 1973), p. 41.

7. Arnold Brecht, *Political Theory* (Princeton: Princeton University Press, 1959), p. 117.

8. Ibid., pp. 160–62.

9. Milton Konvitz, "Sidney Hook: Philosopher of Freedom," in *Sidney Hook and the Contemporary World*, ed. Paul Kurtz (New York: John Day, 1968), p. 25.

10. Charles E. Lindblom, *The Intelligence of Democracy* (New York: Free Press, 1965), p. 276.

11. Konvitz, "Hook," in Kurtz, ed., *Hook*, p. 25.

12. Lindblom, *Intelligence*, p. 269.

13. Sidney Hook, *Political Power and Personal Freedom* (New York: Criterion, 1959), p. 182.

14. Purcell, *Crisis*, p. 65.

15. For example, see Ruth Benedict, *Patterns of Culture* (New York: New American Library, 1960–1934), ch. 2, pp. 45, 53, 235, and 239–40.

16. For example, Richard Cox, *Ideology, Politics and Political Theory* (Belmont, Calif.: Wadsworth, 1969), p. 86.

17. Karl Mannheim, *Ideology and Utopia* (New York: Harcourt, Brace and World, 1959).

18. Daniel Bell, ed., *The Radical Right* (Garden City, N.Y.: Doubleday-Anchor, 1964–1963).

19. Richard Hofstadter, "Pseudo-Conservatism Revisited: A Postscript" (1962), in Bell, ed., *Radical Right*.

20. Murray Edelman, *The Symbolic Uses of Politics* (Urbana: University of Illinois Press, 1964), pp. 50–51, and 69.

21. Gabriel Almond, "Politics and Ethics: A Symposium," *American Political Science Review* 40 (April 1946): 293.

22. Hans J. Morgenthau, *Politics Among Nations* (New York: Knopf, 1960–1948), p. 213.

23. John Berryman, "The State of American Writing, 1948," p. 857.

24. Richard Rovere, *The American Establishment* (New York: Harcourt, Brace and World, 1962), pp. 307–8.

25. Judith Shklar, *After Utopia* (Princeton: Princeton University Press, 1957), pp. ix, viii, and 292–93.

26. Ibid., p. ix.

27. Peter Gay, *Voltaire's Politics* (New York: Vintage, 1965–1959), p. viii.

28. Max Lerner, *America as a Civilization* (New York: Simon and Schuster, 1957), p. 451; Rovere, *Establishment*, pp. 149–54.

29. Peter Gay, *The Enlightenment*, vol. I (New York: Vintage, 1968–1966), pp. 418–19.

30. Peter Gay, *Loss of Mastery* (Berkeley: University of California Press, 1966), p. 122.

31. Purcell, *Crisis*, ch. 11 and p. 209.

32. Paul Tillich, *The Courage To Be* (New Haven: Yale University Press, 1952); Tillich, "The Conquest of Theological Provincialism," in *The Cultural Migration* (Philadelphia: University of Pennsylvania Press, 1953).

33. William Barrett, *Irrational Man* (Garden City, N.Y.: Doubleday-Anchor, 1962-1958), pp. 273, 277 and ch. 11.

34. Ibid., p. 18.

35. Chester Eisinger, *Fiction of the Forties* (Chicago: University of Chicago Press, 1963), p. 308.

36. Reinhold Niebuhr, *The Irony of American History* (New York: Scribner's, 1952), p. 121.

37. David Riesman, "Our Country and Our Culture: A Symposium," *Partisan Review* 19 (May-June 1952): 314.

38. Lerner, *Civilization*, p. 371.

39. Murray Kempton, *Part of Our Time* (New York: Simon and Schuster, 1955), p. 325.

40. Henry David Aiken, "The Revolt Against Ideology" (1964), in Cox, ed., *Ideology*, p. 144.

41. See *Partisan Review*, August 1948.

42. See Stephen Toulmin and Allan Janik, *Wittgenstein's Vienna* (London: Weidenfield and Nicolson, 1973), for a good introduction.

43. A.J. Ayer, *Language, Truth and Logic* (New York: Dover, 1952-1936).

44. Ibid.

45. Marcus Singer, in *Skepticism and Moral Principles*, ed. C. Carter (Evanston: New University Press, 1973).

46. Barrett, *Irrational Man*, p. 21.

47. T.D. Weldon, *The Vocabulary of Politics* (Baltimore: Penguin, 1953).

48. Ibid., pp. 30-33, 84-87, 146-56.

49. Robert Dahl, *A Preface to Democratic Theory* (Chicago: University of Chicago Press, 1956), p. 63.

50. Weldon, *Vocabulary*, pp. 175-77.

51. Felix Oppenheim, *Dimensions of Freedom, An Analysis* (New York: St. Martin's, 1961), p. 8.

52. Ibid., ch. 1 and p. 4.

53. Gerald MacCallum, "Negative and Positive Freedom," *Philosophical Review* 76 (1967): 312-34.

54. Stephen Toulmin, *Reason in Ethics* (Cambridge: Cambridge University Press, 1968-1950), p. 28.

55. Ibid.

56. Ibid., p. 39.

57. Hook, *Political Power*, p. 183.

58. Ibid., pp. 49-50.

59. Ibid., p. 41.

60. Giovanni Sartori, *Democratic Theory* (New York: Praeger, 1965-1957), p. 168.

61. Edward Shils, "Ideology and Civility: On the Politics of the Intellectual" (1958), in Cox, ed., *Ideology,* pp. 236–38.

62. Toulmin, *Reason,* p. 28.

63. Ibid., p. 223.

64. Ibid., p. 153.

65. Herbert Marcuse, *One-Dimensional Man* (Boston: Beacon, 1964), p. 199 and ch. 7.

66. Ibid., p. 187.

67. James W. Smith, *Theme for Reason* (Princeton: Princeton University Press, 1957), p. 109.

68. Ibid., for a full discussion.

69. Thomas J. Thorson, *The Logic of Democracy* (New York: Holt, Rinehart and Winston, 1962), pp. 139–53 and ch. 9.

70. Mayo, *Introduction,* p. 276.

71. Ibid., p. 309.

5 Pragmatic "Realism"

American intellectuals had a marked taste for pragmatism and "realism" in the postwar period and they showed it most famously by the support they gave to John Kennedy's so-called pragmatic presidency. It is not surprising that pragmatism became attractive when grand rationales for political action proved elusive. Nor was affinity for "realism" remarkable among a group of people who had seen enough of the results of totalitarian dreams to last more than a lifetime.

The familiar appeal to pragmatism that was so much a part of the landscape of political thought in the two decades after the war was not often based upon any formal theory. It was rarely a formal philosophical doctrine self-consciously derived from the work of American pragmatists such as Peirce, James, or Dewey. Most often, *pragmatism* was an attitude; it involved a determination to approach politics and decision making in politics with an awareness of the limits of human action, an openness to change, and a willingness to experiment. Above all, it involved a commitment to being empirical and practical and rejecting utopian visions.

This attitude, of course, had a long history in the course of American political theory. It was an approach with which many political thinkers and actors, such as James Madison, Abraham Lincoln, and Franklin D. Roosevelt, felt comfortable. In the twentieth century in particular it was the legacy of the Progressive tradition of political thought, the message Franklin Roosevelt and many of those around him had sought to institutionalize during the New Deal. Certainly it was in the New Deal era that the pragmatic attitude reached its zenith of popularity, especially among many social scientists.

There were always many opponents to this view and the struggle of World War II strengthened these adversaries, who did not believe pragmatism was an adequate basis for justifying America's effort in the war. Natural-law theory, which often specifically repudiated both philosophical pragmatism and the pragmatic attitude, gained new strength during the war.[1] Consequently, the remarkable growth of pragmatism in the postwar decades was at the same time an expansion of an old trend and the development of a new one. It is evident that pragmatism was not as influential in early postwar thinking as it was to become later. Indeed, in the late 1940s and early 1950s there continued to be marked uneasiness among a number of political intellectuals about pragmatism as an adequate approach to political values and political action. Some more philosophically inclined intellectuals, such as James W. Smith, remarked that pragmatism was rather too anti-intellectual in its overtones. To be sure, Smith like almost everyone else had no affection for sweeping systems of abstract thought, but this did not mean the only alternative was pragmatism and its celebration of experience and consequences as the tests of truth. To Smith it seemed obvious that pragmatism was no doctrine for those who cared about the life of the mind or who believed in ideals. Smith complained that its attention focused immediately on the practical and it undoubtedly could lead one away from the realm of the mind, the traditional concern of the intellectual.[2]

Such a judgment made sense to other intellectuals in the 1940s such as Richard Hostadter, Eric Goldman, and Lionel Trilling. Each asserted his admiration for the practical dimensions of human life but quailed before a thoroughgoing pragmatic domination of politics. In part this was surely because these intellectuals were then more confident of their liberalism and of its virtues than they were to be later. In part it was because they were emerging from a war-time situation in which militant liberalism rather than pragmatic liberalism had appeared appropriate. In part it was dread of anti-intellectualism that made them hesitate. A good illustration may be found in Hofstadter's *The American Political Tradition* (1948). Hofstadter assayed the pragmatic approach in the hands of Franklin Roosevelt and judged it imperfect. Hofstadter admired Roosevelt and certainly did not consider his presidency a failure, but

Roosevelt was too pragmatic for Hofstadter. Roosevelt wandered about depending on pragmatic decisions rather than adhering to a coherent program of liberalism.[3]

Even Daniel Boorstin, shortly to become the most outspoken advocate of American pragmatism in politics, was not so enthusiastic at first. In his *The Lost World of Thomas Jefferson* (1948), Boorstin expressed open sympathy for a Jefferson who, although hardly impractical, had a genuinely philosophical orientation to life and politics and grounded his norms in something a good deal more absolute than pragmatism.[4] Similar reservations can be detected in some social science literature as well. They were only to be expected from Adorno and his associates of *The Authoritarian Personality* (1950), dominated as they were by a continental aversion to pragmatism that might almost be called tempermental. Their argument was a somber warning that the "pragmatization of politics . . . ultimately defines fascist politics."[5] One cannot so easily explain the enthusiasm among some political scientists for a more disciplined political system. From the Report of the American Political Science Association's Committee on Political Parties (1950) to the work of James MacGregor Burns, there were momentary, if distinctly nonphilosophical, signs that some social scientists had little confidence in the American pragmatic style and wanted a more coherent party system to accomplish definite goals.[6]

At the same time, there were many other voices that praised pragmatism and, in the long run, the strength of pragmatism proved overwhelming. This development was certainly concurrent with the reaction against the Communists abroad and the McCarthys at home who represented radical commitment and seemingly fanatical certainty. In contrast, pragmatism along with other "skeptical" treatments of the problem of justification in politics looked more promising and more persuasive. In fact, in the postwar era there were a host of intellectuals who insisted that a pragmatic disposition was a substitute for problems of ultimate rationale they linked to the terrors of totalitarianism. Morton White, sensitive to criticisms of pragmatism, entered the lists of those who defended philosophical pragmatism.[7] Daniel Bell called for replacing "principle" and "praise and blame" with pragmatic judgments.[8] Arthur Schlesinger praised the pragmatic "doers" who knew "experience is a better master than any social myth" and were not inclined to degenerate into "wailers."[9] He contrasted the dangerous example of the closed world of the pre-Civil War South with the sterling example of the pragmatic style of Reinhold Niebuhr.[10] Niebuhr certainly had considerable admiration for the pragmatic side of America, where "without a consistent social philosophy [we had] . . . muddled through with a genius."[11] Surrounding the Kennedy administration were a plethora of self-consciously pragmatic intellectuals from Richard Neustadt to Richard Rovere[12] who would have agreed that "one of the glories of American political history is that our approach to politics has been pragmatic rather than theological."[13]

Sidney Hook was particularly insistent about the virtues of pragmatism. The great choice for postwar thought, he believed, was the selection "Between the absolutist and the experimental temper of mind."[14] He wanted to associate himself only with the latter, with "an empirical approach to meaning and truth."[15] Absolutism, of course, was rejected for familiar reasons. It "converts its unreflective prejudices into first principles . . . into a fanaticism of virtue which closes the gates . . . against all who disagree." Hook thought pragmatism, on the other hand, "knows that the finality of judgment is not possible to men and is therefore prepared to review the evidence on which it stakes its ultimate commitments."[16] Hook stressed that a willingness to experiment, a pragmatic attitude, and a fundamental openness meant testing even the most basic political and personal principles—as well as their alternatives—for their consequences. Did they lead to desirable outcomes? This was the skeptical question Hook and other pragmatists claimed they asked.[17] He proposed to operate in politics by this means, "instructed by experience but without recipes."[18]

The popular heroes of the pragmatic cause in the 1930s were easy to identify. They were Oliver Wendell Holmes and John Dewey. Although Morton White discoursed on both men's ideas after the war, expressly to demonstrate their continuing philosophic credibility as formal pragmatists, he overemphasized Dewey in comparison with Holmes for the fashion of the time.[19] Dewey's star seemed to set after World War II. In comparison with Holmes he was less often cited as a paragon of pragmatism in action. Perhaps

Dewey's continuing commitment to socialism was a factor in an age in which advocates of socialism appeared to be dated figures, reminiscent of the bygone days of the 1930s and less than skeptical. It has been argued that Holmes, too, suffered a decline in popularity in the years after the war. Certainly it is true that his "deification" was a fact of the 1930s when he did indeed become a "demigod" for many American intellectuals.[20] Yet it is hard to accept the thesis that his popularity declined after the war in the face of the repeated invocations of his name in the 1940s and 1950s and beyond. Sidney Hook lauded Holmes as a pragmatist who stood for intellectual freedom.[21] Skeptical historian Leonard Levy honored Holmes as a man who "believed that the first mark of a civilized man was the capacity to doubt his own first principles" and Levy pointedly contrasted him with Thomas Jefferson.[22] Henry Steele Commager in *The American Mind* expressed his delight that so many people in America appreciated Holmes and consequently recognized that the choice in politics always lay between those who depended on fixed, mechanical concepts and "dynamic progressive ideas."[23] Although the Holmes whom Commager saw was not always as "progressive" as Commager wished, no one earned greater respect from him. Commager was convinced that no one in American history was a more magnificent example of pragmatism at its best, skeptical and yet "positive and affirmative" and devoted to "experience" as a guide.[24]

By the 1950s, however, it was Daniel Boorstin who more than anyone else sympathetically interpreted the United States as the pragmatic land that had learned pragmatism could replace traditional political theory. Although many had thought, for instance, of the American Puritans as ideological, deeply motivated by Calvinist theology, Boorstin argued that the real import of the Puritan experience was quite different. In his telling, the Puritans became pragmatic conquerors of the wilderness and builders of civilization. They were practical, down-to-earth men and women.[25] Similarly, colonial society in general was largely pragmatic: it "preferred relevant truths to empyrean Truth and would always retain a wholesome suspicion of the private highfalutin' multilingual witticisms of the salon."[26] The American Revolution could not be comprehended, according to Boorstin, unless one granted that it did not produce "a single important treatise on political theory." It "was, happily, a revolution without dogma." It was a practical and conservative revolution, a kind of pragmatic effort to preserve what existed.[27]

If, as Louis Hartz asserted, America had made only one gift to the history of the mind, and that was pragmatism, Boorstin felt that the gift deserved to be celebrated highly. In his view pragmatism was a mode of common existence that took for granted both our institutions and our inherent practicality. It was less a justification for value choices in politics than living proof that we did not require any such thing. Boorstin's purpose was no secret. As he said from the beginning in *The Genius of American Politics* (1953), his aim was to note and to laud "our lack of interest in political theory, and why we are doomed to failure in any attempt to sum up our way of life in slogans and dogmas."[28]

Boorstin went too far for men like Morton White and Henry Steele Commager when he denied the need for any philosophical thought about political action and justification for it. They believed that pragmatism was something more than a dashing description of current American political practice. They did not disagree with Boorstin's favorable judgment of the United States and they were scarcely hostile to pragmatism, but they did not share his belief that pragmatism was inherently nonphilosophical. Although Boorstin certainly went too far in abolishing any theoretical dimension to pragmatism, there was little postwar interest in a philosophical approach to pragmatism. Pragmatism in postwar thought was more than anything else a spirit. It was a spirit of determination to test norms and institutions by their practical consequences, informed by a sense that concrete experience rather than formal theories or sweeping universals was the only realistic strategy for men and women.

Such a casual disposition made it reasonable for theorists like Stephen Toulmin, Robert Dahl, David Braybrooke, and Charles Lindblom to weave what were certainly pragmatic elements into their work with an informality that did not stimulate much comment. Toulmin wrote that the best of all "good reasons" were "estimated consequences" and this more or less conscious linkage of good reasons and a pragmatic-utilitarian perspective fit well enough for his purposes.[29] Similarly, Dahl invoked pragmatic consequences to test various types of democratic polities. Did these systems work out by the sovereign test of experience: Did they deliver? Dahl's answer was that the current American government was by an examination of experience the best.[30] Like many pragmatically inclined social scientists, his method kept leading him back to the worth of existent institutions. After all, weren't they likely to pass the pragmatic test by the fact of their continued existence?

Braybrooke and Lindblom were two thinkers who did not class themselves as pragmatists, but there was a large admixture of pragmatism in their formal theory. They were concerned with the difficulty of making thoughtful policy choices and their conclusion was that this objective could be facilitated by a rigorous adherence to the results of experience and a strict aversion to any flights of fancy or abstract theory.[31] They never made apparent why they thought pragmatism addressed any central intellectual dilemma (in a convincing fashion) including the problem of erecting a rationale for political action. The crucial difficulty pragmatism could not successfully treat was: who was to decide what consequences and which experiences ought to count? Which ought to count on the favorable side of the ledger and which on the negative? One could collect all the experiences in the world and measure consequences endlessly, but from such a bewildering mass someone still had to make choices of significance and attach indicators of preference. Pragmatism or pragmatism allied with utilitarianism might direct one's attention to the empirical world, but after that there was no escape from the imperative of choice and no solution to the problem of justification.[32]

This trouble was certainly perceived by many political intellectuals besides the pragmatists, but for the pragmatically disposed this difficulty usually melted into nothingness in the emphasis on consensus in postwar political thinking. Consensus allowed the questions to stay in the background at best and provided an agreement on significance that did not have to be defended. Consensus joined with pragmatism was an alternative to a self-conscious rationale for value choices, and together they minimized the limitations of pragmatism. Boorstin in this context was the archetype of postwar pragmatism, for he was aware of this truth and he gloried in it.

FACTS

The attractiveness of pragmatism should be seen in a larger framework. It was part of a much broader interest of political intellectuals in the empirical world and in a "realistic" relationship with it. Certainly after 1945 there was a great excitement among many American intellectuals at the prospect of great discoveries about human behavior, not the least in politics. There was a tremendous sense that the world if not the heavens was open to investigation and that much could be learned. Corresponding to this feeling was another, that the realm of fact was a solid place where one could put one's feet down and accomplish something. The result was an enormous outburst of enthusiasm for facts, a remarkable expansion of the sway of social science, and a powerful transference of this attitude to political thought.

It is perhaps fitting that we begin with mention of Peter Gay, historian of the Enlightenment, for Gay was an appropriate symbol of the hopes and passions of social science that characterized the era. Gay's frequent, almost lyrical praise for empirical reason and science was typical of that of many others. The old Enlightenment hopes were hardly dead: "the world needs more light than it has . . . the cure of the shortcomings of enlightened thought lies in further enlightenment."[33] The way lay through science, including social science, and this was the only way. Quoting Freud, Gay proclaimed that "No, science is no illusion. But it would be an illusion to suppose we could get anywhere else what it cannot give us."[34] Our model was to be the Enlightenment, a group of sensible thinkers who much preferred the realm of "facts" over the foolishness of "fancy."[35]

The confidence of postwar social science was brash, but it was only the culmination of a process that had begun early in the twentieth century, especially in the United States. More and more social scientists had chosen to see "most previous scholarship as metaphysical, value-laden, deductive."[36] After 1945 came the final triumph, the behavioral revolution that in the name of fact and realism swept to victory. It may be that as Lionel Trilling mused there was a fundamental paradox in the broad affirmation of fact, a paradox that threatened the mind and imagination at the same time it affirmed reality, but such musing was left far behind in the general rush toward facticity.[37] Certainly the attraction to facticity went very far on occasion. Some social scientists became suspicious of any theory whatsoever and clung with unshakeable conviction to empirical facts in a kind of undifferentiated heap. Others who did not really belong to the dominant empirical revolution, such as Hannah Arendt, nonetheless manifested their own mystical faith in facts. She objected that the "modern masses . . . do not believe . . . in the reality of their own experiences; they do not trust their own eyes and ears, but only their imagination . . . . What convinces masses are not facts."[38]

Daniel Boorstin turned the enthusiasm for facts into an entire theory of American history, a paean to one set of masses who did exactly what Arendt did not think they could, made fact their king. Here in "America the 'is' became the yardstick of the 'ought.' Was not the New World a living denial of the Old?"[39] Boorstin thought so, and reported gleefully that in success "American facts were destroying European theories." Of course, as we know, Boorstin thought that this respect for facts had long characterized the American people and was what was unique to their history. Other intellectual historians agreed.[40]

FACTS AND SOCIAL SCIENCE

Franz Neumann observed developments in American social science from the continental tradition and what he saw was a wave of empiricism and almost servile regard for facts. The social science intellectual climate—"optimistic, empirically oriented, ahistorical"—made him somewhat uneasy, for it appeared to him to be overly empirical and blind to the necessary theoretical dimension of human activities. But Neumann was like other social science emigres to the United States in the 1930s and 1940s in cheerfully admitting that his own inclination for theory had received a bracing and influential empirical tonic from contact with such a contrasting atmosphere.[41]

The truth was, though, that in time many fact gatherers in American social science lost their conviction that facts were enough. Gradually the mainstream developed more and more interest in doing something with facts in the building of empirical social and political theory to understand the real world. This movement proceeded in two directions and carefully eschewed a third. But it is good to remember that it did so only by means of a framework that made the acquisition of factual data and the scientific method sovereign. George Boas, the anthropologist, insisted that there could be no going back, that the empirical scientific method was all that American intellectuals could depend upon now.[42] William Whyte, the sociologist, felt that it was obvious that in the contemporary world social science had no competition from those who wanted to proceed more philosophically. The day of those who dallied in the "sterile field of social philosophy" was done.[43] Many social scientists sought to distinguish the enterprise of normative philosophy from the possibility of theory building in empirical social science. They consciously rejected the former while gradually and often cautiously welcoming the latter.

One path some social scientists followed, despite considerable suspicion from many of their colleagues, was what has been called "grand theory."[44] *Grand theories* were elaborate and complex intellectual systems that purported to reflect the nature of empirical social or political reality, allowing for the inevitable distortions of abstraction. They represented the architectonic attempts to construct a series of behavioral laws that could constitute a sophisticated, theoretical social science. They were often so abstract that their meaning, much less their value, to practicing empirical social scientists was usually in dispute in postwar social science. Nonetheless, leading social scientists like Lewis Dexter were certain that in the long run complex theoretical structures and behavioral laws were not only the best means to advance human knowledge, but also invaluable in aiding people to make informed and realistic choices in public and ethical life.[45]

Among the most famous examples of grand theory in our period were the works of Talcott Parsons, undoubtedly the leading sociological theorist, the "systems analysis" of the political scientist

David Easton, and Harold Lasswell and H. Kaplan's *Power and Society—A Framework for Political Analysis* (1950). The endeavors of these men clearly were attempts to interrelate theory and facts, but although they took the objective of developing a sophisticated model of the empirical world much more seriously than many social scientists, they did not tarry with the normative dimensions of existence. They were devoted to theory, too much so for a goodly number of their American social science associates at that time, but they were not interested in ideas about what ought to be. Like other social scientists of their age, they went in other directions.[46] Sometimes, as with Arnold Brecht in his *Political Theory*, they did not dismiss traditional political theory out of hand. They sometimes had a lingering attraction to old ideas, but they were mainly bent on producing an empirical science of politics and old interests naturally took second place.[47]

No matter how much controversy surrounded these theoretical endeavors, especially the impatience with their tendency to depart from empirical data, their significance for us is in another direction. For these thinkers saw their efforts as very much a part of a general shift to the empirical world. They claimed that their empirical theory was well-grounded in what data was available and thus a useful contribution in organizing facts into a larger universe of meaning. They also hoped that their theories would provide social scientists with hypotheses to go out in the field and test, advancing empirical knowledge. To them their work was a stimulus as well as a product of empirical social science.

A second path was far more directly related to data and far more modest theoretically. We may aptly call this approach *abstracted empiricism*, since its practitioners molded their cautious and limited theory without elaborate systems and from a focus that always remained deeply involved in empirical data. This was, in truth, the ordinary aspiration of most American social scientists at leading institutions. Robert Dahl, for instance, tried to be careful to stick extremely closely to the results of his study of New Haven politics in constructing his empirical theory of pluralism. He was at home in his rich data and unhappy whenever theory slipped away into abstraction.[48] Similarly, Gabriel Almond and Sidney Verba, in their oft-admired *The Civic Culture* (1963), sought to theorize only with the most faithful adherence to their survey findings. There was no other really acceptable procedure in their opinion "if one holds to the view that theories of politics should be drawn from the realities of political life."[49]

The path that was not chosen by most social scientists, of course, was engagement in normative theorizing. "Let us not be first of all ideologists . . . . Let us rather be social scientists first."[50] They did not see their job to be to pursue what they deemed to be ideology or flights of moral fancy. This role might best be left to others, if indeed it should be attempted by anyone. The agreement among the lovers of raw facts, the grand theorists, and the more restrained empirical theorists came down to this: Whatever their conflicting notions about what was necessary for a developing social science, all agreed that the only worthwhile task of the present was to explore "reality," the realm of the fact. In the end, as David Riesman said, it was a choice between those intellectuals who were interested in "dogmatism and fanaticism" and those who sought "openness, pluralism, and empiricism."[51]

This dominant trend, which carried all the social sciences and much of American intellectual life with it, did not go uncriticized. There was genuine division among American intellectuals concerning the role and methods of social science. Some intellectuals shared Arthur Schlesinger's barely restrained contempt for a social science they considered appallingly ignorant of human psychology and dynamics of history.[52] Certainly important questions were raised and debated, but it would be erroneous to confuse the debate, lively as it was for a time, with the reality of the postwar direction of the social sciences. Debate or no, they moved almost inexorably toward a greater commitment to empirically based "reality" and away from concern with normative aspects of politics. Fact gathering and empirical theory received the honors and moral thought in politics did not in an intellectual world in which the only answers most American intellectuals looked for and found were factual and in which the alleged evils of ideology were vividly remembered.

Some critics were bothered by the obsession with techniques that seemed to pervade modern social science. They asserted that mindless concern with methodology and special languages might prove satisfying for those within their confines, but it was doubtful if these things had any other utility. There was more than a hint of suspicion that methodology and special languages came to the front to replace a missing purpose. Some wondered whether social science was counting its toes with increasingly elegant means but doing little more.[53] Critics made modest appeals for political philosophy as part of the larger search for "reality," giving it a role as advisor and analyst without claiming there should be guidance through a great normative vision. For them, apparently, political philosophy also had to respond to the passing of the age of ideology.[54] There were even a few who demanded a much greater place for political theory within social science. For example, John Hallowell, among the most uncompromising, scoffed at the notion that politics could be studied scientifically, or any other way, without a guiding vision of the good. Ethical evaluation was absolutely vital since the true goal of any science of politics must be location and achievement of the good. Hallowell's protest against modern social science was rooted in a "conservative" politics that did not approve of the drift of liberal America.[55] So was the famous indictment by Leo Strauss, who singled out Max Weber as a concrete symbol of the failure of modern social science to take normative purposes seriously. But the complaints came from more than one political direction as David Riesman's suspicions that contemporary fashion in America had gone too far toward enshrining "realism" at the expense of the vital realm of ideals illustrated.[56]

Such critics were, in fact, echoing the ascerbic remarks of the redoubtable Harvard social scientist William Yandell Elliott written well before World War II. Elliott foresaw that social science would eventually have no explicit "normative program." "The appeal is to 'facts,' and these facts . . . rule out considerations of an *a priori* 'ought.'"[57] Certainly what he predicted came to be an accurate description of the purposes of American social science in the decades after the war, but the question is why? What effect did this eventuality have on political thought after 1945?

The question becomes even more salient when we consider that another controversy that took place after 1945 concentrated on the connection between postwar social science and the goal of service to society or to humanity at large. Would the new social science at least assist in the practical business of living? Post-1964 critics of social science were to charge that American social science was only too eager to offer services to the world around it, especially the world of established political and socioeconomic elites. But this was not at all the impression dominant among leaders in postwar social science. They did not see themselves as particularly service oriented nor did they envision service as the proper role for social science. Neither service nor ethics were concerns. Instead, the goal was—again—the construction of a science of politics, a pure enterprise of the empirical intellect. To be sure, this objective was naive. There could be no science of politics that did not have substantial implications for every functioning political system. Service and ethics cannot be escaped so easily. Government distributors of research money turned out to be able to command a good deal of "service" from many social scientists, and social science, disinterested in ethical and policy questions, conceded to the operative status quo an implicit legitimacy. But these effects were rarely noted.

Critics in the postwar period did exist. They rarely objected to the empirical and behavioral revolutions, but they usually wanted to use them for more mundane aims, for assisting in the resolution of contemporary policy issues. Gabriel Almond was a prominent spokesman for this point of view. No one could accuse him of animus toward the empirical norms of modern political science, but he thought there was more to be done than elucidating empirical laws of reality. He said that modern social science had to assume a second task and had to become "animated by purpose and devoted to service."[58] Arnold Rogow, in a famous article in the *American Political Science Review* in 1957, asked the decisive question: "Whatever happened to great issues?" He none too kindly suggested that modern social science had lost a close relationship with vital and lively contemporary issues of practical politics and policy making. Didn't any social scientists care about these matters anymore? Didn't this mean that, ironically, the earnest devotees of empirical reality were separating themselves from the world of practical politics they purported to understand and were necessarily becoming abstract and irrelevant?[59]

Harold Lasswell went much beyond the hope of Rogow that social science would become policy relevant. Lasswell thought social science by spreading its norms throughout society had the potential to realize "democracy" and human dignity to an unmatched extent.[60] His praise of the potential of social science, however, attracted little interest. Its resonance was of the reform-minded social science of the 1930s and was not the route most postwar social scientists favored. Lasswell's status in postwar social science became that of an elder statesman, whose important work lay in the prewar decades, even as Arnold Rogow's more modest faith received little reinforcement.

BEING "REALISTIC"

Along with the tremendous accent on facts and empirical theory by postwar intellectuals went the norm that politics must be "realistic." Indeed, the two decades after 1945 were the heyday of "realism" among American political intellectuals. We have observed the popularity of realism before. Realism was the rallying cry that led intellectuals away from the "illusory" absolutes in political theory toward what Reinhold Niebuhr described as "moral realism."[61] We have seen it also in the claim made by many intellectuals that optimistic perspectives on human nature were inspiring schoolboy fables, hopelessly far from the mark and not at all realistic. Thus Herbert Deane could label St. Augustine's perceptions of human weakness "realistic" without attracting comment.[62] Realism also became the standard applied to political dispositions that involved practical and hard work rather than flighty, utopian pronouncements. It was a term of honor for the pragmatic politician who was praised as a study in contrast to the utopian. Daniel Bell, for instance, was even able to find a "realistic" Socialist in Congressman Berger of Milwaukee of fifty years earlier; at least there was one practical soul in a movement that Bell felt was profoundly addicted to utopianism.[63] Murray Kempton contrasted A. Philip Randolph and Thomas Patterson of the Brotherhood of Railway Porters with the radical Paul Robeson in his study of the blacks in the 1930s to make the same point. To Kempton the first two were hardworking, dedicated men who had a realistic command of the way the world was and they accomplished things; but Robeson was a beautiful person, full of empty slogans and futile postures.[64] Kempton, like so many other political intellectuals, was impressed with those who stopped talking and went beyond "words" to confront the harsh contours of "reality."[65]

Arthur Schlesinger was another prominent voice who defended realism in politics. He was always convinced that the "great need of our time is liberation from the fanaticism of abstraction and a new concern for the empirical realities of life."[66] His most discussed attempt to follow his own norm was his famous article on the Civil War. There he attacked previous historians who were unable to understand what World War II and the Cold War had apparently taught Schlesinger. "Realists" knew that all conflicts could not be resolved by better compromises or more talented leaders. Violence was part of the real world and sometimes it was a necessary part. Schlesinger suggested that no one who truly understood human nature could disagree. It followed, he contended, that realistic men knew violence was the only possible route in the Civil War. It was the only way to end slavery. Consequently, it was time to stop apologizing for our civil conflict and honor it as an eminent expression of the politics of realism.[67]

The general mood was summarized by Leslie Fiedler in his memorable phrase: "an end to innocence." Like Schlesinger, Fiedler hoped that a politics of realism would be "a liberalism of responsibility" recognizing the hard choices that must be made in politics and accepting the sometimes harsh contours of the real world. He acknowledged, as Schlesinger did, how much his perspective had gained from an honest appraisal of the Soviet threat. No one could be politically naive any more, he felt, after America's encounter with Communism. Liberal naivete or the "liberalism of innocence" had floundered permanently on the tragic guilt of Alger Hiss. This was a sober truth for Fiedler as for Schlesinger, but it promised great ultimate benefit. "These years since 1940 have been for writers and critics in America a time of disenchantment, marking, one hopes, the passage from the easy enthusiasms and approximate ambitions of adolescence to the juster self-appraisal of maturity."[68]

One of the most important areas where realism held sway in the postwar decades, of course, was the field of international relations.[69] Here influential intellectuals adopted a frankly "realistic" perspective and were harshly critical of those who did not or would not admit that what mattered in international affairs were the facts of international life, not any "romantic" aspirations or goals. Hans J. Morgenthau earned a well-deserved reputation in those days as an advocate of realism. He self-consciously described his approach as "a realist theory of international politics" and he lived up to his own standards.[70] He argued that Americans and American intellectuals in particular had to learn to see international politics as they took place, not as they might wish to see them. What this meant, above all, was the fact that "international politics, like all politics, is a struggle for power."[71] Pretty concepts like international morality and public opinion were not significant factors in the decision-making process and were not likely to become so. World government, and similar utopian fantasies, were nowhere in sight, and Morgenthau advised that no one should hold his breath for their appearance. Although a political philosopher himself, Morgenthau urged more time be given to comprehension of the actual forces of political power.[72] He felt rather sorry for those whose outlook was primarily moral, just as he considered such an orientation among national policy makers sheer madness. Realism told him: "A man who was nothing but 'moral man' would be a fool, for he would be completely lacking in prudence."[73]

In the late 1960s Morgenthau, unlike many other professors of international relations, emerged as an active opponent of the Vietnam War. It was his opinion that it was an egregious and costly example of the danger of forgetting the goal of a realistic devotion to national self-interest, an indulgence in an ideological anti-Communist crusade. His reputation rapidly declined in his profession, because there were other estimates of realism's dictates. Many who had learned about realism in international politics from him denied Vietnam was unrealistic and charged that Morgenthau had become a crusader. The lesson, of course, is that realism in international politics as elsewhere was an attitude and implied little agreement in terms of concrete policy.[74] Realism's use as a rallying cry was nonetheless great in intellectual assessments of foreign affairs. Kenneth Waltz defended "realism" as ardently as Morgenthau. National interest was the salient variable in international relations and there was no sense in trying to wish away this reality. "Each state pursues its own interest, however defined, in ways it judges best."[75] Some people might not approve of balance of power politics, but to Waltz it was "neither moral nor immoral, but embodied a reasoned response to the world around us."[76] From Waltz's view the sad truth was that many liberal intellectuals had never reconciled themselves to these realities. They kept on treasuring illusions: the idea that reason could somehow brush aside force, that international crusades or self-righteous isolation would solve problems. They often just did not want to escape their comfortable naivete.[77]

George Kennan achieved great prestige in this period as a symbol of the wise diplomat-analyst, one whose thought carried weight because he was a practitioner as well as a student of international relations. He was the experienced voice whose call for realism somehow rang the loudest. Kennan constantly endorsed the "realism" of national interest in the bluntest possible terms with no concessions to those who wanted their international actions justified by idealism. He regretted what he erroneously thought to be general unwillingness of intellectuals to agree with him: "we find no greater readiness, so far, to admit the validity and legitimacy of power realities and aspirations, to accept them without feeling the obligation of moral judgment, to take them as existing and inalterable human forces, neither good nor bad, and to seek their point of maximum equilibrium rather than their reform."[78] He recognized all too well that his advice might be unpalatable and contrary to liberal norms and might "seem to smack of cynicism and reaction. I cannot share these doubts. Whatever is realistic in concept, and founded in an endeavor to see both ourselves and others as we really are, cannot be illiberal."[79] Although George Kennan lauded Reinhold Niebuhr as "the father of us all,"[80] Niebuhr saw himself in a somewhat different light. Certainly he took Kennan to task. He claimed Kennan was guilty of substituting one error in foreign policy for another by replacing dangerous idealism with sheer egoism and self-interest.[81] In retrospect Kennan's judgment appears more plausible than Niebuhr's dissent. Pursuing themes after the war that he had begun long before it, Niebuhr contended in *The Irony of American History* (1952) that Americans continued to be unwilling to accept and use power with "realism" and "patience." Power was a fact of life. It often had to be used and there could be no guarantee that idealism could always accompany it. Indeed, power was best kept separate from idealism, for the crusades of the powerful were often moral and political disasters.[82]

For Morgenthau, Waltz, and Niebuhr ours was a hostile world, one in which virtue alone would not help and could indeed hurt in the struggle for survival. We had to face the world armed with this "realistic" attitude. Their admonitions against the illusions of world government and perpetual peace were the counterpart of the rejection of utopias and ideal societies by those whose thought concentrated on domestic issues. The world of possibilities for American political intellectuals was now increasingly a limited one. The sense of boundaries was great and there was naturally no interest in dancing to the tune of "fantasy."

Realism in foreign relations is the model I have chosen here to illustrate the long-run significance of the turn to the empirical world. Realism had undeniable virtues. Realists urged people to understand their world situation and the fallibilities of human behavior. Less obviously beneficial was the tendency of realists in foreign affairs, as in so many aspects of politics in America after 1945, to slip from pointing out present "realities" to reifying them into fixed and apparently unchangeable laws of nature. Time and again in the study of international politics or in constructing a revised democratic theory, their assumption was that the realities were rigid "givens" and it was the job of policy makers or political philosophers to work with whatever was left. A realist's outlook was taken to be the view of the way things are and were going to be. The choice posed was always whether one was going to accept this state of affairs or wander off into dangerous and fallacious illusions.

This conclusion is certainly at odds with the self-image of many intellectuals in the United States after World War II. For them there was nothing particularly conservative about their enterprise, particularly those who were engaged most directly in the efforts to advance the cause of realism. They saw themselves, in a sense rightly, as advocates of substantial change, undertaking to pry people loose from their misconceptions about the world around them. The role of the *legal realists* is an apt illustration. Their effort to get people to perceive the legal process as they thought it was, a world mixed with a great deal of politics rather than one composed simply of marble columns and blindfolded justice, had begun as far back as the 1920s.[83] It picked up momentum after 1945. More and more political scientists and even legal theorists appreciated that instead of an abstract and objective justice system, we had all-too-human judges and courts, possessed by prejudices and pressured by interests. More and more the realistic study of judicial process came to replace formal constitutional law or at least to maintain a respected position along its side.

Judith Shklar's *Legalism* (1964) represented a high point of the judicial realist perspective at a theoretical level. Shklar's book was a blistering polemic excoriating legalism. It denounced those who seemed to have a mystical faith in law. They hated politics and would not concede that the law and legal processes were inevitably creatures of politics. Shklar cited the Nuremburg Trials as a remarkable example. Here was an obvious abuse of due process and legalist norms smoothly justified with an apparent straight face by legalists. They could not see that, of course, legalist standards had yielded to political aims at Nuremburg and they reacted with horror at Shklar's suggestion that the trials could be justified only on the basis of their *political* accomplishments. If the trials achieved desired political purposes, Shklar said, they were fine, but if they did not, we should not have sponsored them. All of the legalist rationales might as well be thrown into the trash can, and Shklar did so with no hesitation.[84]

Would it make sense to analyze Shklar's "realism" as a defense of the status quo? The same query might be raised about another style of realism that was occasionally fashionable after 1945, the debunking of selected myths of American history. Richard Hofstadter, for instance, self-consciously set out to correct the historical record of America. He was a determined realist and sometimes a brutal one. In *The Age of Reform* (1955), he relentlessly exposed the "agrarian myth" of American history, showing that behind the romance of agrarian Populist movements lay the cold self-interest of farmers as businessmen. He dared to attack the Progressive movement, the ancestor of modern liberal intellectuals, and he demonstrated its responsibility for the adoption of Prohibition after World War I and the mood of fanatic patriotism during the war. He tried to show how much progressivism was corrupted and distorted by its obsessive moralism and self-righteousness.[85] In his earlier even more corrosive *American Political Tradition* (1948), Hofstadter brought to light unattractive and well-forgotten sides of American heroes from the Founding Fathers to Franklin D. Roosevelt. Lincoln more than anyone had the greatest grip on American sentiments, but Hofstadter attempted to draw a "realistic" Lincoln, one who turned out to have many warts. In the ambience of the age, Hofstadter was merely serving as a realist telling the truth, bringing out the facts. It was a matter, Hofstadter remarked, of the need in American history as elsewhere for a hardheaded factual disposition. Sentiment had to take a distinctly second place to realism."[86]

Shklar and Hofstadter, like others, were dedicated and sometimes persuasive revisionists. Yet we need to reflect on the nature of their revisionism. They were skeptics of the ways in which people tended to conceptualize experience, to see the empirical past or present, but they were not skeptical of the "real" in the slightest. This is why Shklar and Hofstadter could campaign just as hard against ideology as they did against legalism or a romantic view of the American past. These were different battles in a single war. People had to lay aside all myth and take the empirical world as it was. This was the twin message of revisionism in ideas and conservatism in defending the reified boundaries of the real world that underlay the focus on facts by so many intellectuals and technicians in social science, political theory, and history.

One of the most frequent, and certainly most revealing, phrases that dots the work of intellectuals in America after 1945 evokes the common mood unusually well. The phrase was "toughminded realism" and it was a constant yardstick by which intellectuals measured others. Were thinkers and politicians ready to be what Arthur Schlesinger termed "toughminded?" Were they prepared to make hardheaded decisions based on brutal facts or did they lapse into utopianism?[87] Were they able to appreciate what the liberal tradition of Peter Gay taught: that there was no escape from the inexorable circumstances reality imposed and that one had to adopt "toughminded realism?"[88] For them it was not in any sense a choice of conservatism over radical change or anything of the sort. It was a matter of intellectual integrity, of being honest and courageous enough to deal with "reality" as a mature adult.

REACTION TO THE CONSERVATIVE IMPLICATIONS

The conservative overtones of toughminded realism were hard to avoid even in the years from 1945 to 1964. Sometimes, as Niebuhr noticed, the widespread infatuation with "reality" reached a state that made it fair to describe it as a "metaphysic" of its own.[89] Certainly in the hands of a rhapsodist like Daniel Boorstin, who claimed that "Americans who knew the reality did not need the dreams," this was unmistakably true.[90] It was a paradox of considerable significance that the metaphysic of toughmindedness could lead its ardent proponents into illusions of their own. Toughmindedness could mean many things. It could encourage fatal policy errors. Toughmindedness may have succeeded in the Cuban missile crisis, but it was to fail in Vietnam.

Even in the twenty years after World War II, the turn to "the facts" and "the real world" did not go on without thoughtful, if sometimes sympathetic, criticism by those who experienced more than a modicum of reservation. Some theorists who had argued eloquently against the adequacy of deductive systems of values for politics went on to include the fallacy of inductive, fact-oriented solutions as well. Men such as J. W. Smith in *Theme for Reason* (1957) and Thomas Thorson (1962) did not hesitate to remark that all the empirical data in the world, all the "realism" in the world, could not provide a secure rationale for any normative system, including the status quo.[91]

Others worried about where the endless thirst for facts and realism might terminate. It was perhaps fitting that the most famous spokesman for this point of view, this anxiety, was Richard Hofstadter, whose credentials as a realist could hardly be challenged. Specifically, he feared that unadulterated respect for practicality and the realm of the fact might slight the deeper reality of the many dimensions of human experience, the role of theory, and possibly even intellectuals themselves. He thought he discerned too much "realism" in American politics as it was, too much departure from the ideal the Founding Fathers represented: the intellectual in politics. Yet for him the Kennedy administration was a final reassurance, for here was his ideal reborn. Here were "realism" and the intellectuals in partnership once again at last.[92]

Hofstadter's doubts were akin to those of intellectuals who wondered about the effect of so much complacent realism on the creative side of American civilization. They were inclined to suggest that there was always a need for criticism in the United States, as elsewhere, to keep the cultural imagination alive. Without intellectuals fomenting a dialectic with their environment, the uncreative forces of mental torpor were likely to sweep the plain. Philip Rahv appreciated that American intellectuals now accepted the "realities of American life," but too much realism might be leading to mental stagnation.[93] Lionel Trilling, whose book *The Liberal Imagination* was itself an example of the life of creative intellect, had more than a little uncertainty about whether practicality and "realism" as a constant diet might not starve out the literary life, leaving us without the essential benefit of "the emotions and the imagination."[94] There were those who specifically assailed the mood in the context of American social science. C. Wright Mills charged that modern social science had wandered off into pure theory or more or less mindless fact gathering with little concern for the intellectuals' traditional role as agents of criticism and reform.[95] Even sympathetic outsiders could regret the same trend. Did social science any longer have any "engagement with reform?" It was impossible to dispute the argument that social scientists were no longer very "critical in their uses of social science."[96]

It took rare souls indeed to go further and probe the very nature of the heart of the postwar focus on "the real world." It took a gadfly like David Riesman to warn his fellow social scientists: "How rare a thing empiricism actually is . . . how often it is simply an ideology or rationalization."[97] It took a pervasive skeptic like Murray Edelman to ask the ultimate question. He wondered whether the emperor had any clothes and whether there was any reality out there. "Observation of politics is not simply an effort to learn what is happening but rather a process of making observations conform to assumptions."[98] If Edelman was right, the entire faith of postwar social science in "the facts," in measureable consequences, and in "realism" would have been faced with a need to reexamine its faith in social science and its empirical epistemology. But no such reexamination came in the decades after 1945; for postwar intellectuals were not basically skeptical about any aspect of their turn to pragmatic realism.

NOTES*

1. Edward Purcell, *The Crisis of Democratic Theory* (Lexington: University of Kentucky Press, 1973).

2. James W. Smith, *Theme for Reason* (Princeton: Princeton University Press, 1957), p. 21.

3. Marian J. Morton, *The Terrors of Ideological Politics: Liberal Historians in a Conservative Mood* (Cleveland: Case Western Reserve, 1972), p. 114. This book influenced me greatly on this general point.

4. Ibid., p. 78.

5. Theodore Adorno et al., *The Authoritarian Personality* (New York: Harper & Row, 1950), p. 7.

6. Morton, *The Terrors*, pp. 3–5; American Political Science Association, Committee on Political Parties, *Toward a More Responsible Two-Party System* (New York: Holt, Reinhart, and Winston, 1950).

7. Morton White, *Social Thought in America* (Boston: Beacon, 1957–1947), p. 275.

8. Daniel Bell, "Ideology: A Debate," *Commentary* 38 (October 1964).

9. Arthur Schlesinger, Jr., *The Vital Center* (London: Andre Deutsch, 1970–1949), pp. 155 and 160.

10. Arthur Schlesinger, Jr., "The Causes of the Civil War: A Note on Historical Sentimentalism" (1949), p. 43, and "Reinhold Niebuhr's Role in American Political Thought and Life" (1956), in *The Politics of Hope* (Boston: Houghton Mifflin, 1962).

11. Reinhold Niebuhr, "Our Country and Our Culture: A Symposium," *Partisan Review* 19 (May–June 1952).

12. Richard Rovere, *The American Establishment* (New York: Harcourt, Brace and World, 1962), p. 307; Richard Neustadt, *Presidential Power* (New York: Wiley, 1964–1960).

*Some books listed here have two dates: the first is the date of the edition referenced here; the second is the date the work was originally published.

13. William E. Leuchtenberg, "Anti-Intellectualism in the United States," *The Journal of Social Issues*, no. 3 (1955): 15.

14. Sidney Hook, *Political Power and Personal Freedom* (New York: Criterion, 1959), p. 183.

15. Ibid., 10.

16. Ibid., p. 183.

17. Ibid., pp. xii and 7.

18. Ibid., p. 268.

19. White, *Social Thought*, p. xxii, passim.

20. G. Edward White, "The Rise and Fall of Justice Holmes," *University of California Law Review* 39, no. 51 (1971): 51-77.

21. Sidney Hook, *Heresy Yes, Conspiracy No* (New York: John Day, 1953), pp. 19-20.

22. Leonard Levy, *Jefferson and Civil Liberties* (Cambridge: Harvard University Press, 1963), p. 64.

23. Henry Steele Commager, *The American Mind* (New Haven: Yale University Press, 1959-1950), p. 374.

24. Ibid., ch. 18.

25. Daniel Boorstin, *The Americans: The Colonial Experience* (New York: Random House, 1959), part one.

26. Ibid., pp. 315-16.

27. Daniel Boorstin, *The Genius of American Politics* (Chicago: University of Chicago Press, 1953), p. 66.

28. Ibid., pp. 1, 8, and 9.

29. Stephen Toulmin, *Reason in Ethics* (Cambridge: Cambridge University Press, 1968-1950), p. 148.

30. Robert Dahl, *A Preface to Democratic Theory* (Chicago: University of Chicago Press, 1956), p. 47, passim.

31. David Braybrooke and Charles Lindblom, *A Strategy of Decision* (New York: Free Press, 1970-1963), pp. 206 and 210-11.

32. For a case of Braybrooke and Lindblom doing this, cf. *Strategy*, p. 240.

33. Peter Gay, *The Enlightenment*, vol. II (New York: Knopf, 1969), p. 240.

34. Ibid., p. 166.

35. Ibid., p. 160.

36. Purcell, *The Crisis*, p. 17.

37. Lionel Trilling, *The Liberal Imagination* (New York: Viking, 1950), ch. 1.

38. Hannah Arendt, *The Origins of Totalitarianism* (New York: Meridian, 1958-1951), p. 351.

39. Boorstin, *The Americans: The Colonial Experience* (New York: Random House, 1958), p. 158.

40. Ibid., p. 156; Louis Hartz, *The Liberal Tradition in America* (New York: Harcourt, Brace and World, 1955).

41. Franz Neumann et al., *The Cultural Migration* (Philadelphia: University of Pennsylvania Press, 1953), pp. 19 and 24; Martin Jay, *The Dialectical Imagination* (London: Heinemann, 1973).

42. George Boas in *Partisan Review*, May–June 1950, pp. 461–66.

43. William Whyte, "Politics and Ethics: A Symposium," *American Political Science Review* 40 (April 1946) : 302–04.

44. See C. Wright Mills, *The Sociological Imagination* (New York: Oxford University Press, 1959), whose classification I have used.

45. Lewis Dexter, "Politics and Ethics," *American Political Science Review* 40 (April 1946): 297.

46. David Easton, *The Political System* (New York: Knopf, 1953); Harold Lasswell and H. Kaplan, *Power and Society: A Framework for Political Inquiry* (New Haven: Yale University Press, 1961–1950); Talcott Parsons, *The Social System* (Glencoe, Ill.: Free Press, 1951), and *The Structure of Social Action*, 2nd ed. (Glencoe, Ill.: Free Press, 1949); 1st ed. was prewar.

47. Arnold Brecht, *Political Theory* (Princeton: Princeton University Press, 1959).

48. Robert Dahl, *Pluralist Democracy in the United States* (Chicago: Rand McNally, 1969), p. 22; Dahl and Charles Lindblom, *Politics, Economics and Welfare* (New York: Harper & Row, 1963–1953), pp. 3–6; Dahl, *A Preface*, ch. 3.

49. Gabriel N. Almond and Sidney Verba, *The Civic Culture* (Princeton: Princeton University Press, 1963), p. 475.

50. Bernard Barber, "Anti-Intellectualism in the United States," *The Journal of Social Issues*, no. 3 (1955): 28.

51. David Riesman et al., *The Lonely Crowd* (New Haven: Yale University Press, 1961–1950), p. xxxiii.

52. Schlesinger, "The Statistical Soldier" (1949), in *Hope*, pp. 55 and 58.

53. David Smith, "A Symposium," *American Political Science Review*, September 1957; *Partisan Review*, May–June 1950.

54. Smith, "A Symposium."

55. John Hallowell, *Main Currents in Modern Political Thought* (New York: Holt, 1950), p. 1; Hallowell, "Politics and Ethics: A Symposium," *American Political Science Review* 40 (April 1946): 302.

56. Leo Strauss, *Natural Right and History* (Chicago: University of Chicago Press, 1953); and David Riesman, "The National Style," in *The American Style*, ed. Elting Morison (New York: Harper and Bros., 1958), p. 361.

57. William Yandell Elliot, *The Pragmatic Revolt in Politics* (New York: Fertig, 1968–1928), pp. 23 and 225.

58. Gabriel Almond, "Politics and Ethics: A Symposium," *American Political Science Review* 40 (April 1946): 285 and 293.

59. Arnold Rogow, "A Symposium," *American Political Science Review*, September 1957.

60. Floyd Matson, *The Broken Image* (New York: Braziller, 1964), pp. 102–15.

61. Lionel Trilling, *The Liberal Imagination* (New York: Viking, 1950), p. 222.

62. Herbert Deane, *The Political and Social Ideas of St. Augustine* (New York: Columbia University Press, 1966–1963), p. 221.

63. Daniel Bell, *Marxian Socialism in the United States* (Princeton: Princeton University Press, 1967–1952).

64. Murray Kempton, *Part of Our Time* (New York: Simon and Schuster, 1955), ch. 8.

65. Ibid., ch. 10.

66. Schlesinger, "Varieties of Communist Experience" (1960), in *Hope*, p. 290.

67. Schlesinger, "The Causes of Civil War: A Note on Historical Sentimentalism" (1949), in *Hope*.

68. Leslie Fiedler, *An End to Innocence* (Boston: Beacon Press, 1952), pp. 24, 191, and ch. 1.

69. For the best survey of "realism" in international relations see Kenneth Thompson, *Political Realism and the Crisis of World Politics* (Princeton: Princeton University Press, 1960).

70. Hans J. Morgenthau, *Politics Among Nations* (New York: Knopf, 1960-1948), p. 3.

71. Ibid., pp. 15 and 27.

72. Ibid., pp. 259 and 340-42.

73. Ibid., p. 14.

74. See Thompson, *Political Realism*, pp. 156-60, for a good discussion of Morganthau's reservations about "anti-Communism."

75. Kenneth Waltz, *Man, the State and War* (New York: Columbia University Press, 1965-1954), p. 238.

76. Ibid.

77. Ibid., pp. 111, 119-20, and chs. 4 and 5.

78. George Kennan, *American Diplomacy 1900-1950* (New York: Mentor, 1951), p. 49.

79. Ibid., p. 89.

80. Quoted in Thompson, *Political Realism*, p. 23.

81. Reinhold Niebuhr, *The Irony of American History* (New York: Scribner's, 1952), p. 148.

82. Ibid., pp. 5 and 128-29, passim.

83. Purcell, *The Crisis*, ch. 5.

84. Judith Shklar, *Legalism* (Cambridge: Harvard University Press, 1964).

85. Richard Hofstadter, *The Age of Reform* (New York: Vintage, 1962-1955), ch. 1 and pp. 276-82.

86. Richard Hofstadter, *The American Political Tradition* (New York: Vintage, 1959-1948), p. v, 93, and ch. 6.

87. Schlesinger, *Vital Center*, pp. 41 and 161.

88. Peter Gay, *Voltaire's Politics* (New York: Vintage, 1965-1959), p. 18; Gay, *Loss of Mastery* (Berkeley: University of California Press, 1966), p. 37; Gay, *Party of Humanity* (New York: Knopf), ch. 9; Gay, *Enlightenment*, p. 108.

89. Niebuhr, *The Irony*, p. 13.

90. Boorstin, *The Colonial Experience*, p. 122.

91. Smith, *Theme*, p. 17; Thomas L. Thorson, *The Logic of Democracy* (New York: Holt, Rinehart and Winston, 1962), pp. 34, 41 ff., 50, and 135.

92. Richard Hofstadter, *Anti-Intellectualism in American Life* (New York: Knopf, 1963), pp. 145-46, 228-29, and 237.

93. Philip Rahv, *Partisan Review*, May–June 1952, pp. 304 and 307.

94. Trilling, *Liberal Imagination*, pp. xii–xiv and 11.

95. The burden of Mills, *Sociological Imagination*.

96. Gay, *Enlightenment*, pp. 321–23.

97. Riesman, "The National Style," p. 366.

98. Murray Edelman, *The Symbolic Uses of Politics* (Urbana: University of Illinois Press, 1964), p. 186.

6 The Decline of Classical Democratic Theory

The skepticism that pervaded American intellectual life from 1945 to 1964 had many important effects besides the attack on political ideologies and utopias. One of these was a challenge to the framework of what many intellectuals termed *classical democratic theory.* This framework assumed that democracy depended on the rationality and interest of the average citizen and it held that democrats should encourage his or her participation. Many intellectuals assumed that these beliefs were a part of the American liberal democratic ethos, a part that postwar political intellectuals challenged. After 1945 the mood of American political intellectuals became decidedly skeptical about the average citizen's political capacities, the benefits of active citizen participation, and the wisdom of any democratic theory that was not similarly skeptical. They became more and more impressed with what Richard Hofstadter characterized as "our enhanced feeling for the nonrational side of politics."[1] They agreed with Lionel Trilling's observation that liberalism could no longer be naive and believe in human innocence.[2] There was a new respect, as Daniel Aaron observed, for old conservative suspicion of the mass person.[3] There was an often almost evangelistic appeal to other intellectuals to revise optimistic notions of human nature, an appeal often coupled with considerable incredulity at the fact that "Even after reading Swift, Burke, Nietzsche, Dostoyevsky, Freud, and Yeats, many Anglo-American progressives still cling on to their Rousseauistic faith in the infinite perfectability of human nature."[4] The new perspective claimed to be more realistic, more honest, and more practical:

> The classical theory . . . pre-supposed the alert and impartial citizen, always thirsting for knowledge and ready to discuss political questions, always moved to vote on principle for the "public good." . . . All of this approach appears to be empirically false, and it can scarcely be wise for us to conduct our political affairs upon a false orthodoxy.[5]

It has never been clear exactly where "classical democratic theory" came from or who believed it. Perhaps this is not important, although the fact that numerous postwar intellectuals and social scientists perceived it as an illusion that must be swept away certainly is. Yet it helps us to appreciate this expression of skepticism to understand as best we can what tradition of democratic theory came under so severe an attack. Sometimes critics focused their arguments on specific thinkers, even to the extent of placing some rather disparate political philosophers together, to construct the "classical democratic theory." When they did, it was clear that they had in mind the democratic ideas of John Stuart Mill, J. J. Rousseau, and, above all, Pericles and the Athens of fifth century *B. C.* These men and the tradition they exemplified were repeatedly identified with the mainstream of past democratic thinking, creating an image of previous democratic ideals as participatory, optimistic, and sanguine in estimations of citizen competence.

The paradox was that few political intellectuals believed the operations of American democracy had anything to do with classical Athens and not a great deal of connection with John Stuart Mill's aspirations for democracy. Moreover, the history of American democratic theory hardly appeared to conform to the classical theory either. There was, without doubt, one stream of American political thought running from Paine to Jackson to the Populists that did accent so-called classical themes, considerable enthusiasm for the ordinary voter, and support for active citizen participation. There were, however, other currents. The most significant surely was not the classical one at all, but rather the pluralist current with its belief in group competition and bargaining, its dependence on group elites, and its skepticism of the altruism and often the interest of the average person in dealing with politics. This skeptical approach to politics dominated Madison and Adams at the Constitutional Convention, produced the Clays and the Calhouns of the pre-Civil War era and continued to be at the heart of American democratic practice (if not always theory) right through the New Deal.

Although occasionally a political theorist such as Robert Dahl acknowledged there was no single classical theory in the American political tradition, even he appeared to believe that what he called the "Populist" view was basic to the American ideology about democracy. This was "the classical theory" of others under another label and for Dahl, too, its illusions were no longer bearable. The belief that the classical theory had to be replaced was the common perception that followed from the widespread belief that it dominated traditional American and contemporary democratic thinking. That many intellectuals incorrectly perceived the historic strength of classical democratic theory does not alter the fact they chose to campaign against it or the deeply skeptical attitude toward the individual political actor that underlay their efforts. The campaign may have proceeded against an exaggerated enemy, but the campaign was a characteristic and important aspect of postwar skepticism.[6]

Marked skepticism about human behavior was central to the assault on the classical democratic theory in the United States after World War II and it was as prominent a theme in intellectual discourse as was the decline in confidence in ideologies and absolutes. One cannot understand the political theory of that era without appreciating this fact and the cast it gave to so many arguments that derived from it. This mood of skepticism about human political activity flowed from two main sources. First, it was influenced greatly by the continuing rise to prominence of American social science in the intellectual life of the United States. We will see that social science findings were at the core of much of the skepticism. But it was also influenced by the empirical events of recent European history. Intellectuals' observations of Stalinism and Fascism were obviously among the most important observations American intellectuals ever made. Arthur Schlesinger noted, reflecting the opinion of a great many others, that European totalitarianism taught him once and for all that the human being was no foundation for optimists and perfectionists to build upon.[7] Indeed, the great deficiency of many modern liberals seemed to Schlesinger to be their "soft and shallow conception of human nature."[8] It was a deficiency rooted in the Enlightenment and its afterglow, but forever denied by the armies and concentration camps of totalitarianism. Others remarked that "the optimistic beliefs of many nineteenth-century liberals and Marxists . . . strike us as hopelessly irrelevant as guides to present and future action."[9] They were founded in what was frequently characterized as "the ideology of the Enlightenment . . . thin, abstract, and therefore dangerous."[10]

The anxiety over European totalitarianism, of course, like the supposedly shallow optimism of assorted American intellectuals, was not entirely an abstract concern to many thinkers in the United States, especially in the 1950s. The shadow of Senator McCarthy and his following and later the Birchers lay over much of the mood of skepticism regarding citizen behavior. Intellectuals often explicitly connected McCarthy with Populist optimism about people and suggested that in the past "Populistic predispositions" had led some people to a fateful embrace with totalitarianism. Edward Shils is a good example of the political intellectual who had the terrifying experience of European totalitarianism in the back of his mind when he viewed McCarthyism or unbounded confidence in people. *Fear* of the mass of people was a surprisingly prevalent intellectual attitude and it was one that intellectuals expressed in their *skepticism* about human action or even human nature.[11]

SKEPTICISM REGARDING HUMAN NATURE

Disillusionment sometimes took the form of an analysis that pictured human nature as seriously marred by original sin. The extent of the religious revival among postwar intellectuals in the United States has been much exaggerated, but it is no exaggeration to note that ancient religious language served to describe the disappointments of some. Sometimes the language could be oblique, as when Hannah Arendt suggested that so many people had trouble understanding concentration camps because they could not "conceive of a 'radical evil.'"[12] Arendt did not think there was any more basis for such naivete about humans than Reinhold Niebuhr did.

Niebuhr, in fact, emerged as the most outspoken critic of human nature who openly employed the concept of original sin, and it can be no accident that he obtained a wide audience. It was his conviction that all people were afflicted with original sin, which they could not overcome and which no polity dared ignore. By original sin he meant, above all, innate selfishness, leading to certain social conflict. Niebuhr criticized ideologies, including classical liberalism and Marxism. He felt they had too long encouraged hopeful visions of human harmony that did not correspond with the eternal reality of our flawed natures. They had given support to those leaders and fanatics who sought to make people and societies perfect at enormous human cost and inevitable failure.[13] Niebuhr also applied his critique at home. He charged that for too long Americans had believed they were special and their country was special, hiding from themselves their participation in human sin and error. America and Americans were not "innocent," there were no innocents, and it was dangerous to believe the contrary. Those who did were all too likely to become overwhelmed with pride and leave many dead victims in their wake.[14]

Niebuhr was part of a modest revival of interest by some political intellectuals in the insights of Christian pessimism, a movement Herbert Deane enthusiastically encouraged in his able *The Political and Social Ideas of St. Augustine.* Deane obviously admired St. Augustine because he, like Sigmund Freud, was a "realist" about human nature and politics. Augustine understood human evil, its irrationality, its greed, its selfishness. He knew politics had to deal with these unbearable realities and not gloss them over with pleasantries about human nobility and grandeur. He never failed to suggest that such a realistic stance was simply common sense, eminently purposeful for those who wanted a peaceful and decent polity.[15]

Deane was only a rather political example of a movement by many American scholars of religious history toward emphasizing the folly of overestimating the good nature of human beings. It was at this time that Perry Miller completed the rehabilitation of the American Puritans that others had begun and he transformed the once despised Jonathan Edwards into a thinker for modern times. It is hard to imagine how Edwards, whose bitter warnings about the sinfulness of man rang from many an eighteenth-century Puritan pulpit, could have undergone such a revival, without appreciating the extent to which some intellectuals were open to "realistic" perspectives in a rather disillusioned age. The Progressive historian V.L. Parrington had authored the standard treatment of Edwards before Miller's classic *Jonathan Edwards* (1949). He was as harsh as any of Edwards's sermons, giving an unrelieved denunciation of a man who misunderstood human beings and their potential. The day for such a view was long gone by the time Miller's classic revision appeared in 1949.[16] This is why Peter Viereck was wrong when he described American intellectuals as trapped with a "dogma of Original sinlessness."[17] Many were increasingly as convinced as Jonathan Edwards was that "evil is as instinctive as love."[18]

So extensive was the renewed fascination with human sin that it produced some unusually strange converts. It was rather remarkable to read Murray Kempton, liberal intellectual of the *New York Post* and a former Communist, maintaining that the greatest mistake of the Communists was their endeavor to teach men and women the falseness of any sense of sin. His program now was the opposite: "if it were possible, we should pass a law forbidding a man to live without the sense of sin."[19]

Arthur Schlesinger made the same point in virtually the same words in his *The Vital Center* (1949), although he avoided outright theological language. He insisted that every modern intellectual must recognize the postwar insight, that people were not particularly goodwilled, that they were swept by aggressive drives that resulted in conflict and doomed utopias. There were no magic formulas such as socialism that could, or should, fool us into believing we could overcome our human weaknesses; we were stuck with them and politics had to face this fact.[20] No doubt he appreciated the reality of what one intellectual called "the furies" within humankind and their eternal durability.[21] On the other hand, Schlesinger and most other political intellectuals were unprepared for the views of Walter Lippmann, well described as "bitter pessimism" regarding human nature.[22] A balance was required, but it was not a noticeably happy balance. "We conclude with Pascal: 'Man is neither angel nor brute, and the unfortunate thing is that he who would act the angel acts the brute.'"[23]

What Schlesinger called *aggression* and Niebuhr *original sin* was a phenomenon alike in consequence and in apparent permanence. Schlesinger and Niebuhr also agreed in noting the tremendous temptations of power in fallible human hands. Fear of power was central to postwar political thinking. In the popular view any normal person, with the usual complement of human frailty, could become a genuine monster once in power, as European totalitarianism had so often tellingly demonstrated. Schlesinger felt this delicate act of "squaring the temptations of power . . . with the weaknesses of man" was a basic modern problem.[24] He was not optimistic, for he believed there "is a Hitler, a Stalin in every breast."[25] He did not see how there could be any conclusion drawn from the shocking Western encounter with "totalitarianism" except a deep skepticism of human beings and their record of "aggrandizement and destruction."[26] Clinton Rossiter sadly agreed. As always, he singled out Marx as the most naive of all. Marx had not the faintest understanding of the human proclivity for evil when entrusted with the reigns of power.[27]

These warnings from intellectuals such as Niebuhr and Rossiter were advanced with self-consciously political implications. Their implications for the citizen and democratic theory were assumed to be obvious. Others were less direct and overt in expressing their opinions, but their views about human nature played an important role in forming a milieu in which a new "realism" about human nature was evident. This was the case, for example, among many postwar literary figures. Much of post-1945 American fiction was obsessed with the individual person outside of any direct political arena, but much of the psychological reflection that interested authors from Faulkner to Shirley Jackson could hardly have given hope to participatory Democrats. Fiction in the 1940s and 1950s was filled with proclamations by disparate figures such as Robert Penn Warren and Truman Capote concerning the absurdity of belief in human innocence. Complex, distinctly ambivalent, and often downright pessimistic images of human life dominated, reaching their height in works such as Salinger's *Catcher in the Rye* and Golding's *Lord of the Flies*. The popular and disturbing gothic fiction of the era, with its exploration of the mysterious and subterranean dimensions of human existence through the eyes of writers such as Carson McCullers, Truman

Capote, and Shirley Jackson, was hardly a moment of reaffirmation of human rationality. Nor did the strong rebirth of critical interest in Freudianism in literary interpretation, practiced by men such as Lionel Trilling and Leslie Fiedler, bolster "classical" confidence in the rational faculties of the individual. Without doubt, there was broad agreement among dominant literary intellectuals "that there are deeper perceptions of man's plight than the brash optimism of a Rousseau."[28]

HUMAN BEHAVIOR

Many intellectuals, who looked at people in a framework that demonstrated to them that man was a flawed, selfish, power seeking, and exceedingly complex being, often argued as if there was something they could call human nature. They usually assumed that human nature was a constant, unlikely to improve and unlikely to change in any fashion. Yet most intellectuals who were social scientists were uneasy with analyses such as Schlesinger's or Niebuhr's that spoke of human nature in fixed and eternal terms. They preferred to talk about human *behavior*, a less rigid and supposedly more empirically measurable phenomenon. They also stayed clear of phrases like original sin and innate aggressiveness.

Moreover, a number of social science intellectuals did not consider the criticism of self-interest particularly apposite. Certainly they did not deny that self-interest was typical of human behavior, but they did not always agree this was regrettable. Robert Dahl could remark with a certain worldly cynicism in his *A Preface to Democratic Theory* (1956) that politics operated on self-interest, that the "essence of all competitive politics is bribery of the electorate by politicians," with the intention of disabusing those who might still think people were noble, self-sacrificing souls in politics, but he did not think the fact that selfishness motivated them was particularly unfortunate.[29] Seymour Martin Lipset shared the same opinion. There was no doubt in his mind that the key to understanding why people voted as they did was economic self-interest, but this did not disturb him.[30] Milton Friedman carried this idea to the furthest extreme, predictably, defending a laissez-faire society. He insisted that people were normally selfish and he did not see why anyone should assume this was tragic. He suspected that many people forgot too easily how often self-regarding interest encompassed quite elevating actions.[31] Or, as he sometimes put it, there was a good deal of evidence in his opinion to show that human beings often expressed "enlightened self-interest."[32]

In part we may suspect that the unwillingness of many intellectuals to deplore the reality of self-interest reflected a longtime liberal conviction that self-interest was not necessarily bad, that at its best individual pursuit of self-interest could produce a satisfactory—and free—social order. After all, liberalism involved individualism and that meant granting each individual a large area in which to follow his own wishes. It was not, then, the rediscovery and in some cases the reaffirmation of the legitimacy of self-interest in human beings that always promoted disillusionment among all skeptical intellectuals as they reflected on the individual in politics. The Niebuhrs and the Schlesingers may have found this fact shocking, but theirs was not the only perspective.

Social science-oriented intellectuals joined the postwar movement toward greater skepticism regarding the human person at another point. For them the crucial question was whether people in their roles as citizens demonstrated much enlightened interest, information, or rationality as opposed to "goodness." Their conclusion made them unmistakably pessimistic.

THE FOCUS ON THE IRRATIONAL

This conclusion about the limited rationality of citizen behavior had long been foreshadowed. The pioneering work of some social scientists in the 1930s and even the 1920s that investigated citizen political behavior challenged any assumption of rationality regarding the average American citizen. They knew the effect of their work was to undermine the "classical" democratic hope.[33] But it took time for the work of these empirically oriented pioneers to gain a dominant voice in the political science profession in particular, a victory that was coincident with the behavioral revolution in the social sciences. These victories were completed after World War II and the findings of modern social science rapidly entered the broader intellectual environment to exercise substantial influence. There they coalesced with the reflections of postwar democratic theorists. Social scientists and skeptical democratic theorists spoke to and through each other, echoing the same message of "realism." Democratic theorists who were well-acquainted with the results of the new research early began to indicate skepticism about classic democratic theory. J. Schumpeter manifested great contempt for the so-called will of the citizenry in democracy. It was nothing but "an indeterminant bundle of vague impulses playing about given slogans and mistaken impressions."[34] Henry Mayo was convinced that research revealed the ugly truth that the "majority may be brought to agree to any absurdity."[35] Hannah Arendt observed that we had to learn from the fact that totalitarian regimes retained mass support right to their end and she seemed to think the lesson about the modern citizen justified her frequent references to the "mob."[36] George Kennan did not hide his scorn for the "populist mood," when he wrote of what he felt was the unfortunate history of public input into foreign affairs.[37] They all appreciated that their dissatisfaction was significant in terms of democratic theory, and they accepted the blunt assessments of Clinton Rossiter who claimed that the failures of American political parties were really the failures of the American people or Giovanni Sartori who remarked that it "is high time, therefore, that we realized that when we complain about democracy, we are complaining about the *demos*."[38]

The disappointment with *citizen rationality* in politics derived from two sets of findings. One was the voter studies; the other was assorted psychological investigations. There is no doubt about the seminal contribution of the surveys and panel studies of voter attitudes that poured from the presses after 1945. The most important early study was *Voting* (1954) by Bernard Berelson et al. and it was notably more pessimistic than some other works. But the most ambitious and most influential study was Campbell et al's *The American Voter* (1960), a report on voter attitudes in the Eisenhower elections. Its findings were a revolution in themselves, albeit only because they thoroughly confirmed what other studies had suggested and what informed democratic thinkers knew.

The authors of *The American Voter* established that not only were most voters quite misinformed about candidates and issues in presidential elections, but more important in this context, they often did not appear very rational as they participated in the democratic electoral process. There was overwhelming evidence that voters seemed to care vastly more about candidates' personalities and political parties than they did about issues. Sometimes they could not offer reasons for their support or opposition to candidates beyond inchoate feelings about candidates picked up from the media. Moreover, they often had no coherent approach to politics and the issues it raised. They not only had no discernable political philosophy, but frequently they lacked a systematic set of political attitudes. In some cases they supported one party or candidate for no discernable reason at all. They were hardly "rational citizens."[39]

These findings joined others until it became a staple of postwar social scientific wisdom to note the widespread apparent irrationality of voter behavior. Herbert McCloskey announced similar findings, that even the most superficial perspectives on issues, or any reflections that might be considered intellectual, simply were not an ordinary element in a voter's behavior.[40] Philip Converse in a famous article argued that people's political views often could not be predicted in any coherent manner, for from one issue to the next there frequently was scant consistency. Often, in fact, all Converse could discern was flagrant inconsistency. For example, there were numerous people who blithely advocated a reduction in taxes while urging an expansion of governmental services, with no sense that these two goals were not compatible.[41] Moreover, as Greenstein remarked, studies demonstrated that citizens seemed unable to proceed consistently from whatever abstract values they did hold to logical policy conclusions. Above all, there was great unease among many social scientists over what Greenstein described in social science understatement, the "scarcely encouraging" evidence that the American people endorsed such rules of the game as free speech as general norms and then turned around and held that they should not be permitted in a number of concrete cases, including the cases of Fascists and Communists.[42]

There was, it is fair to say, a dilemma in the midst of all the criticism that few citizens could escape. On the one hand, they were found to be less than coherent and consistent in what political norms they had and none too subtly criticized for that fact. At the same time they could have read the work of almost any important political intellectual in the postwar era and learned the dangers of ideology. Could the individual person win? Was he not likely to be faulted either for being too coherent and therefore dangerously ideological or for being too muddled and therefore utterly irresponsible?

Such reflections rarely arose in the period, especially when the subject of voter irrationality was under discussion. The classic document *The Authoritarian Personality* drew on its psychological discoveries to echo the general mood. Its authors announced there was no doubt there were major indications of "widespread . . . confusion of our subjects in political matters, a phenomenon which might well surpass what even a skeptical observer should have anticipated."[43] The authors were not happy about these findings precisely because most of their subjects were ordinary Americans. Perhaps it was no wonder, Robert Lane suggested, given data that made clear most political discussions never addressed basic matters of principle or issues. People generally talked about politics in terms reminiscent of Hollywood gossip magazines, stressing personalities to an astonishing degree.[44] Nor were most people likely to be startled out of their patterns of thinking even when they were not merely indulging in gossip. The data showed that people did not gain their perspective from debate and discussion with those who disagreed with them and challenged them, since they talked almost exclusively to people who shared their opinions and prejudices.[45]

Often confused and illogical in their thinking, loving political gossip more than serious political reflection, most citizens were incapable, Lane concluded, of being particularly rational in the pursuit of their, or any other, interest. "Instrumental approach to political change is a minimal feature of electoral activity."[46] Instead citizens followed personalities and especially parties more or less blindly. "Party identification has more influence over a person's vote decision than any other single factor."[47]

It was not a pretty picture. But Gabriel Almond and Sidney Verba in their widely praised *Civic Culture* (1963) asserted that one could accept no other. What they termed the "rationality-activist" model was not descriptive of American (or other Western) political normality. The truth about "citizens in democracies" was that "the process by which they come to their voting decision is anything but a process of rational calculation."[48] So it went.

Voting studies were strongly supported by the findings of much political psychological research and theory. This aspect of social science, in particular through the work of Harold Lasswell, Stuart Rice, Floyd Alport, and others, had been a ready source of skepticism long before 1945,[49] but it gained in strength and respect after World War II. Harold Lasswell was the leading figure in political psychology and his analysis of personality research as it applied to politics was not reassuring:

> the findings of personality research show that . . . the individual who chooses a political policy . . . is usually trying to relieve his own disorders by irrelevant palliative. An examination of the total state of the person will frequently show that his theory of his own interests is far removed from the course of procedure which will give him a happy and well-adjusted life.[50]

The authors of *The Authoritarian Personality* (1950) agreed that subjects attracted to Fascism, racism, or authoritarianism, uncovered by the famous F. scale, were not usefully understood as rational citizens in control of their minds and destinies. There were many who were swept by irrational needs, especially a need to obtain "blind belief in authority," while at the same time they were impelled to want to crush those who appeared weak.[51] Although the authors concluded that most Americans were not really irrational, authoritarian personalities, the broader significance of their epochal findings was congruent with Lasswell's; "differences in ideology are significantly related to personality differences," rather than to conclusions reached through rational thinking.[52]

Political scientist Robert Lane, who was intensely engaged in personality research, shared the general conclusion that political activity often could best be explained as a manifestation of "intra-psychic tensions."[53] He particularly noted that escape from sex and sexual problems was "a normal and perhaps frequent source of political drive."[54] He observed that politics was often especially attractive for those bursting with hostile aggression, since it provided many outlets for those who desperately sought to express their hates.[55] Nor was it a surprise to him that most letters to congressmen were "expressive" rather than really rational and frequently grossly "misinformed" about the subjects they discussed.[56] Lane left the impression that Freud had been correct all along. Politics was an activity all too often suited to the mentally disturbed.

Another popular theory of the time was the *cognitive dissonance theory*. According to this doctrine people had a low capacity for managing conflicting messages their minds might receive. They found ambivalent personal or political relationships and ideas a source of personal anxiety. Consequently, some thought people were not particularly well-suited to operate in a realm like politics, which was necessarily complex and had many conflicting pressures and ideas in it. The problem was not merely the anxiety that resulted. Much more dangerous for politics was the fact that people so strongly resisted situations of cognitive dissonance that they were likely to seek to obliterate (in their minds) whatever facts made for cognitive dissonance. This drive for irrational simplicity and unity in people's outlook was yet another factor that encouraged reservations about popular rationality.[57]

The bestselling works of Eric Hoffer, especially *The True Believer* (1951), brought to popular consciousness the common pessimism, of which Lasswell and *The Authoritarian Personality* were only the two most prominent illustrations. Hoffer unsystematically linked a host of psychological attitudes and situations to the hatred, fanaticism, and irrationality that found a ready voice in the mass movements of politics. Hoffer was particularly attracted by the idea that radical politics gathered in those who sought to compensate for deep-seated personal feelings of failure.[58]

Even before the postwar era Lasswell had been interested in the role of *symbols* as a central feature of political life, a phenomenon that revealed people were easily manipulated and suggested just how vulnerable they were to irrational inner needs and tensions. His interest was shared by other pioneers in the 1930s, especially Thurman Arnold whose books *The Symbols of Government* (1935) and *The Folklore of Capitalism* (1937) were landmarks in the investigation of symbolic influences in political life.[59]

After the war attention to symbolic aspects of human behavior rapidly expanded. This was evident in literary themes of the era from the novels of William Faulkner to the haunting tales of the writers of gothic fiction. But it was especially noticeable among political intellectuals who often implied that people's tendency to act out their psychic needs in politics and their weaknesses for responding to manipulating symbols interfered with citizen rationality and undermined classical democratic theory. Ernst Cassirer documented the powerful and destructive influence of the "myth of the state"; Richard Hofstadter suggested that America's past adventures in imperialism could be understood as an interplay between myths and frustrations; Clinton Rossiter interpreted political parties as vital allegiance symbols most citizens needed.[60]

Perhaps the best single book of the postwar period that undertook a comprehensive psychological examination of the citizen was Murray Edelman's *The Symbolic Uses of Politics* (1964). Edelman's purpose was unusual in that he undertook to attack elite manipulation of the mass of people, but in the process he drew a devastating picture of the average citizen whom he gently preferred to describe as "non-rational." Edelman claimed that it was

> characteristic of large numbers of people in our society that they see and think in terms of stereotypes, personalization, and over simplifications, that they cannot recognize or tolerate ambiguous and complex situations, and that they accordingly respond chiefly to symbols that oversimplify and distort.[61]

Put more sharply, Edelman declared the unpleasant truth was that the "mass public responds to currently conspicuous political symbols: not to 'facts,' and not to moral codes . . . but to gestures and speeches that make up the drama of the state."[62]

Edelman's view was little short of cynical, but the application of that label does not weaken his conclusions nor discredit the literature on which it was based nor discount the ready acceptance Edelman's portrait obtained. The art of governing, according to Edelman, was to be understood mostly in terms of elites who either did or did not skillfully manipulate the masses by symbols. If they were wise, they knew they had to master the techniques of "symbolic reassurance," which was about all most of the citizenry needed to keep them happy. Certainly elites rarely had to worry about satisfying the actual needs of the masses as long as they could provide symbolic reassurance.[63]

THE UNINFORMED VOTER

Although one picture social scientists drew depicted an irrational citizen, another outlined a typical citizen who was appallingly ignorant politically. A massive amount of well-documented evidence challenged not only the classic democratic image of a rational voter, but also the image of an informed citizen who had the knowledge necessary to make a rational decision.

Social scientist after social scientist reported the same dreary data, reported that people were usually uninformed and at times shockingly ignorant about candidates, policies, and even the most elementary characteristics of American government. This was the burden of *The American Voter*, documented in painful tables and excerpts from interviews. In the judgment of its authors, the electorate had "a substantial lack of familiarity with . . . policy questions" and "the public's understanding of policy issues" was "poorly developed."[64] They saw no reason to avoid the most direct language in presenting their conclusion: "We have then, the portrait of an electorate almost wholly without detailed information about decision making in government."[65] Others could not disagree, nor did later surveys. Warren Miller and Donald Stokes presented evidence that led them to the inescapable conclusion that voters had only the slightest information about the behavior of their representatives in Congress.[66] Greenstein cited data that indicated only half of the adult population even knew there are two senators from each state; less than half could give the length of congressmen's terms or the number of judges on the Supreme Court; and less than one-quarter of the citizenry could identify even one of the provisions of the Bill of Rights.[67]

The implications for democratic theory were hardly subtle and they were taken to heart in the postwar era. There was wide agreement that it was past time for democratic thinkers to reexamine "impossible" standards that idealistic theorists once demanded of citizens.[68] There was also a determination to relegate as "one of the myths of democracy" the notion of the "impartial informed voter."[69] Thinkers perceived very well how significant a retreat this was in the light of "classic" democratic optimism; yet they were convinced the data made it dangerous to allow "democracy to rest on voters' competence" any longer without giving "away the case for democracy entirely to its critics."[70] Instead, there was a crying need for a new and more realistic democratic theory, one that made extensive voter knowledge "not necessary either for the validity of democratic theory or for the practical success of democracies."[71] We explore in chapter 7 the creation of this new democratic theory, which was the major work of American political theory after 1945.

STRUCTURAL PROBLEMS

On top of the doubts about the rational and informed citizen came yet another set of problems that seemed to doom any practical chance for participatory democracy, even to the modest extent of majority rule through elections. Thinkers wondered how any thoughtful person could overlook the tremendous barriers that now existed due to the *structural demands* of size and time.[72] For instance, huge populations in the United States and elsewhere seemed to render opportunities for much popular input nil. The enormous complexity of public issues was quite beyond the capacity of the average person to understand what was taking place and thus made it impossible for him or her to influence policy questions in a meaningful manner. Part of the difficulty here, too, was time, but it was also a matter of the intrinsic complexity of many public questions in highly populated and differentiated modern states. Such issues could be comprehended only by those with considerable professional expertise. "The simple fact—and it is a fact—is that the bulk of the voters are quite incompetent to judge complex details of public policy."[73] Richard Hofstadter did not see how the average citizen could find this state of affairs very remarkable, since

> "he cannot even make his breakfast without using devices, more or less mysterious to him, which expertise has put at his disposal; and when he sits down to breakfast and looks at his morning newspaper,

he reads about a whole range of vital and intricate issues and ac-
knowledges, if he is candid with himself, that he has not acquired
competence to judge most of them."[74]

Another structural problem, one that was fundamental to
democratic theory, also emerged from the data of the expanding
discipline of political science. The problem was that there did not
often appear to be a majority "out there," which was quite contrary
to every classical democratic theory. Robert Dahl claimed that a
realistic glance at the electoral process did not, and could not, tell
us much about the preferences, much less the existence, of any
alleged majority. To be sure, in general elections one candidate
obtained a majority of votes, but the evidence suggested that usually this majority agreed on nothing else, including the reason
they employed in deciding to vote for the same candidate. Often
enough, they strongly disagreed with each other on many major
issues, so it was exceedingly misleading to suppose that an electoral
victor represented an issue majority. Even worse was the fact that
many members of the majority had few, or no, discernable positions on any issues.[75] As Dahl and Lindblom described the situation
in *Politics, Economics and Welfare* (1953): "the greater number of
people often do not have definite preferences on a given issue; or
when they do, often they do not act on them; or their preferences
are often so ambiguous and conflicting."[76] Consequently, it was
logical to remark that in "practice, then, the democratic goal that
governmental decisions should accord with the preferences of
great numbers of adults in society is extraordinarily difficult to
approximate." The majority was a myth.[77]

Henry Mayo, among others, pointed out what investigation had
demonstrated, that even when one could identify a majority, it did
not last long, since majorities were almost perversely "fickle."
Majority opinion fluctuated so much and so often that even if he
wanted to, the most dedicated leader or representative could not
move fast enough to translate into law what a majority wanted.
Mayo argued that the data formed a picture that had scant relation
to the classical democratic model of the majority taking and holding
a clear stand. Real majorities were, in fact, too fleeting and too
"transient" to be accorded much serious respect.[78]

PARTICIPATION

The discoveries described above produced much skepticism about the assumptions of classical democratic theory. The totalitarian experience, the rediscovery of original sin, the progress in personality research in politics, and the voter studies with their gloomy message about voter rationality and information could hardly excite postwar intellectuals about *citizen participation*. Together they constituted a virtual tidalwave that swept down upon optimistic visions of democracy with a force that would not be, and was not, denied.

The intellectual mood never turned openly antidemocratic and never turned toward overt sympathy toward oligarchy. That was hardly possible in postwar America, but it did become distinctly hostile to any definition of democracy that sympathized with participation as the central defining and legitimating element. Occasionally, there was an extremely cautious voice like Seymour Martin Lipset's which favored more participation if it increased gradually and brought into the political system unrepresented elements. But the key word was *gradually*, for Lipset shared the general fear that rapid increases in participation were signs of danger and decay and a potential prelude to dictatorship.[79] The great concern of many political intellectuals was that stability would be threatened by a heavily participatory political order. As they saw it, their data gave no grounds for anything but the deepest reservations about participation by an electorate who were often ignorant and nonrational.[80]

It was equally predictable that there would be a more or less frontal assault on those who might want the United States to move toward a more participatory political system. This was exactly the wrong move, many social scientists thought, in the light of their empirical and structural research. It was never exactly clear whom they argued against so anxiously, since the voices in postwar America proposing expanded participation in our government were few until the 1960s but the theme was often repeated. Edward Shils, was alarmed at the idea of expanded political participation. Rossiter warned that greater participation meant bringing in the more uneducated voter and lowering the "quality" of the electorate, and Almond took pains to demonstrate the sadly irrational and impulsive record of popular attitudes when turned toward foreign policy.[81]

To be sure, many democratic thinkers in the two postwar decades did not treat the alternative participatory, or Athenian, model of democracy at length, as they were to do so often and so vigorously during the days of the New Left after 1965. Robert Dahl, for instance, did not consider participatory democracy as one of his models of democracy in his *A Preface To Democratic Theory*. Nor did David Spitz, who was another important democratic theorist of the era. These omissions were striking in themselves and told an unspoken but revealing story about what was considered outside the paradigm.

On the other hand, some thinkers did take note of the participatory alternative. There were a few who had considerable regard for it. Hannah Arendt stands out in this regard. Ordinarily the reaction was quite different and consisted of an attack on the participatory ideal and its commitment to radical political equality. Many insisted on a "deprecation of the equality principle as a criterion for decision making." Most also assumed that "ancient democracies cannot teach us anything."[82] It was commonly assumed that Athenian standards for democracy were irrelevant in the modern world and therefore could not serve as a serious model.[83] John Stuart Mill's earnest celebration of the ideal of self-government, too, "was impossible then as it is now, and—I am not afraid to predict—will be just as impossible in one or ten centuries."[84] The behavior of the voter, the complexities of modern America, and much else led many theorists to agree that equal and intense participation were inappropriate democratic ideals for postwar America.[85] There was broad agreement with Sartori, who declared that if "democracy is threatened from without . . . it is even more seriously threatened from within by perfectionists," those who desired much more participation.[86] The test as always was the empirical world as they perceived it, a world whose permanence was taken as given. By this restricted test they were sure they were right. Participatory democracy was impossible.

It was only natural that the critique of participatory politics was often accompanied by a candid appreciation of a politics of popular apathy. It was a fitting, if not always happy, conclusion to the discoveries of the age. Certainly there was considerable indication that many social scientists were pleased at the marked apathy of the American electorate. This was a quite acceptable situation in a democracy as long as access to those who were interested remained open, since many, or most, citizens were too lacking in information and rational development to be valuable participants in a democratic polity. James Prothro and C. Grigg argued that political elites in America usually had a greater commitment to democracy and civil liberties than the masses did anyway, so the irony was that apathy preserved democracy better than supposedly democratic high participation would.[87] Henry Mayo perfectly summed up the wisdom of the age:

> "It is not an established truth that democracy suffers from voting apathy, or that any democracy has fallen because of it . . . the evidence points overwhelmingly the other way, that there has always been wide, almost feverish public interest in politics and voting in countries where democracy has collapsed, e.g., in the Weimar Republic."[88]

THE DISSENTING DEFENDERS

Not everyone shared the thesis of social scientists and others in the intellectual community who absorbed the conclusions of modern social studies. It was not merely a matter that openly endorsing apathy did not seem democratic to social scientists such as E.E. Schattschneider, or that the data could be read in a far less pessimistic manner as it was by V.O. Key in *Public Opinion and American Democracy* (1961).[89] There were those who went much further and called for a participatory democracy that in their view would transform American practice and put it in touch with its classical democratic origins. They were the genuine dissenters in the decades after 1945. There were not a great many of them in fact, but they represented several rather different traditions of thought that were not quite silent from 1945 to 1964. Carl J. Friedrich spoke out of his affection for the New England town meeting and his belief that this was a type of government that

could be widely used for much, though not all, of the matters involved in the governance of men and women. He remained enthusiastic about the potential for human self-government, affirming an
optimistic *New Image of the Common Man.*[90] Christian Bay and
before him C. Wright Mills spoke out of an anger that greatly
spread in the 1960s, an anger that accused intellectuals of being
shameless apologists for the postwar surrender of the ideal of an
active democracy and cheerfully approving its replacement with
elitism. The formation of the Students for a Democratic Society in
1960 and the issuance of their famous Port Huron Statement in
1962 were other signs of the quickening interest in participatory
politics in the early 1960s.[91] Some intellectuals saw participatory
democracy primarily in psychological terms, lamenting the waste
of human potential incurred by the absence of self-government.
Erich Fromm was the most famous and the most zealous proponent
of the view that apathy was a mark of failure and participation
an essential objective for human growth.[92]

There were other dissenters, but they did not articulate any
common ground or constitute any formal or informal movement.
They were present, but strictly on the fringes of intellectual life
until the 1960s, sometimes uneasy with each other and always
viewed uneasily by the mainstream. They evoked another ideal in
an era in political thought in which the present had become the
standard, and they could hardly have expected much serious
attention.

CONCLUSION

The judgment of many postwar intellectuals, led by prominent
social scientists, was that investigation of human nature or typical
political behavior did not bear out the faith of classical democratic
theory in a rational, informed, interested citizen nor in an established majority. The data of modern social science condemned
it to the dreamy world of sentimentalism. Skepticism toward the
old claims and the actual citizen became the new orthodoxy. It was
the building material for American political intellectuals after 1945
who determined to "erect a vigorous and realistic theory" of
democracy. As with the development of skepticism regarding
absolute answers in politics, so with the rise of skepticism about

the rational voter, the crisis came quite without a trace of panic. Skepticism did not lead to pessimism about the condition of American democracy. It was, the intellectuals thought, obviously in good health even though it was based on "real" voters, not the illusory individuals of past democratic theoreticians. The truth could be accepted without regret. As B. Berelson remarked in *Voting* (1954): "This is the paradox. *Individual voters* today seem unable to satisfy the requirements for a democratic system of government outlined by political theorists. But the *system of democracy* does meet certain requirements for a going political organization," which they took to be sufficient.[93] The real world was satisfactory.

Latter-day critics sometimes suggest that these conclusions were not so much skeptical as they were pessimistic, even misanthropic, in their assessments of human potential.[94] From the perspective of an advocate of a more equalitarian and participatory polity, this conclusion is true, but it is not really accurate to portray the postwar skeptics as basically unhappy with the American people. Moreover, if they were, it certainly was not because they did not fulfill the "classic" standards for a more participatory democracy. Since most political intellectuals were notably pleased with the American political system and the modest role the ordinary citizen played in it, they did not see themselves as thinkers bitterly disappointed with human behavior. They claimed to be skeptical realists who accepted real people rather than hated them. They were convinced, indeed, that "it is striking how often making a fetish of an ideal people goes hand in hand with a contempt for real people, for actual people. Marx was certainly not a humanitarian, and from Robespierre to Stalin we have ample evidence of how easily a mystique of the ideal works out, in practice, in reverse, as a ruthless and merciless Realpolitik."[95]

NOTES*

1. E. E. Schattschneider, *The Semi-Sovereign People* (New York: Holt, Rinehart and Winston, 1960), pp. 130–31 and 139; Richard Hofstadter, *The Paranoid Style in American Politics and Other Essays* (New York: Knopf, 1965), p. ix.

*Some books listed here have two dates: the first is the date of the edition referenced here; the second is the date the work was originally published.

2. Chester Eisinger, *Fiction of the Forties* (Chicago: University of Chicago Press, 1963), p. 137.

3. Daniel Aaron, "Conservatism, Old and New," *American Quarterly* 6 (Summer 1954).

4. Peter Viereck, *Shame and Glory of the Intellectuals* (New York: Capricorn, 1965–1953), p. 56.

5. Henry Mayo, *An Introduction to Democratic Theory* (New York: Oxford University Press, 1960), p. 112.

6. Some famous works: Robert Dahl, *A Preface to Democratic Theory* (Chicago: University of Chicago Press, 1956); Gabriel Almond and Sidney Verba, *The Civic Culture* (Princeton: Princeton University Press, 1963); Giovanni Sartori, *Democratic Theory* (New York: Praeger, 1967–1962).

7. Arthur Schlesinger, Jr., *The Vital Center* (London: Andre Deutsch, 1970–1949)), pp. xxii–xxiii.

8. Ibid., p. 40.

9. Herbert Deane, *The Political and Social Ideas of St. Augustine* (New York: Columbia University Press, 1966–1963), p. 242.

10. William Barrett, *Irrational Man* (Garden City, N.Y.: Doubleday-Anchor, 1962–1958), p. 275.

11. Michael P. Rogin, *The Intellectuals and McCarthy* (Cambridge: M.I.T. Press, 1967); Edward Shils, *The Torment of Secrecy* (Glencoe, Ill.: Free Press, 1956) pp. 46–47, 98–104, 128, and 132–33.

12. Hannah Arendt, *The Origins of Totalitarianism* (New York: Meridian, 1958–1951), p. 459.

13. Reinhold Neibuhr, *The Children of Light and the Children of Darkness* (New York: Scribner's, 1944), pp. 10–11, 17, 39, passim.

14. Reinhold Niebuhr, *The Irony of American History* (New York: Scribner's, 1952), ch. 2.

15. Deane, *St. Augustine*, pp. 242–43.

16. Perry Miller, *Jonathan Edwards* (New York: Meridian, 1959–1949); Robert Skotheim, *Intellectual History and Historians* (Princeton: Princeton University Press, 1969), pp. 205–6 and 252.

17. Viereck, *Shame*, p. 127.

18. Skotheim, *Intellectual History*.

19. Murray Kempton, *Part of Our Time* (New York: Simon and Schuster, 1955), p. 33.

20. Schlesinger, *Vital Center*, pp. 45–46, 63, and 161–162.

21. Barrett, *Irrational Man*, pp. 276–80.

22. William Newman, *The Futilitarian Society* (New York: Braziller, 1960), p. 216.

23. Schlesinger, *Vital Center*, p. 156.

24. Ibid., p. 6.

25. Ibid., p. 250.

26. Ibid., p. 165.

27. Clinton Rossiter, *Marxism: The View from America* (New York: Harcourt, Brace and World, 1960), p. 186.

28. Besides authors and works cited in text, cf. Eisinger, *Fiction*, pp. 16–17, 231–232, 290–292, passim; Leslie Fiedler, *An End to Innocence* (Boston: Beacon Press, 1955), pp. 197, 198, 202–3, ch. 9, and ch. 13.

29. Dahl, *A Preface*, p. 68.

30. Seymour Martin Lipset, *Political Man* (Garden City, N.Y.: Doubleday-Anchor, 1963–1960), p. 239.

31. Milton Friedman, *Capitalism and Freedom* (Chicago: University of Chicago Press, 1962), p. 200.

32. Ibid., pp. 288 and 291.

33. Edward Purcell, *The Crisis of Democratic Theory* (Lexington: University of Kentucky Press, 1973), ch. 6.

34. Joseph Schumpeter, *Capitalism, Socialism, Democracy*, 3rd ed. (New York: Harper, 1950), p. 254.

35. Mayo, *Introduction*, p. 176.

36. Arendt, *Origins*, pp. 206 and 306, passim.

37. George Kennan, *American Diplomacy 1900–1950* (New York: Mentor, 1951), p. 22.

38. Clinton Rossiter, *Parties and Politics in America* (Ithaca: Cornell University Press, 1960), pp. 173–74; Sartori, *Theory*, p. 91.

39. Angus Campbell et al., *The American Voter* (New York: Wiley, 1964–1960), p. 282, passim.

40. Herbert McCloskey, "Consensus and Ideology in American Politics," *American Political Science Review* 58 (June 1964).

41. Philip Converse, "The Nature of Belief Systems in Mass Publics," in ed. David Apter *Ideology and Discontent*, (New York: Free Press, 1964).

42. Fred Greenstein, *The American Party System and the American People* (Englewood Cliffs, N.J.: Prentice-Hall, 1963), pp. 7–9.

43. Theodore Adorno et al., *The Authoritarian Personality* (New York: Harper & Row, 1950), p. 658.

44. Robert Lane, *Political Life* (New York: Free Press, 1959), pp. 86–87.

45. Ibid., p. 33.

46. Ibid., p. 173.

47. Ibid., p. 300; Greenstein, *Party System*, pp. 33–34.

48. Almond and Verba, *Civic Culture*, pp. 473–74.

49. Purcell, *Crisis*, ch. 5.

50. Harold Lasswell, *The Political Writings of Harold Lasswell* (New York: Free Press, 1951), pp. 193–97.

51. Adorno et al. *Authoritarian Personality*, pp. 759–62 and ch. 7.

52. Ibid., p. 891.

53. Lane, *Political Life*, p. 102.

54. Ibid., p. 122.

55. Ibid., p. 119.

56. Ibid., p. 71.

57. Robert Lane and David Sears, *Public Opinion* (Englewood Cliffs, N.J.: Prentice-Hall, 1964).

58. Eric Hoffer, *The True Believer* (New York: Harpers, 1951), part one, ch. 14.

59. Harold D. Lasswell, *Politics: Who Gets What, When, How* (New York: Peter Smith, 1950–1936); Thurman Arnold, *The Symbols of Government* (New Haven: Yale University Press, 1935) and *The Folklore of Capitalism* (New Haven: Yale University Press, 1937).

60. Eisinger, *Fiction*, pp. 16, 234–35; Fiedler, *Innocence*; Hofstadter, *Paranoid Style*, pp. ix and 185; Rossiter, *Parties*, p. 50; Ernst Cassirer, *The Myth of the State* (Garden City, N.Y.: Doubleday, 1955).

61. Murray Edelman, *Symbolic Uses of Politics* (Urbana: University of Illinois Press, 1964), p. 31.

62. Ibid., p. 172.

63. Ibid., pp. 164–67.

64. Campbell et al., *Voter*, p. 281.

65. Ibid., p. 282.

66. Warren Miller and Donald Stokes, "Constituency Influence in Congress," *American Political Science Review* 57 (1963).

67. Greenstein, *Party System*, p. 12.

68. Schattschneider, *People*, p. 136.

69. Mayo, *Introduction*, p. 76.

70. Ibid., pp. 111–12.

71. Ibid., p. 76.

72. Sartori, *Democratic Theory*, p. 61.

73. Mayo, *Introduction*, p. 93.

74. Richard Hofstadter, *Anti-Intellectualism in American Life* (New York: Knopf, 1963), pp. 34–35.

75. Dahl, *Preface*, pp. 129–30.

76. Robert Dahl and Charles Lindblom, *Politics, Economics, and Welfare* (New York: Harper & Row, 1963–1953), p. 309.

77. Ibid.

78. Mayo, *Introduction*, p. 87.

79. Lipset, *Political Man*, p. 229.

80. For example, see Lester Milbraith, *Political Participation* (Chicago: Rand McNally, 1965), pp. 142–54.

81. Shils, *Torment*, p. 21; Rossiter, *Parties*, pp. 24–37 and 184–86; Gabriel Almond, *The American People and Foreign Policy* (New York: Harcourt, Brace and World, 1950), pp. 29–65.

82. Sartori, *Democratic Theory*, p. 251; Charles E. Lindblom, *The Intelligence of Democracy* (New York: Free Press, 1965), p. 262.

83. Mayo, *Introduction*, ch. 3.

84. Sartori, *Theory*, p. 62.

85. Lindblom, *Intelligence*, pp. 252–58.

86. Sartori, *Democratic Theory*, p. 51.

87. James Prothro and C.M. Grigg, "Fundamental Principles of Democracy: Bases of Agreement and Disagreement," *Journal of Politics* 22 (1960).

88. Mayo, *Introduction*, p. 123.

89. Schattschneider, *People*; V.O. Key, Jr., *Public Opinion and American*

Democracy (New York: Knopf, 1961); also see Key's *The Responsible Electorate* (Cambridge: Harvard University Press, 1966).

90. Carl J. Friedrich, *The New Image of the Common Man* (Boston: Beacon, 1950); perhaps it is significant that an earlier edition of this book appeared during World War II.

91. Christian Bay, "Politics and Pseudopolitics," *American Political Science Review* 59 (1965); and Paul Jacobs and Saul Landau, *The New Radicals* (New York: Random House, 1966).

92. Erich Fromm, *The Art of Loving* (New York: Harper, 1956).

93. Bernard Berelson et al., *Voting* (Chicago: University of Chicago Press, 1954), pp. 311–23.

94. Thomas Hartshorne, *The Distorted Image* (Cleveland: Case Western Reserve, 1968), ch. 8.

95. Sartori, *Democratic Theory*, p. 20.

7 The New Democratic Theory

The creation of a new theory of democracy was the central part of the reconstruction of political philosophy accomplished in the twenty years after World War II. We have noted the very intense skepticism many liberal thinkers felt in those years about the validity of classical democratic theory. They were convinced that the old ideal rested on a false conception of human nature or behavior. Moreover, the marching of "totalitarian" masses in Europe in the 1930s had confirmed for them the ominous truth that feckless majorities and mass societies created monsters that did not reflect liberal values. There was a need for a fresh conception of democracy to fit reality and yet save democratic government.

From the first, one of the most interesting features of the *new democratic theory* was the normative assumption that lay behind it. Political intellectuals in America continued to take for granted that "democracy" was a good thing that ought to be defended once it was reformulated in theory to accord with satisfactory practice. No matter how much they denounced the masses, or majoritarianism, or mass societies, intellectuals insisted on their loyalty to the democratic idea, defined as popular election and responsibility of rulers to citizens. It is with this in mind that we may characterize the common position as *democratic liberalism.* Liberal values came first, to be sure, but there was no doubt that American political intellectuals did not see liberal values in conflict with a reformed democratic theory, or with ongoing political practices in America.

Critics then, and even more often later, charged that this was mere pretense. Liberals were accused of developing a theory of democracy that in effect did away with the vital elements of the old ideal. They were accused, as we will see, of preaching democracy even while constructing a theory of democracy they knew was not really democracy at all. These charges were not entirely accurate. There was a genuine commitment to democracy in a vague and general sense. So strong was this commitment that it sometimes led to peculiar results, as intellectuals sought to link democracy with everything they thought was good. For example, consider the case of historian Peter Gay, a keeper of Enlightenment liberal values. He struggled with all his energy to make Voltaire, the great liberal hero of the Enlightenment, into a Democrat. Indeed, dubious as the case was, Voltaire had to be a Democrat because liberalism and democracy went together in the political thought of the postwar period.[1] Gay's argument is perhaps plausible and balanced, but this is not the point. His concern to show Voltaire's democratic side and his inclination to give it the benefit of the doubt are what is so significant.

Such questionable manipulations of "democracy" were not the usual practice. Thinkers who earnestly undertook to define and defend a new democracy were more characteristic. Their view was colored by their affinity for "realism" and it is no surprise that the call for realism resounds through the democratic-theory literature of the postwar years. Critics charged that the liberal reformulation of democratic theory to meet what they considered to be reality proved that most American thinkers preferred American reality above classical democratic principles. Certainly this was a momentous choice and one that laid bare the deep conservatism of American intellectuals. But liberals interpreted their efforts to create a democratic theory that accorded with American political reality as a statement of their enduring and hardheaded devotion to what democracy could exist in an age when so few nations had what could even faintly pass for democracy. It was to them evidence of their determination not to lose what America had in a myopic chase after an impossible dream.

J. Schumpeter, one of the most influential democratic theorists in the 1940s, set the dominant tone. The goal was not a renunciation of democracy, but a democratic theory that was "truer to life" than the classical one.[2]

Giovanni Sartori's important work *Democratic Theory* (1957) contended that the problem with most previous thought about democracy and the difficulty with many radical Democrats in his own time was that both "demand the impossible." They were not realistic. They refused to respect the implacable power of the facts of human fallibility in politics. He gave no thought to the idea that the facts might ever change, much less that they could be made to change.[3]

Henry Mayo was yet another democratic thinker, among so many, who developed the argument along familiar paths. In his *An Introduction to Democratic Theory* (1960), he emphasized in particular the central significance of the findings of modern social science about American political behavior. Classical democratic theory required a high degree of voter "competence," but this competence did not exist. Therefore, classical democratic theory must fall to one that is "more realistic," one that will not require so much citizen knowledge.[4] This did not mandate any abandonment of the democratic perspective. Although we should forget all about classic fantasies regarding popular concern for the public interest, we still had to be Democrats of some sort. The reason was, of course, the need to be "realistic." "Self-protection is a strong argument for the vote" and, indeed, given their image of human behavior, it made sense for political theorists of the age to make the strongest of cases for checks on rulers.[5]

Robert Dahl, the most celebrated political scientist of the period, also argued in his *A Preface to Democratic Theory* (1957) that the proper route for contemporary democratic thinkers was to approach democracy empirically. He was quite convinced that the best, if not the only, way to formulate an adequate democratic theory for the postwar era was not to tarry with the realm of ideals and principles. It was much better to examine nations that political scientists took to be democratic and to cull from them what they had in common. This was democracy, an empirical reality solidly rooted in human fact.[6] This was also a sadly circular approach that failed to explain the norms political scientists used to decide which countries were "democratic." Nor did Dahl explain why we should take political scientists' word about the nature and existence of democracy over anyone else's. But Dahl's position was significant as an instance of the dominance of the ethic of "reality" in the outlook of an influential postwar political thinker.

REALISM AND THE MAJORITY

The realists constructed the groundwork for new democratic theory by their attack on the concept of *majoritarianism* and theories of democracy disposed to either majoritarianism or participatory politics. Part of the attack was explicitly normative, although perhaps the most intriguing part was the technical arguments social scientists made against majoritarianism. Of course, the normative arguments about majoritarianism derived from the perceived behavior of masses in politics. Their behavior made an uncritical enthusiasm for majoritarianism dangerous to liberal values we know always came first. One of those values, and a principal aspect of the new democratic theory as well, was *constitutionalism*. Regular systematic checks on popular power were necessary to preserve civil liberties and individual choice. Constitutionalism was not a form in which the majority might proceed regularly so much as it was a check on the masses. Dahl specifically attacked Populist, or majoritarian, democracy because he thought it could so easily upset a constitutional, liberal order.[7] Carl J. Friedrich, one of the most sympathetic observers of human beings in politics, was nevertheless also an ardent supporter of constitutionalism understood as a set of limitations on popular will. He conjured up the image of Jean Jacques Rousseau and majority tyranny as the enemy (perhaps with Nazi Germany and its mass rallies in mind).[8] Hans Morgenthau spoke similarly about international relations. Majorities were often foolish and could be dangerous. Expert diplomats and national self-interest were better guides.[9]

Conservatives such as Russell Kirk and William F. Buckley had no particular inclination to support democracy in any form. Yet even Kirk in his *Program for Conservatives* (1954), after archly ridiculing universal suffrage and the democratic ethos in general, allowed that if majorities were restrained by constitutional impediments in America, it was endurable.[10] The conservative suspicion that the mainstream of intellectual opinion was locked in the most intimate embrace with an intensely democratic ethos seems curiously mistaken in retrospect. "The commitment by the Liberals to democracy has proved obsessive, even fetishistic," Buckley claimed, but he was quite wrong. To be sure, democracy in a vague sense was part of postwar American political thought. Yet democracy in the sense of majoritarianism and mass culture most certainly was not. Buckley heard the words democracy and democratic, but he did not understand that postwar political intellectuals had in mind a special meaning.[11]

Robert Dahl propounded the most important normative argument that undermined majoritarianism. He contended that majoritarians did not realize genuine representation cannot be achieved on the one-dimensional scale of one person, one vote, nor could a majority be considered simply the majority of votes. Dahl sought to understand democracy on what we may call a two-dimensional scale. He insisted that the one-person, one-vote principle simply overlooked the fact that people have varying intensities of feeling and commitment to individual issues or candidates. Dahl maintained that a person who cares desperately about candidate X should not be easily overruled by the almost indifferent preference of two other citizens who prefer candidate Y. If he is, how can one say the system that will elect Y addresses the actual levels of preference or intensity?[12]

Dahl was not just making up problems for the sake of playing games. He was quite right to indicate the real difficulty posed to majoritarianism by the intensity factor. Perhaps he was also right in concluding that nothing much can be done about it. But the significance of the intensity dispute goes in quite another direction. For Dahl thoughtful consideration of it raised the most fundamental reservations about majoritarianism. It did not mean he was prepared to abandon the principle, but it clearly made him look at it in a new and a more skeptical light.

The greatest stimulant to skepticism was the potential significance of the intensity argument for minorities. Dahl, among others, was quite sensitive to this question. It may have been his liberal concern with minority rights that led him to the matter of the intensity factor in the first place. Certainly his discussion of intensities in politics raised the spector of casual majorities overriding minorities on issue after issue. Yet Dahl's concerns were really upsetting only if one distrusts majorities, that is, people in general. It was a worry that fit well with the liberal fear after 1945, the belief that majorities might well threaten the individual—and often. It completed a picture in which majorities rarely received sympathy. When the majority did care, and did act, political intellectuals often invoked memories of the European totalitarian era and its lessons. As Edward Shils said, at its best democracy would pursue "moderation" and avoid populistic outbursts of "emotional intensity" and an "apocalyptic mentality."[13] Yet when the majority did not care, but naturally overcame intensely concerned minorities, it was faulted because intense concerns were made secondary to numbers. It was always unsatisfactory.

To be sure, there was nothing really new in the desire Dahl and others had to preserve individual political liberties nor in their anxiety about majoritarianism in this connection. Classic thinkers from John Locke to John Stuart Mill, associated with what became the liberal democratic ethos, were aware of the problem; so, for that matter, had been many American political thinkers. From Madison's Federalist paper number 10 to John C. Calhoun's *Disquisition on Government* and beyond, this problem had been a central issue in American political thought. Moreover, political practice in America was hardly a story of unrelieved majoritarianism. Yet Dahl showed the belief that mass, equalitarian democracy was a great threat. Clearly it was more characteristic of the new democratic theorists to notice the American Populists, McCarthy's following, and the unpleasant modern history of Europe than the *Federalist Papers*. Moreover, they realized that popular images of democracy were deeply interconnected with the concept of majoritarianism, *regardless* of the past nature of American political thought and practice. It was to obtain a revision of these images, which some called ideals, that they undertook to construct a "new" democratic theory.

Technical arguments against a majoritarian conception of democracy took several forms, but each served the same cause and each was part of the same movement in postwar thought to break the popular linkage between democracy and simple majority rule. Here again Dahl was a leading figure, especially in probing the most important technical problem, the missing majority. But the assault on the fallacy that a majority of identifiable stability could ever exist took many forms. Over and over the theme was sounded that democracy as majority rule was based on a phantom, for there was, and could be, no majority that could rule. Some insisted that the language of popular "will" was too nebulous to be very useful in any democratic theory.[14] Others such as Dahl dismissed Madison's emphasis on general community interests and popular aspirations: this was a business in which we lacked concrete definitions.[15]

There was much objection that loose talk about general will and popular wishes sounded good, but they were nothing but expressions of sentiment. They were without, if you will, empirical referents. This judgment was a sign of the "realism" of the new democratic theorists who wanted evidence or else they did not want to listen to democratic notions. It was part of a movement that in the hands of Schumpeter among others, slipped into an even more radical view, now taken for granted by many social scientists, that one could not talk of a common good or public interest.[16]

There were limits to the attack on the majority one might not have expected. For to cast doubt on the possibility of majority rule might serve the point of view of those whose purposes were less to formulate a "realistic" democratic theory than to suggest that America's democratic system was fraudulent. This was the danger of the road the revisionists chose to follow. C. Wright Mills was an example of an important radical who joined the revisionists when it came to denying the possibility of majority rule in the America he knew, but he concluded from that fact that America, not popular democratic theory, must change.[17] Later, others agreed. Murray Edelman, for instance, brushed aside the idea of democratic institutions and majority rule in America as symbolism no sophisticated person took seriously. It was simply part of the ideology of a system that claimed to believe in but did not practice majoritarianism, facts that obviously puzzled Edelman.[18] Neither Mills's nor Edelman's views were especially popular, not only because they did not always address the issue of whether there could ever be majority rule, but also because they went too far. They were challenging the American political order itself.

Nor was the argument made by such international relations

"realists" as Hans J. Morgenthau particularly popular, although their views were part of the critique of majoritarianism. Morgenthau scorned the notion that "world public opinion" had any influence. It just was not so. Much more popular, and the apex of the argument in fact, was the view that majoritarianism was fallacious because it simply did not describe the way politics worked.[19] Dahl asserted that "majority rule is mostly a myth" because the study of politics could not locate such majorities. What Dahl found instead were interested group minorities who exercised great influence over various aspects of policy. We had, he said in a famous phrase, "'minorities' rule."[20]

We know that voting studies uncovered the fact that people did not vote for winning candidates because they were part of any self-conscious majority. Indeed, the supporters of one winner or another often did not agree with each other, or with the winner, on many issues. Giovanni Sartori, drawing on yet other modern social science literature, remarked that majorities were no more than "fluctuating aggregates, arithmetical entities whose main function is fulfilled once they have designated their leaders."[21] The idea that even if there were majorities they were made up of diffuse and changing groups and persuasions came to dominate democratic theory. The belief was widespread that there was really no other way to examine the reality behind the majority myth, and few disagreed.[22]

There were perplexing ambiguities in all these propositions. Some thinkers like Dahl seemed to deny there were any majorities at all, and others rested content with observing that majorities were fickle and inconsistent things, and so not deserving of much respect in politics. These two positions were by no means identical. One appeared to be a conceptual-empirical proposition and the other was a frankly normative judgment. Yet their purport was the same: both suggested that majoritarianism was not a satisfactory way to approach democracy and both based themselves on "the realities" as they saw them.

Why were democratic theorists so eager to undermine the majority idea? Did their concern derive from a view of democratic politics that fit the facts of American practice, or did their interest go beyond that? One is bound to ask this question given the opinion of so many intellectuals about the individual in politics. They had scant respect for the behavior of ordinary citizens in political affairs in America just as they had not liked what they saw of mass political behavior in the 1930s and 1940s. The great advantage of the argument that majorities did not even exist conceptually was that perhaps then their worries, and those of fellow intellectuals who pondered European totalitarianism, might be laid to rest. May we not say, at the least, that many modern democratic theorists were relieved to be able to suggest there were no majorities? Yet at the same time that modern social science proclaimed the non-existence of majorities, the worry went on and the memories lingered. Theorists thought technical social science arguments could exorcise a great fear of modern American liberalism. It was not so easy to do.

The most serious imaginable questions for traditional democratic theory were raised by the critique of the concept of majority rule and the desirability of majority rule. Not every one joined, of course, in the attack on majoritarianism. Sidney Hook acknowledged the dangers implicit in majority rule, especially the potential threats to minorities. He agreed that naive faith in idealized individuals was foolish. Yet he continued to insist that majority rule was important and worthwhile, even though it had to be combined with a rigorous system of popular education.[23] Carl J. Friedrich continued to defend majority rule as a desirable reality in local government, above all in his idealized images of New England, and Sheldon Wolin called for a much more participatory democracy in his brilliant *Politics and Vision* (1960).[24] V.O. Key, an important postwar political scientist, expressed another dissenting judgment. He resisted the mood of disenchantment with the masses. He had not in any sense lost faith in the majority. "The masses do not corrupt themselves; if they are corrupt, they have been corrupted. . . . If a democracy tends toward indecision, decay, and disaster, the responsibility rests here, not in the mass of the people."[25]

As we will shortly see, such heretical views were not widely shared by many social scientists, much less other political intellectuals. Yet the problem remained, and it remained large and demanding: what was democracy about if not majority rule? What could sustain democracy if not the principle of majority rule? Too few thinkers faced these awkward questions. Henry Mayo was convinced, in the liberal skeptical manner, that "the majority principle is not the last word in politics—there is no last word."[26] He did not want to do away with the principle completely anymore than Dahl did, but he could not offer much in the way of a reason why not. It seemed to him that the alternatives were worse. He thought that political equality, majority rule, and democracy were somehow all linked together, and he felt that none of them could be abandoned without abandoning the others, but he was somewhat vague and wavered on this point.[27] Nor was Charles Lindblom's reassurance in *The Intelligence of Democracy* helpful. He remained committed to the majority principle, but thought that a useful distinction could be made between the "petty majority" and the "grand majority." The *petty majority* was produced by political structures that encouraged clear and unequivocal choice, but the *grand majority* could be formed only by bargaining and "partisan mutual adjustment," processes that would in practice gain greater support for a political system in the long run. His concern with the broadest popular support suggested characteristic concern for political stability, but it did not constitute a powerful defense of the normative ideal that majority rule is basic to a good polity. It made majority support a *useful* objective, not a basic principle of democracy. Clearly Lindblom was more committed to democracy than that, but again it was not obvious why he was.[28]

Yet democratic theorists continued to insist that one must be realistic. What this admonition meant was skepticism of the majority principle in practice. As one dryly observed: "The link which identifies voters and representatives (even in an arithmetic sense) is . . . more than tenuous; it is often non-existent . . . Hence any theory of democracy which depends for its validity upon the assumption that a majority-supported government is legitimate . . . is clearly at a disadvantage here."[29] Another was a good deal more blunt: "the people's self-government becomes for all practical purposes more and more nominal."[30]

THE NEW DEMOCRATIC THEORIES

The consequences of this conclusion were usually expressed in one of two ways. Sometimes, as in Charles Cnudde and Deane

Neubauer's *Empirical Democratic Theory*, which contained a
number of the best social science articles on democratic theory
from the later years of our period, there was simply no attempt at
all to think about what democracy is in any systematic fashion.
They were under the pleasant but naive misconception that it was
possible to write about democratic theory without knowing what it
is.[31] Far more often there was an attempt to mold a democratic
theory that dispensed with the old-fashioned illusions about democracy modern social science found implausible. Perhaps it marks
the most creative moment in political thought in the United States
from 1945 to 1964, but it definitely does not mark the most skeptical moment. The skepticism of classical democratic beliefs was
rarely matched by skepticism of social science or the "reality" it
found. A new faith only replaced the old one.

Polyarchy

One version of the new democratic theory was polyarchy. *Polyarchy* held that democracy exists when there are competing elites
between whom voters choose at elections, and who thereafter
govern. The average citizen retains ultimate power of leadership
selection, and democracy is preserved, but otherwise the voter
plays little role and certainly none in the policy-making process.
Although polyarchy was first described by Schumpeter, in the
postwar years it was Robert Dahl who pioneered in the formulation
of the theory of polyarchy and the delineation of the characteristics said to be necessary for polyarchy to obtain. Although his
democratic theory was not exclusively polyarchal, certainly polyarchy was central to it. He took it for granted that polyarchy was,
in fact, descriptive of much of the reality of American government
in action and he was pleased that it was therefore quite a realistic
theory of democracy.[32]

The description and praise of American government viewed in a
polyarchal framework was common among postwar democratic
thinkers. Lindblom joined Dahl in *Politics, Economics and Welfare*
in using the polyarchal model.[33] The talk was often blunt. Polyarchy was admired in some circles because it did not get ensnared in
optimistic misunderstandings of voter interest and intelligence.

Polyarchy received praise because it frankly acknowledged the truth about the voter and the resultant decline of popular contribution. After all, it was said: "To talk as though the people actually govern in any modern democracy is to perpetuate a fiction, even though we may call it a 'noble lie.'"[34] Others were even more outspoken. They recognized quite openly that polyarchy implied that great elitism must be incorporated into democratic theory and did not shrink from this conclusion. Democracy was now in large manner an elitist form of government and "Far from being repugnant to democracy, authority is its power formula par excellence."[35] They frankly called for a revision of citizen expectations and urged that we appreciate that "distrust and fear of elites is an anachronism."[36]

Democracy under polyarchy, then, consisted of selection among elites by elections. More and more it was clear, as leading articles demonstrated, modern social scientists took this assumption for granted, even if they did not always explicitly say so.[37] E.E. Schattschneider defined democracy the same way. It was a system where people have choice among competing leadership groups.[38] These polyarchal definitions partly explain why American social science after World War II became so entranced by the electoral process. Since, as Dahl said, the selection of elites was the new cornerstone of American democracy, and indeed of democracy itself, it was only natural that there would be an extraordinary interest in finding out about elections.[39] The great monument of postwar political science was *The American Voter*, a collective project of a number of University of Michigan social scientists headed by Angus Campbell. Their use of the data collected by the Michigan Survey Research Center helped raise it to a position of power and respect in the political science establishment. But Michigan social scientists or their data were not the source of all the numerous voting studies that suddenly appeared in the postwar decades. Prominent political scientists such as Seymour Martin Lipset and V.O. Key, whose landmark work *Southern Politics* was perhaps the single most praised election study before—and after— *The American Voter*, built remarkably successful careers partly through their study of election results and popular attitudes.[40]

No doubt part of this phenomenon was explained by the rising fashion of empirical investigation and the availability of voter attitudes and voting results for quantification in a decidedly empirical fashion. We may be sure, though, that the polyarchal model of democracy gave a good deal of legitimacy to the extensive concentration on electoral studies just as the results of these endeavors led many students of political behavior to become ever more convinced that polyarchy was the realistic model of democracy, that "the purpose of elections is to select leadership, not to maximize [ideal] democracy."[41]

There were several main reasons advanced for polyarchy as an adequate theory of democratic process. The first, as we have seen, was that it was descriptive of what took place in the United States. It was a "realistic" theory in an age that took seriously the maxim that one ought to stay close to the "real world." The second was that it included the necessary minimum of popular control that allowed it to qualify as a form of democratic theory. Dahl and Lindblom, for example, contended that the first problem of politics was the control of leadership. They were sure that polyarchy could accomplish this goal within the limits of reality. "Polyarchy, not democracy, is the actual solution."[42] Yet although there were sincere bows in this direction, the major focus was directed elsewhere, especially to the value of polyarchy in providing the leadership so many American liberals considered vital in the postwar era. Indeed, if the defense of polyarchy had a single theme, it was its provision of the possibility of strong leadership.

Of course, political intellectuals were always careful to distinguish what they sought from unchecked elite rule. Arthur Schlesinger, one of the most aggressive proponents of strong leadership, did not forget to remind his readers that no group of people were "more perfect" than any other,[43] so there was an undoubted conflict between the enthusiasm for leadership and for much democratic control, not to say participation.[44] Even the most zealous advocates of polyarchy knew this: "We want a government that is responsive to the wishes of the people but, at the same time, we want an effective government. . . . There is a high probability of conflict between these two objectives."[45]

Polyarchy in theory and practice was intended, however, to resolve this conflict. Elections would ensure enough control, while at the same time there would be the necessary leadership. The modern world required we accept what Schumpeter called the "vital fact of leadership."[46] It must accept this fact, many social scientists claimed, because most citizens were too poorly informed and disinterested to be allowed to govern. It must accept it because leadership was inescapable anyway. As V.O. Key remarked, "Mass opinion is not self-generating; in the main, it is a response to the cues, the proposals, and the visions propagated by the political activists."[47] Finally, it must accept it because leaders tended not only to be more aware of issues, problems, and basic knowledge, but also because they very often were experts in technical matters needed for policy formulation and implementation or had ready access to those who were. Herbert McCloskey and associates reported their research showed that leadership elites at several levels of government were far more "informed" about relevant issues.[48] Richard Hofstadter dwelt on the vital need for experts in leadership in a democracy and, like many others, based his considerable sympathy for the New Deal partly on its use of experts.[49]

Beyond these reasons, however, lay a certain policy bias of modern liberal thinkers it is important to understand if one wishes to grasp why polyarchy appealed so much to so many American intellectuals after 1945. Only polyarchy as a model of democracy provided for the style of active presidential leadership for which so many liberals yearned because they thought it would lead to the adoption of their liberal welfare programs. James MacGregor Burns was a leading example of the crusader for presidential leadership. He became famous through a series of books that damned Congress for interfering with the liberal welfare program he strongly advocated. Burns also wrote a massive biography celebrating Franklin Roosevelt, the paradigmatic activist leader for so many postwar liberal intellectuals. The message of his biography of John F. Kennedy was the same: presidential leadership is the very core of democracy.[50] Arthur Schlesinger followed the same course. Whether he was collecting Debs's writings or producing an award-winning biography of Jackson, the New Deal ideal seemed to be extraordinarily near the surface and the contemporary import was the value of executive leadership. Schlesinger's later multivolume hymn to Roosevelt made his point even more explicitly, a point

Schlesinger and Burns wanted Eisenhower to hear and Kennedy to practice.[51]

Schlesinger was certainly the most enthusiastic proponent of leadership among the large number of political intellectuals who rallied to this polyarchal cause. Part of his argument was normative. Leaders, who easily became heroes in his mind, properly should provide the direction of our society and guide us to a better society. They had an almost sacred duty to ensure we would have "the politics of responsibility, which tries to define the real issues and present them to the people for decision."[52] At the same time, leaders were obviously functional for any enduring and developing political society. They were the key to growth. For Schlesinger the "real division" in Third World nations was "not between left and right; it is between hard and soft—between leadership which has the will to do what must be done . . . and leadership which falters."[53] America had been lucky. We had had leaders like Hamilton, Jefferson, and Lincoln who appreciated the interrelated moral and functional aspects of leadership. Schlesinger eventually found in John Kennedy another figure who represented his ideal and he made him into another of his heroes.[54] For Schlesinger Camelot was his dream come true and "John F. Kennedy's life nobly embodied reason in politics."[55]

A close reading of the literature of the years after World War II that praises leadership shows there was often a division between two schools of thought. Although men such as Dahl, Schlesinger, and Burns all agreed on the necessity of leadership and the value of what we may term a polyarchal conception of democracy, they did not always do so with quite the same image of the electorate or for exactly the same purposes. Dahl and many of those associated with him did not demonstrate much enthusiasm for the average voter and often thought of leadership as a substitute for the untrustworthy citizenry. Burns and Schlesinger, on the other hand, were far more confident of the electorate, confident, for example, that it would agree with them, with leadership, and support enactment of needed social welfare programs. For these thinkers polyarchy was democracy. Congress and vested interest groups emerged in their analysis as the undemocratic forces in America, and the people under the guidance of vigorous leaders were the engine of democracy. E.E. Schattschneider represented the more openly democratic side of polyarchy, which believed that leadership was the means to accomplish popular wishes in a democracy.[56]

These thinkers were not far from mainstream polyarchy. They were by no means Populist Democrats. Leadership did not consist in automatically translating popular wishes into policy. It was far more active, since it had a moral role. It had to set goals and the pace of accomplishment. People would support such leaders, but there was little that Schlesinger, for example, wanted them to do otherwise and he certainly did not cast them in the role of initiators.[57] He had in mind Franklin Roosevelt, we must remember, a man who was hardly a passive receptor of popular wishes.

The classic manifesto of liberals who wanted more polyarchy in American politics was Richard Neustadt's *Presidential Power* (1960). Written without much theoretical clarity, this book assumed polyarchy was the appropriate aim in democracy and that the problem faced by modern liberals was that polyarchy, although very much present, was imperfectly realized in America. Neustadt's book, supposedly read and admired by John Kennedy, was a sophisticated instruction manual intended to show a president how to gather the power he needed to be the effective polyarchal leader Neustadt so obviously felt he should be. Neustadt included obligatory praise of the style of Franklin Roosevelt and its obvious contrast with Dwight Eisenhower's style.[58] His ringing headings such as "Leader or Clerk?" were intended to stir the heart of every polyarchist.[59] His book was full of popular modern political science distinctions; in particular he laid great stress on the gap between formal presidential powers and actual powers. Neustadt's point was that the presidency could be both much less and much more than formal powers suggested. It all depended on the skill of the incumbent president and his White House to convince us by one means or another that he should be listened to. Only then would the presidency come into its own and polyarchy's possibility be realized.[60]

Plans for domestic programs were not alone in attracting liberal thinkers to polyarchy. If anything, there was broader agreement on the need for polyarchal democracy for the purposes of foreign affairs.[61] Hans J. Morgenthau was an important figure here, and even such participatory Democrats such as Carl J. Friedrich were always careful to support polyarchal values when it came to foreign affairs.[62]

Morgenthau, the leading figure in the study of international relations, did not go quite as far as Kennan but like him he praised the beauty of the nineteenth century before the rise of modern democracy. That was an age, he believed, when international stability was so much better maintained. Then it had a well-regulated order with a well-understood morality. Morgenthau did not concern himself with the quality of that order or its morality. He assumed it was good.[63] He lamented the subsequent appearance of mass "heroes" in international affairs instead of "horse traders" who knew how, through use of the marvelous instrument of diplomacy, to handle the world.[64] Morgenthau, rather like Neustadt, was not at all convinced we had enough polyarchy at the present time, but, on the other hand, he was determined we should have the wisdom to preserve what we did have. Polyarchy was the only feasible variety of democracy, and what made it so attractive was that it removed the arena of foreign affairs from popular judgment.

Realism, the provision of democratic checks on elites, the promotion of needed leadership, were among the reasons political intellectuals offered on behalf of polyarchy, but there was also a fourth reason frequently mentioned. Some suggested that only polyarchy could preserve what amount of popular input remained in American democracy. It was, for instance, noted that Britain's high regard for tolerance of diversity derived from its acceptance of deference to its elites. Was this not an object lesson for the United States, which certainly required a like disposition toward polyarchy?[65] More often, the argument was that the entire constellation of liberal and democratic values had their best protection in elites because social science information suggested the elites in America were more committed to them. For example, a study of the populations of Ann Arbor, Michigan, and Tallahassee, Florida, showed that higher education was definitely correlated with greater support for democratic principles, defined in this case to include a strong sympathy for minority political rights.[66] Herbert McCloskey found in another study that the so-called elites were the true "carriers of the creed" and implicitly deserved great credit for this fact.[67] Perhaps the most famous of all these studies was S.A. Stouffer's *Communism, Conformity and Civil Liberties* (1955). Stouffer discovered at the height of the McCarthy period that community leadership elites were far more disposed to be tolerant of "nonconformity" in political opinion than were average citizens.[68]

This line of evidence was indeed strong armor for the defense of polyarchy. It transformed polyarchy from being "reality" to making it the only way to preserve the ideal of liberal democracy. Opponents might rage against polyarchy as a barely disguised elective monarchy, but they could not escape the closing pincer of the liberal argument: more democracy meant more participation by those who apparently were not very liberal. To be sure, there was no reason why this had to end the argument, for one might still have asked why this was so and whether greater participation by more people might not have increased their commitment in turn. But there is scant treatment of this theme in liberal social science literature of the postwar decades. Instead, quite another interest developed. There was a rise of interest in the advantages of citizen apathy.

Some thinkers who were most attracted to polyarchy openly broached the topic of the positive value of citizen disinterest in politics. It was not illogical to expect, given their obvious affinity for leadership and considerable distress over popular ignorance, that some theorists would do so. One, for example, observed that "the apparently private vice of disinterest in politics may . . . be a public virtue and a sign of social and political stability.[69] Bernard Berelson and associates in *Voting* developed the idea in a most aggressive manner. Although they did not deny that too much apathy would be destructive, their main message was an admiring appreciation of the apathy that so obviously existed in the American political order even then. "The apathetic segment of America has helped to hold the system together and cushioned the shock of disagreement, adjustment, and changes."[70] It was left to Heinz Eulau to offer the most unrestrained celebration of American political apathy. Apathy was a marvelous sign, for it indicated a "politics of happiness." It signified that people were satisfied with America —as Eulau thought they should be.[71]

The open proclamation of the value of apathy was not a common notion, nonetheless, for the very good reason that its tone was awkwardly undemocratic. It was one thing to ascribe considerable utility to leadership by elites, but it was quite another to pronounce solemnly against the very ethic of participation. Moreover, the analysis of theorists of apathy was open to objection. Few raised doubts then, but E.E. Schattschneider was an exception. He suspected that the large numbers of citizens who were not part of the political order were not satisfied, but rather alienated. In Schattschneider's mind apathy was not a good sign, contrary to the view of Eulau, but quite the opposite. It was an alarming danger signal. Schattschneider became an uncharacteristic voice in the postwar era, urging that the United States needed to find the means to get more people into political activity.[72]

His warnings received scant attention in an age of consensus and presumed satisfaction. His participatory instincts were not widely admired either. The usual assumption was that the question of democracy, as Dahl and Lindblom said, was "not so much whether citizens are active but whether they have the opportunity to exert control through activity when they wish to do so."[73] On this score most intellectuals had no doubts.

Conclusion   The theory of polyarchy was no fluke that somehow reached a few minds and books. It received much discussion and support. There were several versions, some more open to popular input than others and some perhaps best understood as an argument for leadership rather than a strict adherence to Dahl's model. But there can scarcely be any doubt that polyarchy democracy in the broadest sense, democracy defined as rule by leaders selected through elections, was a constant theme of American thinkers in the two decades after World War II. To be sure, it failed to convince everyone. A.W. Gouldner might complain that it was a doctrine of pessimism, that: "Instead of assuming responsibilities as realistic clinicians, striving to further democratic potentialities wherever they can, many social scientists have become morticians, all too eager to bury men's hopes."[74] But the last words on polyarchy were usually like those of Giovanni Sartori: "It is not possible to construct a different democratic system."[75]

THE POWER ELITE CONTROVERSY:
AN IMPORTANT CASE STUDY

In 1956 C. Wright Mills published his remarkable study *The Power Elite*. The result was an instant controversy that still continues over his decidedly critical view of the American political process. This controversy was important in its own right, and still is, but it was also enormously revealing in terms of its interaction with mainstream polyarchal views of American politics.

Perhaps one might have expected that Mills's work would receive a warm welcome. After all, Mills's analysis was intensely poly- archal in the sense that he claimed American government was under the sway of elites who made the main policy decisions. Mills singled out political, economic, and military elites as key. He suggested that their loosely coordinated actions were decisive. He did not deny that elites often disagreed with each other, but sug- gested that when the chips were down, and their vital interests or power was at stake, they united. He consciously rejected a Marxian perspective that would have concentrated exclusively on economic elites and he denied that either political or military elites were merely a committee of the wealthy.[76]

But there were three aspects of Mills's approach that made his book shocking and indeed an outrage to many intellectuals. First, Mills explicitly attacked any version of democratic theory that in- tended to see power as at all dispersed in America.[77] Even poly- archists could not accept Mills here, for he painted a picture of American government where power was too tightly oligarchal. Mills seemed to be presenting a simplified picture. Daniel Bell, for example, complained that Mills was dangerous because of the very inaccuracy of his portrait: "terms like . . . 'power elites' often rein- forces a sense of helplessness and belies the resources of a free so- ciety: the variety of interest conflicts, the growth of public respons- ibility, the weight of traditional freedoms, the role of volunteer and community groups, etc. etc."[78] Max Lerner's objection followed similar lines. He granted, cheerfully, that in the United States there were elites, but there was nothing to compare with Mill's fictional image of a power elite. American government was far more open.[79] Richard Rovere of *The New Yorker* was quite willing to acknowl- edge that there was an American "establishment," but Mills made it all-powerful, which was a gross exaggeration.[80] Rovere was at least open to considering Mill's proposition but Yale political scientist Robert Lane was not. He dismissed Mills, snapping that "in point of fact, there is no such national oligarchal structure."[81]

Mills's second controversial point was his suggestion that the reality of the power elite destroyed America's claim to be a democracy.[82] There was almost universal repudiation of this claim by intellectuals and the criticism of Mills in this regard was fierce. One might wonder if it was not also ironic. What was at issue was whether polyarchy, in the extreme form of a power elite, could accurately be described as democratic. Mills did not think so. His critique was simply that elitism could not be papered over by calling it democracy. Was it because Mills was proposing that the polyarchal emperor had no clothes, that polyarchy was really elitism, that the attack was so swift and so severe? Certainly he appeared to be using a rather similar set of facts to arrive at a description not at all remote from polyarchy. His only difference was his assertion that polyarchy was unchecked elitism.

There is a good deal of validity in this suggestion. Yet it is not an entirely fair point to make, for the polyarchists insisted on the importance as well as the reality of a popular role. Rovere was surprised that Mills left out public opinion and most social science opinion insisted that polyarchy must include a stress on the centrality of elections in maintaining the democratic character of modern American government.[83] Tenuous as they knew the electoral link with popular sentiment was, they still held it to be essential. Mills, on the other hand, was not interested in elections. He asserted that they did not select most of the ruling elites and they told us little about power in America. Here was a decided contrast that separated him from the polyarchal theorists.

Daniel Bell's objections were typical and quite interesting. Bell's feeling was that Mills employed a highly participatory definition of democracy that was out of touch with the realm of possibility. He was a utopian engaging in a form of "romantic protest against modern life."[84] Yet Bell did not rest here, for to do so would imply that Mills's description of American government was accurate. Bell went on to challenge Mills's model. Bell charged that Mills went too far: he overdid the elitist element, and he ignored elections. Bell concluded that Mills was not a good social scientist. The power elite theory, Bell suggested, should be dismissed because it was a "confusing and unsatisfactory" failure to follow "an empirical analysis."[85]

Mills's third argument held that the power elite was a dreadful reality not only because it was undemocratic, but also because it produced disastrous policy consequences for the United States and the world at large: "its men of decision enforce their often crackpot definitions upon world reality.[86] This charge was the most fundamental of all, for with it Mills tried to challenge the actual politics of the American experiment. As we will see in the ninth chapter, Mills ran headlong into the sentiments of American intellectuals who, although bothered by McCarthy and the radical Right, were convinced that America was the best hope of the world.

The fight over *The Power Elite* was important, at the least because it clarified the nature of what postwar democratic theorists meant by polyarchy and what they thought polyarchy meant in relation to the American system. For them polyarchy was still democracy, and not a power elite, and recognition of polyarchy was both realistic and an affirmation of the continuing vitality of American leadership at home and abroad.

PLURALISM: THE OTHER HALF

The fight over *The Power Elite* occurred when many democratic theorists believed that a model of democracy that concentrated too exclusively on leadership was neither a plausible model of American democratic experience nor an entirely attractive one. Thus postwar democratic theory that developed the idea of polyarchy rarely offered it in isolation. Although for our purposes it helps to distinguish polyarchy from pluralism, in fact most theorists talked of what Dahl called the "American Hybrid," a combination of polyarchy and pluralism as the operative reality and normative ideal of American democratic politics.

Pluralism, or the notion that competition among political interests and interest groups produced government decisions, nonetheless received much greater emphasis than polyarchy among some thinkers, just as the reverse was often true. It was a much older idea, among social scientists and political thinkers. We should remember, as many social scientists did, that James Madison was the first great American pluralist. His famous defense of the American Constitution in Federalist paper number 10 depended heavily on a pluralist understanding of politics. It is true enough that Madison and many other analysts of "factions" in his period were pluralists more in their empirical theory than in their normative preferences. Pluralism was to them a fact to be dealt with rather than unreservedly celebrated.

On the other hand, as early as John C. Calhoun, America had a thinker who not only used the pluralist model descriptively, but also advanced it as the most satisfactory form of politics. Not surprisingly, there were many thinkers after 1945, such as Daniel Boorstin, who were quite prepared to acknowledge that Calhoun was as great a political philosopher as America had ever known.[87]

The real increase in interest in pluralism came in the decades after 1900. Arthur Bentley's *The Process of Government* (1908) is now recognized as the classic of early modern pluralist analysis. Although Bentley had no normative focus, he rigorously sought to deny that there was any possibility of understanding political and social life outside a group framework. There simply was no such thing.[88] At about the same time, certainly by the 1920s, there was a considerable burst of interest in pluralism in English political thought. G.D.H. Cole advanced pluralist socialism, and Harold Laski, due later to travel quite another road, became an aggressive advocate of the advantages of politics operating within a pluralist paradigm.[89]

The Model

Yet it was not until after World War II that most American social scientists turned to pluralism as the appropriate way to understand American politics. There is much literature to draw on to illustrate the pluralist model, and it would be scarcely accurate to portray all versions as identical. A general outline can be sketched, however, for there was a broad model that most thinkers shared. Consider, for example, Earl Latham's *The Group Basis of Politics* (1952), an able and articulate presentation of pluralism. Latham followed the steps by which a complex bill became law in Washington to argue that only a pluralist view of politics could explain the legislative process. He observed that at each stage in the law-making process numerous group pressures were brought to bear and the different resources and strategies of groups had tremendous impact on what kind of bill emerged. Groups were the decisive factors. He concluded that this case study, and by explicit implication all American politics, demonstrated that "the struggle of groups to write in their favor the rules by which the community is governed" was the truth about American government.[90]

Latham saw government's role in the process as ambiguous. On the one hand, government could be interpreted as a kind of balancing force in the competitive struggle of groups for power and influence. But at the same time Latham argued that one could not really accept in any full way the ideal of government as neutral referee, because it, too, was divided into conflicting groups that disagreed with each other and often were allied with the nongovernmental group interest.[91]

In *American Capitalism* John Kenneth Galbraith proposed a somewhat different model. He was later to lose some of his enthusiasm for it, but it became a part of the intellectual folklore of our period. Galbraith reached out beyond the realm of conventional politics to consider the broader power relations in the American society as a whole. In particular, of course, his focus rested on economic power. His thesis was that the major interests in society encompassing labor unions, large corporations, retailers, and so on blocked and checked each other's power, providing the boundaries that kept the United States free of despotism and maintained a pluralist democracy. Galbraith acknowledged from an economist's perspective the reality of pluralist politics, what Latham and David Riesman, among others, called "veto politics."[92] Unlike many pluralists, Galbraith even in the early 1950s suspected that considerable government action would be necessary to ensure that his countervailing system lived up to its potential, which he did not believe it always did. The state needed to participate and in no way did Galbraith propose to depend on pure market mechanisms to sustain pluralism.[93]

Perhaps the most mature delineation of the pluralist theory of democracy was propounded by David Truman in *The Governmental Process* (1950). Truman studied the operations of group interests in American political life, discussing how they mobilized resources and how they manipulated government to their interests. No one provided so much detail about so many groups as Truman did. No one sketched the picture in such rich variety or with such overwhelming data. No one made a more convincing case for the reality of group interest as the controlling phenomenon of politics. No one more brusquely dismissed the old individualist and public-interest framework with so much evidence to fortify his argument. Significantly, no one was more satisfied with the pluralist democracy he described than David Truman.[94]

The pluralist perspectives of social scientists such as Latham, Galbraith, and Truman were not identical. They were also not the last word. Pluralist thinkers continued a process of refining and reformulating pluralist democracy long after the early 1950s. One of the most heralded attempts, coming at the end of our period, was Charles Lindblom's *The Intelligence of Democracy*. Lindblom proposed that democracy at its best operated through the phenomenon he called "partisan mutual adjustment." He distinguished partisan mutual adjustment from pluralism as it was usually presented, since he felt most pluralists dwelt too much on the role of interest groups. They tended to overlook or to underemphasize that "partisan mutual adjustment" involved legislative bodies, the executive, bureaucratic agencies, and political party elites as well as pressure groups. Nor was bargaining the only technique employed. Reciprocity, calculation, and even authority were sometimes used.[95]

Certainly this theory, which was both descriptive and normative, was a close cousin to pluralism. It was really a more sophisticated form of pluralist democracy, one that respected the multitude of modes of expression and operation in which pluralism took place. Nevertheless, it was an attempt, of some importance, to formulate pluralism in more complete and thus more adequate terms.

Robert Dahl performed perhaps the most creative theorizing because he brought pluralism and polyarchy together into a composite normative and empirical theory of American democracy. He recognized that polyarchy and pluralism were two parts of a single theory, that group pressure and elections of elites were the twin features that distinguished modern democracy. Both deserved mention because both were crucial. In terms of day-to-day politics he felt that pluralism was the operating reality, but it had to be modified substantially by the regular polyarchal aspect. Moreover, both depended on each other in "the American Hybrid." Elections were crucial because they ensured that pluralism would work. If there were no polyarchy then leaders would not have to take pressure groups into their calculations and would not have to allow other competitive voices and wills to be heard. Pluralism and polyarchy, therefore, formed a kind of ideal partnership out of which issued democracy.[96]

This was the critical link. For social scientists did not need to consider the pluralism they saw as central to democracy any more than polyarchy had to be similarly considered. But there is no doubt that they did. Lipset, for instance, was convinced that pluralist democracy was the good society in itself, and Dahl described the "American Hybrid" as a splendid form of democracy.[97] Gabriel Almond and James Coleman went even further, using the pluralist model of government as the ideal toward which less-developed countries all over the world ought to aim. Modern societies, they affirmed, offered the appropriate model of interest groups and parties "competing, pragmatic, and bargaining."[98]

Henry Kariel's critique *The Decline of American Pluralism* spoke out pointedly about the collapse between "is" and "ought," which described so much of the pluralist writing about democracy. He complained that most social scientists who characterized the American political system as pluralist easily slipped into the assumption that pluralism was also *the* normatively satisfactory conception of democracy, without bothering to offer much defense. He noted that this did not allow them to be critical or even reflective about pluralism and thus their own supposedly objective findings.[99] Kariel was undoubtedly correct that too many social scientists shifted comfortably from their social scientific theories of pluralist political behavior in America to a casual acceptance of its normative worth, but this was not the case with *all* the democratic theorists. No one can read Dahl's *A Preface to Democratic Theory*, among other works, without agreeing that this was a straightforward closely argued attempt to close the gap between "ought" and "is." To miss this point is to miss the extent to which much of the postwar democratic theory was a self-conscious creation.

The Power Elite Controversy Revisited

Although there was an undoubted normative aspect to the discussion of pluralism, it received most attention as an empirical model. The first case made for pluralism was always a justification of pluralism as an accurate picture of the operations of American government and politics. In this task much of the exploration of pluralism was done by studying local governments. For example, Edward Banfield's study *Political Influence* was a sympathetic study of pluralism in action in Chicago.[100] But the classic work was carried out by the Yale school of political science in the late 1950s and early 1960s. Its dominant figure was Robert Dahl and he was assisted by numerous disciples, including Nelson Polsby and Aaron Wildavsky. Their materials were heavily, but not exclusively, derived from study of the local politics of New Haven. Their stance was an aggressive defense of a pluralist model and a harsh attack on sociological interpretations, such as Floyd Hunter's study of Atlarta *(Community Power Structure* 1953*)*, which claimed that local governments were governed by small cohesive elites. C. Wright Mills's later *The Power Elite* came out of this sociological tradition and merely applied it to the national level.

Dahl's *Who Gcverns?* (1961) was the great opening shot in the campaign to show that pluralism was the correct model of local politics. He argued that to find out who ruled, it was necessary to study how decisions were actually made in concrete issue areas. When he did so in New Haven, he discovered that elites or, as he preferred, minorities, did make the crucial decisions. But the fact was, he said, that in different policy areas, different minorities ruled. Moreover, these minorities were influential in every case because they were interested and chose to expend their resources in this arena. There was no evidence that when others wanted to do so they could not be influential. There was no single power elite and no closed political system to be found, only the reality of pluralism.[101]

Dahl's efforts were often replicated in later years, for instance by Aaron Wildavsky,[102] but it was Nelson Polsby who made the most articulate pluralist case in theoretical terms. This was particularly true in his critical perspective on the sociological-elite school. He accused them of adopting a research technique that guaranteed they would "discover" that an elite ruled. Their method, called the *reputational approach,* involved asking people who was influential in local politics assuming in the question that there was such an influential elite. He was convinced that this method was completely inadequate in comparison with observation of the actual processes of decision making. Polsby also charged that the power elite school was completely unwilling to take seriously cases that, even by their own flawed methods, did not fit their elitist model. They invariably offered dubious "explanations" to justify every gap between theory and data instead of honestly rethinking their theory. Polsby objected in particular to the suggestion in the power elite literature that when data did not fit, the reason was that a local elite was simply clever enough to hide behind a veil of secretness. This kind of assertion seemed to him to be unscientific and a weak and lamentable attempt to paper over theoretical anomalies.[103]

What Dahl, Polsby, and others did was wage a persistent and thorough campaign on behalf of the pluralist paradigm of American politics. They did so with two great advantages. First, they had the advantage that their analysis claimed democracy was alive and well in the United States in a time when many political intellectuals agreed and welcomed such reassurance. Second, they had what they judged to be the master weapon, the appeal to their facts. Over and over they emphasized that they took into account the facts of decision making. They told a story that only blind theorists and, implicitly, blind radical ideologues could serenely avoid.

By the mid-1960s the brief dominance of the pluralist paradigm had begun to crack, but only slowly. The main preliminary thrust came from social scientists, above all Peter Bachrach and Morton Baratz, who thought that complete reliance on studying observable decisions was a trap. There were, they said, really "two faces of power," only one of which empirical analysis of decision making could detect. They suggested it was important to explore the aspects of policy and broader social and economic structure that were not matters of discussion and decision. Many questions appeared closed. Why was this so and did it tell us something deeper about who ruled than any of the perhaps relatively petty controversies that entered the public arena?[104] But these queries were to come late and only after the pluralist model swept the field of analysis of American political behavior. They came as questions addressed to a newly dominant model, as acknowledgments that for the moment the pluralist paradigm was in the commanding position.

Other Problems with the Model

There were two additional aspects of the model of pluralist reality that were to become centers of controversy in the postwar period. Perhaps they may be said to be the dark side of the pluralist model from the perspective of later days. How they were viewed by pluralist thinkers is perhaps as good a test as one could have of how complete the support was for pluralism—even with its faults.

One aspect was the fact that such disparate social scientists as Seymour Martin Lipset and David Truman noted that most groups were actually under the control of elites themselves. That is, groups that allegedly opened access and representation up to so many diverse elements of the population were often not governed internally by electoral procedures and almost never by participatory democracy. Truman coined the term "active minority," a pleasant euphemism for these elites, but they did not pose any problems to him in his affirmation of pluralism.[105] Lipset was less happy about the absence of much democracy in the unions he studied, but he considered this a price worth paying for their pluralist contribution to making democracy work in the larger political order.[106] Perhaps there was not more concern here because the rather elitist nature of most groups appeared to be quite congruent with the popular analysis that saw both pluralist and polyarchal dimensions to American political life. From this perspective, the "active minority" in groups was only one more element of polyarchy in the American system.

There was more disagreement even in our period about the question of the unorganized groups in the American population. Were all groups organized? Was pluralism in practice really representative of the population as a whole? Could all groups get organized? In the 1960s critics began to pose these questions with an insistence that foreshadowed what was to follow in the next ten years.

Murray Edelman scoffed at the idea that American pluralist politics benefitted the many. He insisted that democratic myths, including pluralism, did little more than sustain present "inequalities in wealth, in income, and in influence."[107] Kariel blasted the pluralist system for producing "a plurality of entrenched oligarchies" rather than any viable representative system.[108] Even Sidney Hook wondered how full a political democracy we could have, given substantial inequalities in economic resources, and he suggested more democracy in industrial life partly for this reason.[109] Herbert Marcuse and the Students for a Democratic Society, in those days the far Left, suggested that equal access was greatly delimited by class structure and even police activity.[110]

Even so established a social scientist as E.E. Schattschneider did not fail to remark that something was wrong with pluralism in practice in the United States. He thought it was undoubtedly true that there was a "business or upper-class bias" in the pluralist reality.[112] "The flaw in the pluralist heaven is that the heavenly chorus sings with a strong upper-class accent. Probably about ninety per cent of the people cannot get into the pressure system."[112]

By 1960s many pluralists did recognize there were inequalities in practice. Charles Lindblom agreed, but declared that assertions of inequality in pluralism did not bother him: "the allegation that the values of different persons are unequally weighted in partisan mutual adjustment is . . . an allegation of very dubious relevance . . the allegation appeals to a criterion of equality that is not at all suitable for appraising democratic systems like partisan mutual adustment."[113] But most of the postwar democratic theorists had no intention of granting the critics' point and simply dismissed it as irrelevant. They denied that pluralism ensured unequal political influence. Earl Latham recognized that the organized had a natural advantage over the unorganized, but he felt the evidence showed that organization led to counter-organization and the system continued on in an adequate manner. He did not have any sense that there might be great problems for some groups to get organized and thus represented, although he did mention in a footnote that, of course, some relevant elements will not be represented in any decision.[114] David Truman was even more sanguine. What impressed him over and over was the variety of groups and the "multiplicity of points of access" to the government. He gave little attention to those who were not organized and less to the difficulties one might have in getting organized.[115] Throughout most of these years Robert Dahl agreed, showing no doubt that every "legitimate" interest could get a fair hearing in the American governmental process.[116]

With all the advantages of a retrospective analysis, we must recognize that their uncritical confidence was exaggerated at the least. We must also wonder whether their optimism was not more a result of their normative attraction to pluralism than it was of social science at its most empirical. The democratic theorists' resistance to critics of their model is surprising in men who were so skeptical of the assertions of classic participatory democratic theory. One might have expected more from professed skeptics, especially since skepticism with the performance of pluralism in the United States need not have led to an abandonment of the theory of pluralism. But much skepticism was not forthcoming from within their ranks.

The Defense of Pluralism

Pluralism was praised for its normative attractiveness just as much as, and indeed more than, it was for its empirical validity. Although we know the line between empirical reality and normative soundness was never very clear in American political thinking from 1945 to 1964, we can identify several reasons advanced on behalf of pluralism as a normative theory of democracy by postwar democratic thinkers. Many applauded pluralism because it was uniquely democratic. It allowed organized groups of citizens almost endless points of access to governments. Pluralists argued that unlike democratic theories that concentrated exclusively on elections as their mechanism of democratic representation, the pluralist emphasis on group representation (as well as elections) on a continuing basis in legislatures, political parties, and bureaucracies provided more chance for citizens to influence the policy-making process more often, at more points, on a more frequent basis. Sympathetic intellectuals claimed that at the same time pluralist democracy enshrined in politics the basic liberal values of an open, tolerant, and free political universe. It was the political expression of the liberal norm of diversity.[117]

This theme was pursued by those who defended pluralism because they believed it blocked power and dispersed it throughout the entire political order. This perspective appealed to intellectuals uneasy about the potential for tyrannical democracy, those who feared populism at home or who thought European "totalitarianism" suggested caution about centralized power of any sort. It particularly appealed to laissez-faire liberals, such as Milton Friedman, the capitalist economist.[118] William Kornhauser's fascinating study *The Politics of Mass Society* is a good example of the broader sentiment that feared any great concentration of power. Kornhauser contended that pluralism in a country, the existence of an infrastructure of groups and divided citizen loyalties, could deter the rise of mass movements and irrational crusades such as had befallen Nazi Germany. The absence of such a complex structure in Germany was, he contended, fatal to genuine liberal and democratic experience.[119] This was also the conclusion of Max Lerner. He believed majority tyranny was not an idle threat. It had sometimes flared up in the United States, but he was confident that if we held onto our combination of pluralism and constitutional checks, we would forestall any such event in the future.[120]

It is difficult to convey how strong the anxiety was that majoritarianism might overwhelm what liberal thinkers held dear, and consequently how warm the welcome was for pluralism, which promised to provide both democracy and protection for the individual. Some who were deeply worried about fanatical or foolish majorities concluded happily that pluralism and the Constitution were "in fact such effective safeguards that they often make it difficult for the majority to get its way, except over a long period of time."[121] Sartori in his *Democratic Theory* was less sure of a fortunate resolution, because he was more concerned that liberal values, especially individualism, were in fundamental opposition to majoritarianism. For him there could be no disputing the fact that a "non-liberal democracy is a totalitarian democracy" and hateful to its core. Yet he concluded that the American Hybrid probably provided enough insurance.[122]

It would be inaccurate, however, to suggest that intellectual concern over the prospect of majority tyranny commanded complete attention from pluralists. As memories of the war and even McCarthy faded, the case for pluralism often stressed the advantages its proponents felt it offered as a mechanism for decision making. Robert Lindblom, for example, defended his version of pluralism on this basis alone. He suggested that pluralism was the most functional form of democracy, since it was an unequalled "method for calculated, reasonable, rational, intelligent, wise—except the exact term does not matter—policy making."[123] He had in mind four features in particular that he believed characterized pluralism or "partisan mutual adjustment." It was a complex process of political interactions and pressures that served well as a means not only to represent public sentiment, but also to provide the best policy in an intellectual situation of skepticism about values and justifications. Pluralism was a democratic process that conducted the age-old search for the correct goals through group pressures and accommodations and thus solved this problem. It also was a successful instrument for policy makers to obtain information. Interested parties of all types fed their knowledge and values into the system with the result that there were rarely any isolated, uninformed decision makers. Similarly, the almost endless number of decision makers and forces pressing upon them usually ensured that mistakes could be caught early and rectified. Finally, the sheer multiplicity of actors in the American system of pluralist politics aided, Lindblom thought, coordination and consensus. It guaranteed that movement would be incremental, but that when it occurred it would be informed and supported widely.[124]

This suggests a last and by no means unimportant reason why so many thinkers, especially social scientists, felt so much enthusiasm for pluralism. They had no doubt that it contributed enormously to the maintenance of stability in America. Lindblom admired "partisan mutual adjustment" as a potent force for "social agreement,"[125] and Clinton Rossiter respected the pluralistic nature of our political parties because they were "major contributors" to our "precious national and social unity."[126] Others such as Seymour Martin Lipset celebrated pluralism because it provided the "cross-cutting cleavages" he thought were essential to preserving stability in the United States. They made compromise necessary and encouraged only those in politics who were willing to bargain rather than demand what they considered to be ideologically correct.[127] The happy result, pluralist intellectuals claimed, was that incremental change and public order went hand in hand. As Bernard Berelson put it, pluralism was a perfect balance of consensus and cleavage. It provided enough consensus for the preservation of America and enough cleavage to provide for orderly growth and development.[128] Taken together, a large proportion of postwar political intellectuals thought these reasons provided a full argument for pluralism. They contended that it was democratic and yet it prevented majorities from running wild. It guaranteed a richly diverse society and one that would continue to be stable. The master assumption behind the whole argument was that the United States was both a satisfactory society and blessed by an unusually satisfactory political system. This view was rarely stated, but it certainly was taken for granted. Had these thinkers been as skeptical of the United States as they were of alternative democratic theories, they might have had different opinions on pluralism, but they did not pretend to be.

Conclusion

In 1964, heralding an era that was to see a great storm of criticism descend on pluralism, Henry David Aiken complained that Daniel Bell's definition of pluralist democracy as "bargaining among legitimate groups and the search for consensus" was a horrible desecration of the possibilities of politics. It entirely neglected the realm of human aspirations and ideals.[129] This accusation missed the point that for very many political intellectuals in America, pluralism with polyarchy had become an attainable ideal, indeed the best practical expression of the age-old human aspiration for democratic government. Moreover, it was an ideal that existed. It was democracy and it was democracy in America. Because it was, there was little likelihood it would be probed too deeply in the postwar period. Its weaknesses were rarely seen. Pluralism and polyarchy were not viewed skeptically, no matter how often postwar social scientists stated their devotion to "objectivity" and "realistic" and "skeptical" examination of all positions.

The ordinary mood was quite different. Clinton Rossiter articulated it when he said America's pluralistic political system merited "pride" and a "considerable if not exactly uncritical affection and admiration."[130]

It was not surprising, consequently, that critics such as Henry Kariel charged that postwar democratic theory was a part of the new mood of acceptance of America, a formidable and challenging "resting place of the conservative mood, as sustained by the liberal intelligentsia."[131] They were quite right, but at the same time we must see the emergence of this democratic theory, from Truman to Dahl, as a significant moment in American political thought. For better or for worse, the "American Hybrid" lives on today and many call it democracy.

NOTES*

1. Peter Gay, *Voltaire's Politics* (New York: Vintage, 1965–1959), ch. 4 part 3.

2. Joseph Schumpeter, *Capitalism, Socialism, and Democracy*, 3rd ed., (New York: Harper, 1950), p. 269.

3. Giovanni Sartori, *Democratic Theory* (New York: Praeger, 1967–1962), p. 52.

4. Henry Mayo, *An Introduction to Democratic Theory* (New York: Oxford University Press, 1960), p. 93.

5. Ibid., p. 118.

6. Robert Dahl, *A Preface to Democratic Theory* (Chicago: University of Chicago Press, 1956), p. 63.

7. Ibid., p. 55.

8. Carl J. Friedrich, *The New Image of the Common Man* (Boston: Beacon, 1950).

9. Hans J. Morgenthau, *Politics Among Nations* (New York: Knopf, 1960–1948, p. 555.

10. Russell Kirk, *A Program for Conservatives* (New York: Regnery, 1962–1954), p. 247.

11. William F. Buckley, Jr., *Up from Liberalism* (New York: Hillman, 1961), p. 138.

12. Dahl, *Preface*, p. 48.

13. Edward Shils, *The Torment of Secrecy* (Glencoe, Ill.: Free Press, 1956), p.

*Some books listed here have two dates: the first is the date of the edition referenced here; the second is the date the work was originally published.

226.

14. Mayo, *An Introduction*, p. 89.

15. Dahl, *Preface*, p. 25.

16. Schumpeter, *Capitalism*, pp. 250-54.

17. C. Wright Mills, *The Power Elite* (New York: Oxford University Press, 1961-1956).

18. Murray Edelman, *The Symbolic Uses of Politics* (Urbana: University of Illinois Press, 1964), p. 19.

19. Morgenthau, *Politics*, p. 261.

20. Dahl, *Preface*, pp. 132-33.

21. Sartori, *Democratic Theory*, p. 102.

22. Mayo, *An Introduction*, pp. 87-88.

23. Sidney Hook, *Political Power and Personal Freedom* (New York: Criterion, 1959), ch. 2.

24. Friedrich, *The New Image*; David Spitz, *Democracy and the Challenge of Power* (New York: Columbia University Press, 1958), p. 159; Sheldon Wolin, *Politics and Vision* (Boston: Little Brown, 1960), p. 434.

25. V.O. Key, Jr., *Public Opinion and American Democracy* (New York: Knopf, 1961), p. 558.

26. Mayo, *An Introduction*, p. 203.

27. Ibid., pp. 94-95, 176, 179, and 181-82.

28. Charles E. Lindblom, *The Intelligence of Democracy* (New York: Free Press, 1965), p. 328.

29. Ibid., pp. 81-82.

30. Sartori, *Democratic Theory*, p. 25.

31. Charles Cnudde and Deane Neubauer, *Empirical Democratic Theory* (Chicago: Markham, 1969), pp. 65-68.

32. Dahl, *Preface*, pp. 75-84; Robert Dahl, *Who Governs?* (New Haven: Yale University Press, 1961), bk. 2; Dahl and Charles Lindblom, *Politics, Economics, and Welfare* (New York: Harper & Row, 1963-1953), pp. 171-172 and ch. 21.

33. Dahl and Lindblom, *Politics*, pp. 277-78.

34. Mayo, *An Introduction*, pp. 62, 72-73 and 165.

35. Sartori, *Democratic Theory*, p. 138.

36. Ibid., pp. 118-19.

37. Cnudde and Neubauer, *Empirical Democratic Theory*, p. 153.

38. E.E. Schattschneider, *The Semi-Sovereign People* (New York: Holt, Rinehart and Winston, 1960), p. 141.

39. Dahl, *Preface*, p. 124.

40. For example, see Seymour Martin Lipset, *Political Man* (Garden City, N.Y.: Doubleday-Anchor, 1963-1960).

41. Sartori, *Democratic Theory*, p. 108.

42. Dahl and Lindblom, *Politics*, pp. 272-75.

43. Arthur Schlesinger, Jr., *The Vital Center* (London: Andre Deutsch, 1970-1949), p. 170.

44. Sartori, *Democratic Theory*, p. 167.

45. Lester Milbraith, *Political Participation* (Chicago: Rand McNally, 1965), pp. 142–54.

46. Schumpeter, *Capitalism*, pp. 269–73.

47. Key, *Public Opinion*, p. 558.

48. Herbert McCloskey, "Consensus and Ideology in American Politics," *American Political Science Review* 58 (June 1964).

49. Richard Hofstadter, *Anti-Intellectualism in American Life* (New York: Knopf, 1963), ch. 8.

50. James MacGregor Burns, *The Deadlock of Democracy* (Englewood Cliffs, N.J.: Prentice Hall, 1967–1963); Burns, *Roosevelt: The Lion and the Fox* (New York: Harcourt, Brace and World, 1956); Burns, *John Kennedy: A Political Profile* (New York: Harcourt, Brace and World, 1960).

51. Arthur Schlesinger, Jr., *Age of Jackson* (Boston: Little, Brown, 1945); Schlesinger, *Writings and Speeches of Eugene V. Debs* (New York: Hermitage, 1948).

52. Arthur Schlesinger, Jr., "The Crisis of American Masculinity" (1958), in *The Politics of Hope* (Boston: Houghton-Mifflin, 1962), p. 246.

53. Schlesinger, "On Heroic Leadership" (1960), in *Hope*, p. 14.

54. Ibid., pp. 6–9.

55. Arthur Schlesinger, Jr., in *The Faces of Five Decades*, ed. Robert Luce (New York: Simon and Schuster, 1964), p. 339.

56. Schattschneider, *People*, p. 139.

57. Richard Neustadt, *Presidential Power* (New York: Wiley, 1964–1960), ch. 7.

58. Ibid., ch. 1.

59. Ibid., ch. 2.

60. Ibid., p. 145, passim.

61. The unmistakable message of George Kennan, *American Diplomacy 1900–1950* (New York: Mentor, 1951).

62. Friedrich, *The New Image.*

63. Morgenthau, *Politics*, p. 248.

64. Ibid., pp. 539, 545–70.

65. Herbert H. Hyman, "England and America: Climates of Tolerance and Intolerance," in *The Radical Right*, ed. Daniel Bell (Garden City, N.J. Doubleday-Anchor, 1964–1963), pp. 305–6.

66. James Prothro and C.M. Grigg, "Fundamental Principles of Democracy: Bases of Agreement and Disagreement," *Journal of Politics* 22 (1960).

67. McCloskey, "Consensus and Ideology in American Politics."

68. S.A. Stouffer, *Communism, Conformity, and Civil Liberties* (Gloucester, Mass.: Peter Smith, 1963–1955), p. 27.

69. Mayo, *An Introduction*, p. 124.

70. Bernard Berelson et al., *Voting* (Chicago: University of Chicago Press, 1954), pp. 311–23.

71. Heinz Eulau, "The Politics of Happiness," *Antioch Review* 16 (1956), pp. 259–64.

72. Schattschneider, *People*, pp. 108 and 112–13.

73. Dahl and Lindblom, *Politics*, p. 312.

74. A.W. Gouldner, "Metaphysical Pathos and the Theory of Bureaucracy," *American Political Science Review* 49 (June 1955): 507.

75. Sartori, *Democratic Theory*, p. 24.

76. Mills, *Power Elite* pp. 170, 224, 276, and 277.

77. Ibid., pp. 16 and 259.

78. Daniel Bell, *The End of Ideology* (New York: Collier's, 1962-1961), p. 74.

79. Max Lerner, *America as a Civilization* (New York: Simon and Schuster, 1957), pp. 486-87.

80. Richard Rovere, *The American Establishment* (New York: Harcourt, Brace and World, 1962), p. 3.

81. Robert Lane, *Political Life* (New York: Free Press, 1959), p. 259.

82. Mills, *Power Elite*, p. 361.

83. Rovere, *Establishment*, p. 261.

84. Bell, *Ideology*, p. 74.

85. Ibid., p. 48.

86. Mills, *Power Elite*, p. 360.

87. Daniel Boorstin, *The Americans: The National Experience* (New York: Random House, 1965), p. 218.

88. Edward Purcell, *The Crisis of Democratic Theory* (Lexington: University of Kentucky Press, 1973), p. 17.

89. William Yandell Elliott, *The Pragmatic Revolt in Politics* (New York: Fertig, 1968-1928), ch. 3.

90. Earl Latham, *The Group Basis of Politics* (Ithaca: Cornell University Press, 1952), p. 209.

91. Ibid., pp. 34 and 49.

92. Latham, *Group Basis*, p. 199; David Riesman et al., *The Lonely Crowd* (New Haven: Yale University Press, 1961-1950), ch. 10.

93. John Kenneth Galbraith, *American Capitalism—The Concept of Countervailing Power* (Boston: Houghton Mifflin, 1956-1952), chs. 9-11.

94. David Truman, *The Governmental Process* (New York: Knopf, 1960-1950), p. 502, passim; see Truman's discussion of his theory in David Truman, "On the Invention of Systems," *American Political Science Review*, June 1960, pp. 494-95.

95. Lindblom, *Intelligence*, ch. 1 and pp. 98-99.

96. Dahl and Lindblom, *Politics*, pp. 3 and 12; Dahl, *Preface*, pp. 132, 137-38, 145, and 150.

97. Lipset, *Political Man*, p. 439; Dahl, *Preface*, p. 151.

98. Gabriel Almond and James Coleman, *The Politics of Developing Areas* (Princeton: Princeton University Press, 1960), p. 533.

99. Henry Kariel, *The Decline of American Pluralism* (Stanford: Stanford University Press, 1961), pp. 113 and 137.

100. Edward Banfield, *Political Influence* (Glencoe, Ill.: Free Press, 1961).

101. Dahl, *Who Governs?*

102. Aaron Wildavsky, *Leadership in a Small Town* (Totowa, N.J.: Bedminster, 1964).

103. Nelson Polsby, *Community Power and Political Theory* (New Haven: Yale University Press, 1963), chs. 3 and 5, passim.

104. Peter Bachrach and Morton Baratz, "Two Faces of Power," *American Political Science Review* 56 (1962): 947–52.

105. Truman, *Process*, pp. 139–55.

106. Lipset, *Political Man*, pp. 430–33.

107. Edelman, *Symbolic Uses*, pp. 4 and 18.

108. Kariel, *Decline*, p. 68.

109. Hook, *Political Power*, ch. 3 and p. 325.

110. Herbert Marcuse et al., *A Critique of Pure Tolerance* (Boston: Beacon, 1965), pp. 41, 46, and 92.

111. Schattschneider, *People*, p. 31.

112. Ibid., p. 35.

113. Lindblom, *Intelligence*, p. 264.

114. Latham, *Group Basis*, pp. 31–32, 39, and footnote 36.

115. Truman, *Process*, pp. 36 and 507.

116. Dahl, *Preface*, p. 145.

117. Sartori, *Democratic Theory*, pp. 264–65; Lindblom, *Intelligence*, pp. 229–30.

118. Milton Friedman, *Capitalism and Freedom* (Chicago: University of Chicago Press, 1962), p. 3.

119. William Kornhauser, *The Politics of Mass Society* (Glencoe, Ill.: Free Press, 1959).

120. Lerner, *Civilization*, pp. 398–400.

121. Mayo, *An Introduction*, pp. 201–2.

122. Sartori, *Democratic Theory*, pp. 357 and 377, passim.

123. Lindblom, *Intelligence*, p. 294.

124. Ibid., pp. 151–52, 161, 187, and ch. 11.

125. Ibid., ch. 14.

126. Clinton Rossiter, *Parties and Politics in America* (Ithaca: Cornell University Press, 1960), p. 177.

127. Lipset, *Political Man*, pp. 12–13 and 76–80.

128. Berelson et al., *Voting*, pp. 311–23.

129. Henry David Aiken, "The Revolt Against Ideology" (1964), in *Ideology, Politics, and Political Theory*, ed. Richard Cox (Belmont, Calif.: Wadsworth, 1969), p. 150.

130. Rossiter, *Parties*, pp. 1 and 152.

131. Kariel, *Decline*, p. 336.

8 The Continuing Commitment to Liberalism

The striking fact about American political thought after World War II was that there was little inclination to abandon traditional liberal values. This was a time of eager skepticism about many things, old absolutes, fanatic ideologies, human behavior in politics, the attractions of radical change, but skepticism stopped abruptly before liberalism. Indeed, the thrust of American thought from 1945 to 1964 was primarily a defense of old liberal values by new means and in a realistic framework. As Richard Hofstadter said, perfectly expressing the outlook of most American intellectuals, "what appeals to me . . . is simply the old liberalism, chastened by adversity, tempered by time, and modulated by a growing sense of reality."[1]

The signs of agreement were evident to all. John Kenneth Galbraith observed that "Nothing much divides those who are liberals by common designation from those who are conservatives."[2] They all turned to traditional liberal values almost reflexively. The same unity was present in most significant fiction of the era. Literary intellectuals held on to liberal norms; they "asserted a now sobered liberal spirit."[3]

Even the new democratic theory was no exception. It involved no abandonment of liberal values. It did not challenge the liberal ethic of individualism, nor the norm of tolerance, nor the modern welfare state. Moreover, it transformed classic democratic ideas in a distinctly liberal direction by its emphasis on democracy as pluralist representation and its pointed concern with individual political liberties. Above all, it was intended as a reconciliation of democratic theory with a respected liberal reality. It was a self-conscious tailoring of classical democratic theory to liberal reality.

The usual attitude toward the old liberal values was by no means skeptical but rather quite the opposite. It was an attitude that treated liberalism and its chief norms as what Arthur Schlesinger called "a fighting faith."[4] This phrase was a popular one. It did not mean a faith in the sense that there was any absolute justification for liberalism, but rather that American intellectuals were sure enough of its worth that they thought liberalism deserved a vigorous defense. As Max Lerner phrased it, American liberalism was "a fighting faith for freedom of the person, higher living standards and a more spacious way of life."[5] Sidney Hook urged his readers to battle, with the admonition: "If those who love freedom do not fight for it passionately . . . those who have passion for power, for domination over others, will win their war against freedom."[6] He went so far as to say: "there must be one working absolute . . . about which we must be fanatical: the rules of the game."[7] No student of the period can fail to notice these repeated injunctions to action nor the specific usages of the metaphor (and it was not always meant merely as a metaphor) of fighting. We know that our political language is deeply imbued with the vocabulary of war—we fight everything from juvenile delinquency to cancer and we wage wars on poverty and polio—but one might be surprised to discover such language used in defense of traditional liberal values. But when one understands that postwar American intellectuals were imbued with a great sense of cause—and threat— and were a unique combination of skeptics and fighters, doubters and believers, the mystery lessens.

PLURALISM AND THE OPEN UNIVERSE

At the heart of the liberalism of postwar theorists was the idea of *pluralism and the open universe.*[8] Never, indeed, had pluralism appeared to be more attractive. It fit the world as so many intellectuals encountered it, an ideal that seemed to fit reality. The testimonials were almost endless, their very numbers making the point in undeniable fashion that this was intellectuals' first and most central premise.

Pluralism had several specific meanings, which sometimes varied from person to person. But in them all pluralism encompassed the ideal of moral and social diversity and the idea that America was a nation that embodied this diversity. Since pluralism was about openness, above all, liberal intellectuals were enthusiastic in their praise of the "open society."[9] Peter Gay proudly affirmed that the Enlightenment was the model for "modern liberal politics." It was "a world united by its celebration of diversity, a cosmopolitan harmony orchestrated in free individuality; an open world, not of absolutes or of persecutions, but of pacific and continuous dialogue."[10] Arthur Schlesinger returned again and again to his conviction that "the free play of diverse elements" was essential to the good society and there was no doubt that America met his test.[11] The philosopher James Ward Smith joined the sociologist Edward Shils in insisting that pluralism was the right solution, that "a reasonable conception of the world must make its peace with a greater richness than it can summarize."[12] Of course, Judith Shklar affirmed that "a defense of social diversity, inspired by that bare-bones liberalism which . . . is committed only to the belief that tolerance is a primary virtue and that a diversity of opinions and habits is . . . to be cherished and encouraged."[13] Even Henry Kariel, a self-proclaimed critic of pluralism in American politics, quickly affirmed the pluralist ideal. Diversity was an unquestioned positive good.[14]

But pluralism was not meant as an ideology or new absolute. It is well to realize that for liberal thinkers in America it was just the opposite, since we know they believed liberalism could no longer base itself on absolute claims. This explains why American thinkers could often agree with Lionel Trilling who saw liberal pluralism as a "large tendency rather than a concise body of doctrine."[15] Indeed, as we have seen, the very absence of any absolute justifications in the modern world was a common ground on which American thinkers sought to justify what values they had, and obviously this was never truer than with their endorsements of pluralism. It was the acceptance in principle of the idea that there were no answers. It was the creation of a virtue out of what some might have seen as an unpleasant reality. If there are no answers, then we have pluralism, or ought to. To praise that reality was a main aspiration of postwar liberalism.

There was a widespread belief that intellectual and social pluralism were a reality in the United States. No matter how great the internal threat posed by McCarthyism, no matter how much it sometimes seemed that conformity and mass culture were too strong and menacing, nonetheless pluralism seemed real. Judith Shklar, for instance noted its existence, something that "any liberal should rejoice in."[16] Max Lerner's *America as a Civilization* was an extended essay on the manifold expressions of pluralism in America as an open society.[17] Arthur Schlesinger dismissed the pessimistic views of those who refused to see the vibrant diversity of America.[18] Clinton Rossiter made a somewhat similar point. He suspected that Americans did not appreciate the marvel of American pluralism, of "unnumbered diversities of faith and intellect [who] seek to live together in accommodation."[19] But he was delighted at the success of the experiment, which was ensured by the fact there was "little in the American cast of mind that makes it friendly to absolutes, at least in the realm of politics and human relations."[20] Finally, as we have seen, the study of postwar politics in America produced a descriptive theory of political pluralism that many intellectuals found attractive.[21]

The ideal of pluralism and the reality of pluralism in America were closely allied in postwar political thought. To defend one was to defend the other, which lent a cast of conservatism to the perspective of many postwar intellectuals.

A thinker such as the maverick Peter Viereck—who not only doubted that America and the West in general were shining exemplars of the open universe but even dared to suggest they were too pluralistic, that "ranks must close. Simply must"—stands out as unusual.[22] Perhaps it was because he was even more frightened of Communism than were most of his fellow intellectuals that he cast doubt on the pluralist reality as well as the pluralist ideal. But it is clear that his conclusions were not popular, nor given the extent of theoretical commitment to pluralism could he have expected them to be. The similar conclusions of Herbert Marcuse, more than a decade later, were to receive a no less cool reaction.

TOLERANCE

With pluralism came *tolerance*. Indeed, tolerance was one of the most widely held values of political intellectuals in the United

States after 1945. It was almost a sacred norm for most American intellectuals. For them it was tied with their prior support for pluralism. Intellectuals believed pluralism implied tolerance. An open universe suggested the wisdom of an acceptance of many views. Moreover, the reigning view that there were no absolutes, in politics or anything else, surely meant that one must tolerate all kinds of views, with the assumption that any might be right and that all must receive a hearing. As Edward Shils put it, "The readiness to live and let live is essential to the free society."[23]

Most of the statements about tolerance that constantly, almost ritualistically, appear in the writing of postwar intellectuals were perfectly general in their tone and implied as broad a tolerance as one could imagine. *They were usually without real definition.* At times one senses that tolerance was taken for granted as a good *much more than it was defined or its limits explained.* J.W. Smith, for instance, made a typically vague call for "an ethic of sympathy and toleration."[24] Peter Gay almost endlessly invoked tolerance as a value of inestimable worth.[25] Judith Shklar repeatedly praised a tolerance she, too, did not always define. Her statements were as warm as Henry Mayo's was cool—"Toleration may reasonably be supported"—but both were staunch in their conviction that tolerance was essential.[26] Louis Hartz's *The Liberal Tradition in America* affirmed the central importance of tolerance and the dangers of altering "eccentricity into sin" in America.[27] Richard Hofstadter was for tolerance and so were many more.[28]

Despite the apparent vagueness and expressiveness of many intellectual endorsements of tolerance, there was another side. Many political intellectuals, like the authors of *The Authoriatarian Personality*, undertook careful definition of the term.[29] Others, including some who on occasion appeared ritualistic in their support of tolerance, did outline some justifications for retaining this traditional liberal value in a new age. There were writers like Thomas Thorson and Judith Shklar whose respect for tolerance derived from their belief that there were no absolute justifications in politics. From this perspective tolerance was good because it accorded with the facts of a human existence in which no one had the right to believe he had the truth or the consequent right to impose it on others. This might seem to imply that tolerance was only a consoling value, one that many intellectuals adopted because there was no better solution. Certainly the common perception was that tolerance was a toughminded value, one for those who were able to accept the fact that this lesser good would have to substitute for a higher truth that had proven elusive. But there was scant evidence that Thorson or Shklar and others who agreed really entertained the feeling that there was much that was second-best about the situation. They were enthusiastic about tolerance, just as they were enthusiastic about pluralism. The logic of tolerance in the light of their skepticism merely reinforced their traditional liberal belief that tolerance was good for more positive reasons.

J.W. Smith expressed one aspect of this sentiment when he argued that tolerance as well as democracy incorporated the "principle that the rights of others be respected."[30] Tolerance was a value intended to honor individuals as valuable in themselves, people to be respected for themselves, rather than judged exclusively, or mainly, for what opinions they held or what life-style they lived. Others felt, as John Stuart Mill had, that tolerance was crucial for the development of individualism, itself considered a basic good. This perspective was rarely defended in any detail, but it was common enough to deserve mention.[31] Another frequent utilitarian argument was exemplified by Sidney Hook, who contended that tolerance of "heresy" promoted the discovery of truth, or what degrees of truth, humans could uncover. Hook insisted that in an open universe, potential discoveries and changes always hover about us, and we must be ready to learn and grow in an atmosphere of tolerance.[32] Max Lerner took yet another utilitarian approach, arguing that tolerance was plainly useful in America because ours was such a pluralistic country. If we were not tolerant of the diversity that was the blunt fact of American life, we could only expect severe conflict and social disorganization. Tolerance allowed Americans, different as they so often were, to live with each other in relative peace.[33]

Overall, though, there were few explanations of the importance of the norm of tolerance. In the writings of American intellectuals in our period it was more an assumption than a sharply reasoned conclusion. Perhaps it is because of this fact that there was so little attention given to the limits of tolerance. Generalized celebrations of tolerance were plentiful, but few intellectuals precisely indicated where its inevitable boundaries were. Apart from the great debate over academic freedom in the 1950s, few political intellectuals were interested in probing the treacherous question of limits.

This lack of attention to the boundaries of tolerance was partly due to the perception of some intellectuals that the major battle they had to fight lay in another direction. They spent much more time watching, as Arthur Schlesinger did, for evidence that the practice of tolerance was increasingly diminishing or bewailing any indications that Americans did not prove receptive to heresy.[34]

Yet there was little dispute whenever an intellectual such as Edward Shils announced that sensible limits to tolerance meant that "extremism is excluded."[35] Extremism was usually taken to encompass two tendencies no one wanted to tolerate. Certainly, actions by those who sought to overthrow the United States political order by conspiracy, force, or violence received no tolerance. Yet many political intellectuals carefully distinguished such actions from thought and from other types of political action. They meant to condemn only a specific form of revolutionary action (which usually meant Communist). More broadly, however, there was considerable impatience with those in politics, whatever their beliefs, who proved to be intolerant. Sidney Hook often criticized such people, insisting there was no reason to be tolerant of the intolerant.[36] J.W. Smith agreed and he suggested that the "core of a reasoned ethics is intolerant of intolerance."[37]

But who were identified as the intolerant? They were unfailingly those at home and abroad who did not embrace the liberal belief that there were no answers in politics, the McCarthys and the Communists, the fanatics and the totalitarians. But, again, it is well to be clear about the liberal position. Even those intolerant dispositions, so frequently manifested by those who did not support majority rule and minority rights in politics, were acceptable, if hateful, as long as they did not appear in the realm of political action.

We will shortly see that some critics contended that tolerance for most American thinkers was a different thing in practice than in theory. The point was made that tolerance sounded good and was often pronounced in a grand and sweeping fashion, but that when forces or movements appeared at home or abroad that did not agree with the liberal consensus, liberal tolerance vanished and liberal intolerance appeared quickly and firmly. Yet it is not so clear that postwar liberalism was hopelessly confused and inconsistent to defend tolerance as a value against those who do not think it is worth defending or preserving. The more significant problem was that many intellectuals took too seriously their own association of tolerance with skepticism. For in fact there were few American intellectuals from 1945 to 1964 who were skeptical about tolerance as a norm. For diverse reasons or often for no particular reason, they took tolerance as something they wanted in theory and practice. They were not skeptical about its worth. Thus when they were presented with those who did not respect tolerance, they had no hesitation whatsoever in vigorously opposing them. This is not the same thing as claiming that political intellectuals saw beyond obviously intolerant opponents such as the Birchers, the conspirational Communists, or Senator McCarthy. They rarely asked if their own practice was consistent with their firm dedication to tolerance.

To be sure, some thought was given to evidence of intolerance in American life. There was recognition that the American people were not as tolerant as they should be. Sometimes intellectuals faulted mostly the general population, as was the case with Seymour Martin Lipset's firm conclusion that the American people were not notably tolerant.[38] Samuel Stouffer's study of the extent of popular intolerance in his *Communism, Conformity and Civil Liberties* was especially shocking, although it did reinforce comfortable intellectual suspicions that southerners, rural people, and churchgoers were particularly intolerant.[39] Louis Hartz found the entire American tradition, including intellectual thought, surprisingly intolerant. His famous admonitions about the danger of too much liberal consensus within America, the intolerance of tolerant liberalism, reflected his uneasiness. In his view "the moral unanimity of a liberal society" was not entirely a beautiful prospect to behold and hardly a statement of liberal commitment in practice to tolerance.[40] But Hartz, like Stouffer and Lipset, classed himself in the category of those who were tolerant. None of them

demonstrated much awareness of questions of skepticism and tolerance or the limits of tolerance as it functioned in America. Like the
effort of other commentators who decried the mass society or the
cultural conformity they saw in America, they continued to express
an intense, but unclarified, commitment to tolerance as a norm.

From a left-wing perspective in the middle 1960s, the critical
judgment on American tolerance was far more piercing and fierce.
Herbert Marcuse's *One-Dimentional Man* (1964) challenged the
reality of tolerance in the United States, and more pointedly,
challenged the record of American postwar intellectuals regarding
support of tolerance in practice. Rather than pluralism and
tolerance, what Marcuse saw was a remarkable sameness and conformity, "one-dimensional thought and behavior" operating all the
while under broad banners praising the opposite.[41] Indeed, Marcuse felt conformity was so monolithic in America that he
discerned what he called "totalitarian" tendencies in the United
States.[42] Marcuse singled out many examples of conformity
happily existing under the banner of tolerance, but nowhere did he
hit nearer American intellectual life than in his assault on modern
American philosophy. As far as he was concerned, modern
philosophers were lost in their Wittgensteinian language games,
while studiously avoiding the search for truth and for the proper
political order. The dominance of linguistic analysis not only shut
out philosophers who had other concerns, itself a sign of intolerance,
but it also did not challenge or encourage any challenge to the
ongoing political order. The result was to accept the political status
quo and, backhandedly, undermine genuine pluralism and
tolerance.[43]

Later Marcuse and Robert Paul Wolff returned to the attack by
contending that American political experience showed conclusively
that tolerant pluralism did not exist for those interest groups and
movements that did not conform to the liberal norms and the
operating status quo. Their views, of course, laid the groundwork
for many of the accusations that were to be heard so incessantly
during the New Left period of the late 1960s. Marcuse and others
then repeated and expanded his belief that tolerance in America
was a sham, which existed only for those prepared to go along with
the reigning liberal ideology.[44]

Marcuse's analysis was hardly an accurate description of the perimeters of tolerance in America especially in the arena of intellectual and religious tolerance. There was a good deal of room for diverse viewpoints, if pointedly less than some celebrations of tolerance in the United States perceived. It was true enough, though, that Marcuse's analysis did form a valuable and striking contrast to the liberal self-image, a needed corrective to the real limits beneath the amorphous affirmations of tolerance endorsed by most postwar American intellectuals. Marcuse certainly was right in his observation that no one believes in "pure tolerance" and that the "issue was only the degree and extent of intolerance."[45]

But Marcuse's broadside came late in the two decades after World War II, and it came with too many appendages about "true consciousness" and Hegelian-Marxist dialectics to receive any ready acceptance. Much earlier and less "extreme" was the critique from the Right, produced above all by William F. Buckley in his books *God and Man at Yale, McCarthy and His Enemies,* and *Up from Liberalism.* Buckley observed what he considered to be a major paradox in American intellectual life. Despite widespread intellectual affirmation of pluralism and tolerance, torpor seemed to consume postwar political intellectuals. There were few signs of crackling debates and fewer signs of creative advancements in human understanding. The postwar decades were an "Age of Modulation" where the mood of "tact" was the essence of good form and intellectuals were expected to "modulate and not only our voices, but also our dogmas."[46]

His explanation for this phenomena concentrated on what he took to be the pervasive fact of intellectual consensus, if not outright conformity. This fact, he felt, was good evidence that scant tolerance was actually practiced by most thinkers. Although Buckley was not concerned with the fate of radical Left movements he was deeply involved with the development of a conservative alternative, and he was angered and outraged by the consensual mainstream intellectual response to conservatism. Here the polite tact disappeared and with it any shred of so-called tolerance. "I wondered when else . . . there has been such consistent intemperance, insularity and irascibility as the custodians of the liberal orthodoxy have shown toward conservatives who question some of its orthodox premises."[47] How could liberal intellectuals believe their attitude toward conservative ideas and intellectuals was remotely congruent with their softhearted professions of tolerance and openness? Buckley remarked that "it is not easy to tell whether a) the Liberal really believes that two sides of an issue are being heard, b) is blind to reality, or c) is indulging in a little hypocrisy."[48] But he thought he knew the answer. All the talk about tolerance went exactly as far, and no further, than tolerance of liberal values.[49] It was extremely paradoxical to him that intellectuals repeatedly denounced him when he dared suggest that some conformity and intolerance were justifiable and then blithely turned around and demonstrated in attitude, and often in deed, the rankest intolerance.[50]

THE FIGHT OVER ACADEMIC FREEDOM

It was Buckley's earliest book, *God And Man At Yale*, that most explicitly confronted the question of tolerance and liberalism, stimulating a classic intellectual debate over academic freedom. Buckley charged that American liberals, specifically focusing on the faculty of Yale University, no more believed in tolerance than they did in the man in the moon. They spoke the word, but they avoided the reality. He tried to show that at Yale there was no tolerance for those who were devoted Christians nor for those who were laissez-faire economists and did not like Keynesian "collectivism." He made the point that all intellectual fields had standards that often went beyond technical skills to dogmas of belief. These dogmas effectively excluded those who saw the world differently and they were intended to do just that. Academic freedom was merely a shibboleth in university intellectuals' hands to protect themselves from anyone criticizing them while they busily spread their all-too-conformist version of truth in religion, in politics, and in economics. They wanted tolerance for themselves, but none for those who did not agree with them. They might claim that tolerance and academic freedom were urgent necessities in a situation in which the absolute truth could not be known, but they would not allow those who made absolute claims any tolerance.[51]

Buckley's attack caused even more controversy because Buckley went on to advocate abolishing academic freedom. Yale University was a private college, Buckley reminded his readers, and what was taught ought to be up to its alumni. If they wanted Christianity and capitalism taught, they should be able to have their way. Since liberal intellectuals did not practice tolerance anyway, they should not object. All Buckley wanted to do, he observed, was to change the current orthodoxies to ones he found more congenial. Given that professors were always indoctrinating anyway, the crucial issue was what they will indoctrinate. Buckley preferred his own "eternal" truth to the hypocritical combination of an abstract tolerance and the harsh reality of liberal dogmas. He called on the alumni to organize to get action.[52]

Buckley's book and his reasoning were all but unanimously rejected by academic intellectuals. In reply, books by other intellectuals poured from the presses, all of which agreed that Buckley was shockingly intolerant and an undoubted enemy of liberal values.

Peter Viereck explicitly criticized Buckley in the harshest language. Although he certainly did not think for a moment the United States was under any constitutional or moral imperative to give Communists federal or university jobs, he was determined that academic freedom be preserved inviolate. He was convinced that "Academic freedom is as fragile as it is indispensable. Hands off!" Moreover, he judged it simply preposterous to turn American colleges and universities over to Buckley's alumni, whom Viereck indelicately labeled the "plutocracy."[53]

Perhaps the most famous discussion besides Buckley's was Sidney Hook's *Heresy Yes, Conspiracy No*. Although not conceived as a reply to Buckley, Hook agreed that wherever there were college professors who were under the discipline of a party, and therefore had no commitment to intellectual freedom, they should not be allowed to teach. He had in mind in particular members of the Communist party. They were not deserving of tolerance because they were not free individuals and were not committed to the development of free men.

But Hook was insistent that proscribing from universities those who were not intellectuals seeking the truth and devoted to encouraging such an objective in others did not in the slightest imply that academic freedom in general ought to be restricted. Indeed, Hook was eloquent in defending the value of academic freedom and in urging its preservation. He approached the subject from a utilitarian point of view, arguing that academic freedom was a useful guarantee that those who sought to find truth would be safe to pursue their endeavors wherever they might lead, confident that the result would be a general benefit for society as a whole. To him there was no basis for panic even if honest inquirers who happened to be Communists or Fascists were allowed in universities. He had great confidence that freedom could sustain the presence of error. He did not doubt that freedom was its own best strength, that freedom could win over prophets of totalitarianism in the struggle for the human mind, or that the failure to believe this was really a failure to believe in freedom itself.[54]

Hook welcomed "heresy" then, assured that it promised growth and creativity in the human experience. Later, in other writings he continued to welcome it. He also continued to warn against those, like Robert MacIver in his *Academic Freedom in Our Time*, who in Hook's opinion were unable to recognize the necessary limits on academic freedom. At the same time, Hook specifically singled out Buckley as someone else he did not like, an unfortunate example of an intellectual who, rather like the Communists, thought he knew the truth and had no respect for academic freedom. Buckley was interested in the imposition of his personal dogmas, not in inquiry and freedom.[55] Hook's attitude touched the essential issue that underlay the entire academic freedom debate, whether or not there were absolute answers in politics or any other aspect of human affairs. For Hook as for most of his fellow intellectuals, there were no such answers and academic freedom consisted of the protection of those who did the best they could to discover the partial and changing truths that were all the modern world could offer.

For Richard Hofstadter tolerance and with it academic freedom were every bit as vital as Hook contended. Hofstadter explored the history of academic freedom in *The Development of Academic Freedom in the United States* (1955) and indirectly in the later *Anti-Intellectualism in the United States* (1963). His defense like Hook's rested firmly on the premise that since ultimate truths were absent, freedom was crucial for human development, and therefore fanaticism must be soundly defeated whenever it appears. It did not occur to Hofstadter any more than to Hook that these premises were themselves a powerful orthodoxy whose application in universities and elsewhere had an inevitably discouraging effect on those who did not believe them.[56] It is not a question of whether Hofstadter or Hook were genuinely skeptical or completely tolerant. Certainly they were not, but even if they had been, their adherence to tolerance as a value was bound to frustrate, anger, and impede those like Buckley for whom the ascendancy of the dogma of tolerance meant the defeat of truth.

Another outlook, the most revealing of all, in the dispute over academic freedom was provided by Russell Kirk in *Academic Freedom* (1955). In those days Kirk was not yet totally disenchanted with the academy and he criticized Buckley's *God and Man at Yale* in the most severe terms. As far as he was concerned Buckley did not believe in tolerance or freedom in universities. What Buckley had in mind was sheer indoctrination. Kirk wanted nothing to do with such a position, contending that toleration for scholars must be very broad. He did not want subversion or conspiracies from within the university, or anywhere else, nor did he consider indoctrination by liberals genuine scholarly activity. But tolerance was an attractive value and it should not be replaced by dogmas about Communism *or* the American Way. Although his guess was that enthusiasts such as Sidney Hook and John Dewey were far less committed to free inquiry than they seemed, he accepted the fact that tolerance meant tolerance of those who did not have ideas in accord with one's own.[57]

Kirk's position is so significant because he was a leading conservative thinker of the 1945-64 era. That even he was contemptuous of Buckley's disregard for tolerance demonstrates how general the consensus was on the importance of academic freedom and tolerance. The atmosphere of general suspicion among the various thinkers in the debate, suspicion over who was and was not a threat to academic freedom, should not cloud the abstract commitment to tolerance. Nor should it obscure the boundaries of that tolerance, boundaries that did not extend to those who did not share the postwar orthodoxy of tolerance.

FREEDOM

There is a plausible basis for connecting pluralism and tolerance with the skeptical attitudes of liberal thinkers in America after 1945, although we must note that these norms were obviously also longtime elements of liberalism. Other components of classic liberalism were far more unmistakably defended not because they were a consequence of skepticism, but because they were traditional liberal values appealing to American political intellectuals from 1945 to 1964 as they had long before. This was notably true of freedom.

Liberty was the centerpiece of postwar political intellectuals' beliefs as it had long been the heart of American political philosophy. Freedom is praised so often, and by so many thinkers, that it is an obvious and routine dimension of the work of almost all American political intellectuals after 1945. Intellectuals agreed on the proposition that liberty was the "most basic of the ideals" as they agreed on nothing else. To them what America stood for, above all, was "the fundamental American principles of freedom and tolerance of dissent."[58] The most enthusiastic joined Hook and proclaimed that "the goal . . . should be . . . to expand the world sector of freedom."[59] Almost no one questioned assertions like those of Max Lerner, one of the most ardent advocates of freedom, that "there have been few civilizations in which freedom has flourished as it has in America."[60]

There is a difference, of course, between frequent and sincere invocations of a value like freedom and careful explication of its meaning. Although there is little doubt that among many postwar thinkers the invocation was the meaning, there were also reasonably clear patterns of definition. For example, there were those who thought liberty was properly and essentially economic freedom, room for the business entrepreneur to pursue his or her objectives in a free marketplace. This was true, of course, of most American conservatives, but was perhaps most lucidly argued by Milton Friedman in his *Capitalism and Freedom*.[61] But this definitional focus was distinctly not the one that rallied most, or even much, support from American political thinkers after 1945. Two other definitions of freedom, which were also endorsed by Milton

Friedman, were far more likely to be invoked. One was general intellectual freedom. Daniel Bell was quick to insist that free trade in ideas was absolutely essential and Sidney Hook made one of the most renowned appeals on its behalf.[62] Indeed, the entire academic freedom controversy may be interpreted as an argument over, and eventually in favor of, this notion of liberty.

The most frequently advanced definition of freedom was the right to political freedom, the right to dissent and speak out on specifically political issues. Thomas Thorson suggested that the protection of minority rights to free dissent was the core of American liberal democracy. Arthur Schlesinger aggressively upheld the importance of political disagreement, "the indispensibility of dissent." Even Erich Fromm, critical as he was of so much of the American reality, felt its greatest advantage over the Russians was the commitment to the legitimacy of political criticism.[63]

The assumption of most writers was that political freedom held a prominent place in American experience and that it would not be easily maintained. This judgment was confirmed for some intellectuals after 1945. During the late 1940s and 1950s many thoughtful thinkers expressed alarm at popular attitudes and government actions concerned with the Communist menace. Many political intellectuals felt there were signs of an overreaction that was dangerous to the endurance of political liberty in America. Daniel Bell regretted that Communists in America were not always accorded "scrupulous regard for their civil liberties."[64] Edward Shils deplored the "disturbance and degradation which America had suffered from its own zealots of secrecy and loyalty." The costs of government overzealousness at its worst had been sacrifice of "rule of law" and the disastrous encouragement of a "homogeneity of attitude."[65]

Occasionally a voice during these years could be heard that insisted loyalty to political freedom had to include strong support for the rights of the Communist party to carry on legal work, a disposition open to accepting Communists within the liberal democratic framework as long as they adhered to its norms, and an attitude critics might have thought was more concerned with condemning inconsistencies in the American record of political freedom than in denouncing the enemy of Communism.[66] But it was just at this point that leading thinkers often wanted to make a crucial concession to "reality." Arthur Schlesinger deplored the abuses of government snoopers and prosecutors in the 1950s. He perceived some threat in their actions for a robust political freedom. He wrote an eloquent essay in 1960 on Bernard De Voto that made a great deal of De Voto's impassioned crusade for the preservation of civil liberties in the 1950s. Yet there is no evidence that Schlesinger ever changed his mind from his own judgment of the 1950s that "the indulgence of freedom must inevitably take second place in the real world to the harsh requirements of survival."[67]

What was the line between protection of political liberties and facing the realities of Communism? It never became clear among postwar political intellectuals. There were many opinions and many ambiguous opinions. The general direction was to pursue twin objectives: celebrating political liberty, including criticism of statist actions that appeared inimical to liberty, while at the same time joining the attack on Communists at home and abroad. These twin objectives were not necessarily contradictory, although they were not easily reconciled by men like Schlesinger. He agreed with Peter Viereck's insistence that American intellectuals must not let themselves be manipulated by Communists and their naive dupes into "the most successful communist hoax ever perpetuated: the confusion of communist military conspiracy with the sacred cause of civil liberties."[68]

From a rather different perspective, conservatives like Buckley and Friedman wondered how long political freedom would last unless there was a dramatic reversal of the erosion of economic liberty in the United States. Buckley was disgusted with the statist trend he believed threatened all aspects of freedom. In *Up from Liberalism* he proclaimed his famous manifesto: "I will not cede more power to the state. . . . I mean to live my life an obedient man, but obedient to God, subservient to the wisdom of my ancestors, never to the authority of political truths arrived at yesterday."[69] Milton Friedman expressed genuine shock at John Kennedy's 1961 inaugural address, with its stirring summons to citizens to serve the state. Such a doctrine was anathema to anyone who believed in liberty, he charged, and it ought to be denounced.[70]

Moreoever, especially by the early 1960s, there were complaints from the American political Left that freedom was largely rhetoric rather than reality when it came to political dissent. This was the assertion of the Port Huron statement. It was the view of Herbert Marcuse as well as Robert Paul Wolff, who maintained that the rich had such an advantage in fact that formal pronouncements about political liberty meant nothing in the raw context of political life in America.[71] More orthodox intellectuals, of course, found this an appalling assessment that was far from the mark. "It is absurd to assert that because the rich have easier access to the costly media by which to spread their views, therefore the political freedoms are a 'sham,' or meaningless to the poor."[72]

Another area of dispute between a small minority of radical thinkers and the mainstream concerned the very nature of liberal freedom. For Marcuse, or Erich Fromm, the essence of liberty had less to do with rights to dissent, or with general intellectual liberty, than it did with a dramatic, if imprecise, "liberation" of the human personality. This could only occur through a thoroughgoing revolution in human society that would introduce socialism, participatory democracy, and community.[73] Although these views were expressed in the 1950s by Fromm and in the 1960s by Marcuse, they were only a ripple in the pond of American thought from 1945 to 1964. Their very revolutionary tone, even when presented in the most gentle forms, ensured that they would not receive any serious consideration.

LIBERAL INDIVIDUALISM

Although critics might question the degree and consistency of postwar American thinkers' commitment to basic liberties, this perspective would have seemed incredible to most intellectuals in those years. Their conviction was that in opposing McCarthy and restricting Communists, they demonstrated intense loyalty to a generous range of intellectual and political liberty. What limits they considered or proposed were aimed against those who they were convinced sought to abolish the very principles of intellectual and political liberty. As Hook said, speaking for so many of his intellectual colleagues, there should be no freedom for conspiracies. Nor did Arthur Schlesinger see how anyone could doubt that America was right to apply a clear and present danger test. There could be no right to a government job or any civil liberties at the price of national self-protection.[74]

Devotion to liberty was matched by a respect for the individual as a being possessing the right to choose, one in whom freedom was an enobling quality. The traditional liberal adherence to the ethic of individualism underwent no dimunition throughout the postwar period and, indeed, the general commitment to individualism produced some of the relatively small criticisms of American life that appeared in the thought of intellectuals after the war. Although there was no doubt of continuing support for liberal individualism, there was doubt about its vitality in postwar America.

Expressions of support for liberal individualism after 1945 were frequent and endless. They can be found everywhere, if usually without much definition. Eric Hoffer's *The True Believer* was an essay in defense of people who were authentic individuals, able to stand on their own legs and unwilling to fall into the hands of ideologies and absurd mass movements.[75] Glenn Tinder, writing from a religious perspective, dismissed the communitarian solutions to political order offered by Marx, Rosseau, and Hegel. Each of them denied individualism.[76] Erich Fromm spoke of his belief in the central value of individual autonomy which made genuine love possible.[77] Even in that age of pluralist group analysis, social scientists in great numbers eagerly aligned themselves with individualism. David Riesman, one of those most concerned, was a tireless advocate of the goal of autonomy and his hero was John Stuart Mill.[78] Earl Latham, prophet of group analysis, insisted that to recognize the reality of the group was not to lose sight of the primary worth of the individual. The individual person remained the object of every group and all politics.[79] From quite another side, Lon Fuller, the legal scholar, argued that legalism rested on the assumption of the supreme value of the individual, and Max Lerner believed one could not, and should not, begin to approach *America as a Civilization* without respect for the ethic of individualism that lay at its center.[80]

This warmth toward individualism existed together with a

realization that the decades after 1945 were a time of alienation for many, including not a few intellectuals. There was considerable sense of otherness, of humans separated somehow from their fellows, both in a cosmic sense as well as in the very specific world of the United States. Paul Tillich sounded the great existential theme of alienation and loneliness.[81] C. Wright Mills in *The Sociological Imagination* suggested that many Americans were confused in this alienated age, and Glenn Tinder's remarks about estrangement and alienation in the 1960s were by then commonplace.[82]

Much contemporary fiction expressed the same concern, as literary intellectuals turned from social themes to the individual person. The fiction of important postwar writers such as Truman Capote and Carson McCullers evoked a lonely and rather confused human being, somehow unconnected with the world around them.[83] Yet this trend in fiction, like the broader focus on the alienated American, did not usually indicate a renunciation of individualism as a norm. It was, on the contrary, a manifestation of intense intellectual involvement with the individual above all else. Certainly it did not imply any suspicion that alienation, if it actually characterized the age, was caused by the relentless admonitions of the liberal ethic that one had to be an individual. The energies of intellectuals were directed elsewhere, toward the manifest threats toward the ideal of individualism on the American scene. The greatest threat and one that received extensive scrutiny, especially in the 1950s, was the allegedly increasing conformity in the United States and the emergence of a mass society.

On the one hand this anxiety was directly related to the McCarthy controversy and the rise of a radical Right in America, which provoked many intellectuals to protest that there was too little willingness in the United States to accept individuals who wanted to criticize. Lionel Trilling sternly observed that liberalism could always benefit from criticism and ought to welcome it.[84] Philip Rahv found that there was entirely too great an obsession in America with conformity even among intellectuals.[85] A host of intellectuals spoke out on this question as early as 1952 in a memorable issue of *Partisan Review*.[86] Students of America like Louis Hartz in *The Liberal Tradition*, Max Lerner in *America as a*

Civilization, and Henry S. Commager in *The American Mind* all shared the fear. Lerner worried that the "pressures to conform are strong" for artists in America, and he found this most unfortunate.[87] Even such an unreserved enthusiast for the United States at mid-century such as Commager felt it necessary to acknowledge with no little anxiety that "the pressure for intellectual conformity and growing intolerance with independence and dissent" were too great.[88] Richard Hofstadter did not think the educational system was doing much to counter the trend. He deplored public education's concern, which tapered off after the late 1950s, with teaching children life adjustment. To him this doctrine encouraged conformity and mass culture and did nothing positive for intellectual values.[89]

On the other hand, the anxiety was related to a wave of scholarly and popular sociology and social psychology that purported to demonstrate the United States was moving in an alarmingly conformist direction. Erik Erikson's *Childhood and Society* (1950) warned about the conformist dangers to contemporary American children from "Momism" and "Bossism."[90] Sloan Wilson's *Man in the Grey Flannel Suit* (1955) constituted a chilling exploration of business and suburban conformity, and William H. Whyte's *The Organization Man* (1956) was an equally disturbing report that covered much the same ground in rather more academic fashion.[91] Whyte's chapter "The Fight Against Genius" detailing the animosity toward the creative individual was especially discouraging. Both books received a good deal of consideration in the popular as well as intellectual press. There was great concern for what their findings meant for individualism in the United States.

Laboratory studies of individual and group behavior only seemed to confirm the intellectuals' fears. Two of the most famous, and most painful, were the Solomon Asch and Stanley Milgram experiments. Coming a decade apart, both reported that people in America were remarkably open to suggestion, that they responded with surprising submissiveness to external authority and the desire to conform, and that they could inflict substantial pain and punishment on others at the behest of outer pressures even when they knew what they were doing was wrong. These experiments were inevitably chilling in their influence on some intellectuals' hopeful views of Americans, or perhaps human behavior in general. Certainly they indicated that individualism was scarcely in a healthy condition.[92]

But certainly the most controversial and intriguing of all the contributions to the debate over individualism and conformity after 1945, a debate that revealed the general intellectual commitment to individualism, was David Riesman et al.'s *The Lonely Crowd* (1950). Although Riesman was to make clear later that he did not think the United States was a mass culture,[93] it was difficult to draw that message from his famous book. His argument was that although the myth of liberal individualism remained the American ethos, including considerable respect for the norm of individual competition, our practice was quite different. He claimed he detected more and more signs that the actual stress in American culture was on cooperation and conformity in schools, in homes, and in workplaces. He concluded that, in fact, the ideology and the reality were in opposition, since cooperation and emphasis on social values were now dominant in practice in America.[94]

In terms of Riesman's typology of behavior this meant that Americans were increasingly "other-directed" people. They were primarily sensitive to signals from other people and tremendously interested in being liked and respected by others. Inevitably they were more conformist. Riesman thought that one could also observe the increasing disappearance of people who were "inner directed," who followed moral standards learned at home. He had not much more sympathy with inner-directed persons than he did with other-directed ones, however, since he believed neither could claim to be authentic individuals. In his view, neither was able to act as an autonomous person, using reason and judgment to realize himself in a complex and trying world.[95] This was a point he made more emphatically in *Individualism Reconsidered and Other Essays*.[96] Riesman's goal was autonomy and he consciously intended his work to be a devastating critique of America past and present. His judgment was that the United States did not now produce, and had never produced, nearly enough people who were individuals and he saw scant indication that this truth would soon be reversed.

Riesman's judgments were echoed in the writings of radical social scientists. Erich Fromm bewailed the "inward emptiness" of Americans who were in the grip of "mass culture" that was literally destroying them.[97] Refugee Marxist intellectuals, such as Theodore Adorno and Max Horkheimer from the Frankfurt Institute, agreed and reported that the America they found was far too much a mass society for the good of the individual as well as society itself.[98] Of course, C. Wright Mills drew a devastating picture of a great portion of the middle classes in his influential *White Collar*. Here were the masses of public and private bureaucrats and clerks locked in routine and conformist life patterns. They manifested little indeed of the old American ethic of individualism.[99] Although Fromm and others bemoaned the many "automatons" of conformity produced in America ever more frequently, Herbert Marcuse ten years later vigorously protested the "suppression of individuality" in the reality of "comfortable, smooth, reasonable, democratic unfreedom" of the United States.[100] Marcuse's thesis in *One-Dimensional Man* (1964) became famous. He contended that conformity held sway in the United States not merely because of spineless timid intellectuals or a bad educational system. Rather, the ability of liberalism to absorb any creative departures or radical ideas into the dominant culture made it very difficult for anyone to be a nonconformist in America. No matter how radical an idea might seem and no matter how much effort one might make to break out of the suffocating free unfreedom, the grasp of the liberal pluralist hand would tighten on the effort, turn it into a cultural fascination, and destroy its "subversive force."[101] This process was too powerful for anyone to break, and Marcuse concluded that the prospects for radical change were bleak in the America he knew in 1964. Conformity was too strong and likely to continue to be.

Riesman, Fromm, Marcuse, and many others sounded the alarm about the condition of individualism in the United States after 1945 a good many times. There is no question that many other intellectuals worried about this matter a great deal. Their respective definitions of the value of individualism were often different when they were not merely vague, but the concept continued unshaken as part of liberal and nonliberal intellectual's postwar faith. However, the Marcuses mired in pessimism about the individual in a postwar America were few. Worry was one thing; genuine pessimism was another, far rarer sentiment. As Max Lerner observed, there was conformity in America, and conformists certainly could be found, but there was a wide variety of other personality types.[102] Seymour Martin Lipset suggested there was much reason to wonder if it was even true that there was more conformity in the West, including the United States, today than in the past. Optimist as always, he suspected there was probably more individual political freedom and expression in his America than there had ever been in human history. This was not to deny signs of conformity, but it was to acknowledge another set of signs, those of hope and achievement.[103] Even a sometime pessimist like Richard Hofstadter could, and did, acknowledge the hope.[104]

Yet a sense of uneasiness remained long after McCarthy was dead and the discussion of *The Lonely Crowd* had quieted. Few intellectuals repeated Arthur Schlesinger's onetime charge that contemporary America was in "a time threatened by homogenization,"[105] but there were even fewer thinkers prepared to agree with Clyde Kluckhohn's optimistic conclusion that there was no particular problem in regard to individualism in the United States. Few shared his relaxed assurance that if there was more evidence of other directness among Americans in the postwar years, it was, after all, only a matter of degree. Even fewer appear to have shared his intuition that greater conformity might be good, releasing the tyranny of the superego and overthrowing guilt, producing a human being who was potentially more autonomous.[106]

THE VIEW OF THE STATE

Although there was every indication that political intellectuals in the United States after World War II were eagerly devoted to individualism as they interpreted it, just as American theorists had been for a long time before them, there was a reformulation of classic liberal attitudes about the state. After 1945 the New Deal's vastly increased use of the state's power to provide security and welfare was accepted in liberalism. The controversy that had divided the 1930s was over. The old liberal orthodoxy in favor of a weak state was abandoned. Yet the change came free of any traces of state worship and accompanied by more than a little skepticism of further growth of the state. What emerged was a kind of compromised liberalism, accepting a newly expanded state, but suspicious as of old of a powerful state, including a socialist state. In a sense, the compromise may be described as a reconciliation between the liberal principle of a small state and the "reality" of its necessary modification to deal with imposing practical problems.

More than anyone, Arthur Schlesinger summed up the new orthodoxy, which was a delicate compromise. Schlesinger had some harsh things to say about big businessmen. They were often reactionary in politics and lacked creativity in their own enterprises. But this was only to be expected from most postwar intellectuals. It did not mean at all that Schlesinger was ready to abandon capitalism and turn to the socialist state.[107] Nor did his predictable praise for strong executive leadership in the government mean that Schlesinger was ready to surrender his liberal suspicions of a too powerful state. Schlesinger praised Alexander Hamilton, Teddy Roosevelt, and, of course, Franklin D. Roosevelt as exemplars of governmental leadership. They were all ready to act quickly and with determination to meet domestic difficulties with state power. He contrasted them sharply and quite intentionally with Jefferson. Schlesinger thought Jefferson was as poor an example of leadership as Schlesinger's hero, the Progressive intellectual Herbert Croly, said he was forty years ago. For Jefferson did not really like government, he was afraid of power, and he used it only reluctantly.[108] Yet Schlesinger insisted that the state should not do more in the postwar economy than lay down "ground rules." He warned against the frame of mind that turned to the state at a moment's notice whenever anything went wrong. Schlesinger was optimistic about what people could do on their own and convinced that "experience suggests that the limited state can resolve the basic social questions which were supposed to compel a resort to the unlimited state."[109] He had no reservations in concluding that in the United States faith properly remained in "the limited state."[110]

Although Schlesinger's stance may be taken as a typical effort to combine the old liberal article of faith in a modest state with the new reality of an expanded state, it was obvious that such a compromise depended greatly on intellectuals' views of postwar capitalism. If there was fundamental opposition to capitalism, even to capitalism combined with a newly active welfare state, the liberal compromise would not work for political thinkers of the age.

The fact is that there was almost no opposition. The substantial proportion of American intellectuals who in the name of Marxism or some other form of socialism had cried out in the 1930s against capitalism, was reduced to a tiny number. In the place of Marxist critiques of the evils of capitalism, Max Lerner now offered justifications of the mixed economy of capitalism and an expanded government. His argument was not simple, but surprisingly intricate, stocked with a rich proliferation of statistics that suggested American capitalism was not as good as its most ecstatic defenders asserted, but hardly the dismal failure thinkers like Lerner once had believed it was.[111]

Lerner carefully assayed a number of classic objections to American capitalism, but he judged that few of them were any longer persuasive. Few American intellectuals from 1945 to 1964 disagreed with him. Lerner recognized that some people might have reservations about the huge size of the principal units in the American economic structure or our sharp inequalities in income distribution, but he felt these problems were "on the way to being resolved."[112] He acknowledged there remained a "hard core" of poor that neither capitalism nor government had yet been able to absorb into the American economic mainstream, but there was none of the urgency or outrage in Lerner's perspective of the late 1950s that was to appear at the very end of our period.[113] Clinton Rossiter's eager praise for capitalism's record—"such a good job of production and distribution"—and his admiration for how far America, under capitalism, had come toward achieving a "humane and stable economy" were typical.[114] He did not see how anyone who was fair could possibly disagree, nor did he think one could avoid recognizing the obvious political consequence: "surely we need not rehearse once again the obvious fact that the appeals of radicalism have gone unheeded in America because the promises of radicalism have been largely fulfilled."[115]

The obvious decline of quasi-Marxist interpretations of American experience after 1945 were, according to historiographer John

Higham, traceable to the same obvious fact: "the hugely satisfying performance of the American economy in the last two decades."[116] Even when an economic interpretation did gain attention, as was true of David Potter's *People of Plenty*, it appeared in non-Marxian dress. Potter was certainly uneasy about a number of aspects of modern American economic life, most memorably the role advertising played in shaping consumer wants, but he emphasized the shaping influences of the enormous resources of the United States in a manner that, perhaps unintentionally, cast a favorable judgment on the American economy.[117]

A far more unequivocal assessment appeared in a number of studies of economic and social mobility published in the 1950s. Leading sociologists such as W. Lloyd Warner, Seymour Martin Lipset, and Richard Bendix contended that empirical evidence demonstrated mobility was increasing in the United States. The mixed economy had not destroyed opportunity for entrepreneurs nor locked all who belonged to the lower classes into permanent lower class conditions. The news from America was hopeful and positive.[118] Michael Harrington's *The Other America* (1962) took time to reach the consciousness of intellectuals.[119] It is clear why it constituted a kind of consciousness revolution when it did, for the popular analysis of the performance of the mixed economy was overwhelmingly favorable until the middle 1960s. Richard Hofstadter noted this fact and the associated shift of sympathy by liberal intellectuals toward big business. He did not disagree, but he was not entirely sure that all was well in the mixed economic system of the United States.[120] Adolph A. Berle's *The Twentieth Century Capitalist Revolution* was less hesitant. It was a more characteristic affirmation of the mixed economy and the virtues of bigness in modern economic life, one which had considerable influence.[121] Arthur Schlesinger basically shared this judgment. He steadily adhered to his view that government intervention in the economy had its limited uses, that "the normal man can take government, like liquor, in moderation and benefit from it."[122] He remained convinced that the postwar amity between big business and government was basically beneficial, especially in terms of the vast bountifulness of the American economy. As late as 1960 he was convinced that the central issues of his time were not economic at all. "There still are pools of poverty which have to be mopped up; but the central problems will be increasingly that of . . . individual dignity, identity, and fulfillment in an affluent society."[123]

Certainly Schlesinger agreed with Peter Viereck that American capitalism "happens not to be a sacred religion," and Schlesinger would not have disputed Viereck's conclusion that widespread intellectual reconciliation with capitaism was a fact in postwar American intellectual life.[124]

The major intellectual figure of the era who dealt with economic questions was John Kenneth Galbraith. He consistently praised the success of the mixed economy. In his *American Capitalism* (1952) he had sharply critical words for intellectuals who did not seem to him to appreciate the remarkable record of productivity of American capitalism. Galbraith suggested that the old danger of unchecked capitalist power had diminished because of the modern compromise with the state, which maintained a happy and vital "countervailing power" that often ensured the private sectors of the economy would remain responsive to the larger public interest.[125]

To be sure, in his later work *The Affluent Society* (1958), Galbraith's enthusiasm noticeably waned. He did not deny the productive capacities of the mixed economy nor did he suggest any major alterations in the nature of the American economy. Yet he complained that there was far too much concern with production and consumption for the social health of the American society. The affluence of Americans was daily proving itself to be too much of a good thing. He pleaded that America needed a broader vision than at present "in which the pursuit of goods is paramount." Surely America could do better than simply follow its new "creed" of "more production."[126]

Galbraith contended that the enormous affluence generated by the mixed economy was an unparalleled opportunity for the United States. It constituted an opportunity to address inevitable social needs of the community as a whole. Instead of amassing more and more goods, often at the behest of those who skillfully used advertising to stimulate "wants," Galbraith insisted we ought to tackle neglected social services and redress "the social balance." Galbraith had in mind a wide variety of state-financed activities ranging from a frontal assault on what remained of poverty to a massive improvement in our educational system. Russian triumphs in space Galbraith interpreted as an alarming warning about the fate of a "society which sets as its highest goal the production of private consumer goods."[127]

Although there is no doubt that *The Affluent Society*, reinforced by later books such as David Riesman's *Abundance For What?* (1964), began to turn intellectual thought toward an expansion of the welfare society that Lyndon Johnson undertook to realize in the middle 1960s, Galbraith's position was consistent throughout our period with the main drift of intellectual opinion in regard to the mixed economy. He may have grown less sanguine about *what ends* that economy served, but he never doubted that its historic capacities were immensely valuable nor did he propose any fundamental alteration in the economic structure of modern capitalism.

We can understand this most clearly by observing Galbraith's attitudes toward economic equality. In all his discussions of the need to tax much more heavily to provide government funds to redirect some of the mixed economy's energies to the production of social goods and services, he always carefully distinguished his position from equalitiarianism. However much Galbraith and other intellectuals reflected upon the nature of American economic experience, sometimes critically, they almost always argued that economic equality or a serious effort to move in that direction was not a worthwhile goal.[128] It was widely believed the record of history proved that excessive zeal for equality guaranteed the end of liberty and this assumption drastically limited the appeal of socialism for postwar political intellectuals.[129] As Peter Viereck remarked, "Equality is desirable. A lot of things on earth are desirable. But equality is not the same as freedom."[130] Rossiter wanted some of both liberty and equality, but "in a showdown between liberty and equality, which must often take place in both theory and practice," he opted unequivocally for liberty.[131] The lesson of the tragic "failure" of Marxism lay in the background. As Irving Howe said, quoting Max Scheler, "True tragedy arises" when [ever] the idea of 'justice' appears to be leading to the destruction of higher values."[132]

Yet Rossiter and Howe did not intend their point to be taken as a brief for the return of laissez-faire economics and a night-watchman state. Those days were gone forever and their passing was not regretted in the slightest. President Eisenhower did not dismantle the New Deal and John Kennedy did not much expand the welfare state. They were an expression in policy of the intellectuals' consensus in theory.[133]

The consensus was perhaps more fragile than it sometimes seemed. Angry attacks on the mixed economy in the United States occasionally appeared, most memorably in Erich Fromm's untiring efforts to illuminate his thesis that capitalism diminished human potential for love and caring,[134] but the most important reason why this was so was the criticism conservative intellectuals aimed at it. Perhaps the most discussed side of this dissent came from the so-called Chicago school of economists and its public leader, Milton Friedman. His principal political work, *Capitalism and Freedom* (1962), was a manifesto that has proven to be of enduring interest to libertarians. Through his professional work and a tireless set of lecture appearances, Friedman argued that the creation of a competitive capitalist society could genuinely preserve the liberal values of individualism, tolerance, and pluralism. The alternative was the growth of a government that even then, he thought, threatened basic liberties in many other realms besides economics.[135]

In Friedman's view the only appropriate role for government was to insist that certain rules of the game be imposed on private business to maintain fair competition, including the enforcement of antitrust laws. It certainly was not appropriate for the state to enforce antidiscrimination laws on the basis of race, for if the state could interfere here it could interfere anywhere. Indeed, to Friedman's mind it was interfering far too often already. The progressive income tax was an egregious example of the infringement of human liberty; so was the welfare system, public schools, the licensing of professionals, and the passage of right to work laws. Everywhere Friedman and other economic libertarians looked, they saw the hand of government and consequently the reduction of human liberty.[136]

Of course, Friedman was not alone among "conservatives" in this disposition. William F. Buckley and others associated with the *National Review* complained along with Friedman, although in less sweeping terms, that the state was too massive, posing a threat to human liberty that was too great for one not to voice objections. Buckley suggested that "the conservatives, as a minority, are the new radicals," and his claim was not farfetched here at least.[137] Buckley's famous tale of the capture of the Yale economics department by the Keynesians was a story of the progress of the advocates of the mixed economy into dominant positions in the world of economic analysis. To Buckley it was a sad tale, one heavy with dark meaning for the American future.[138]

Even among American conservatives there was no unanimity on behalf of the capitalist ideal untouched by the state. Russell Kirk, for one, was uneasy about capitalism. After all, capitalist entrepreneurs could forget about some rather important things, such as God and tradition, in their all-too-evident rapacity and egoism. Although Kirk hardly had respect for the state, he did reflect the ambivalence in the very home of conservatism in America regarding the undiluted capitalist ethic. This ambivalence, for example, partly explains why neither Buckley nor Kirk wanted anything to do with Ayn Rand's swashbuckling entrepreneurs. She put the dollar sign ahead of the cross, and that was clearly unacceptable.[139]

If, in general, it was only on the Right that criticism of the postwar compromise between the state and the capitalists was commonly heard, nevertheless there were those who wanted a somewhat different balance between the two that favored the side of the state. This was obviously the case with those who supported the confrontation with poverty that slowly marshalled support in the early 1960s. It was also true of those who continued to worry that private economic power was too great and that Galbraith's countervailing power was not yet sufficient. Some political intellectuals, for instance, called for sharp governmental centralization to mobilize power needed to break up economic structures they felt clearly exercised control well beyond what could be tolerated in a liberal society.[140] Others were frankly for more economic equality, as was Seymour Martin Lipset: "since I feel that inequality though inevitable is *immoral*, I support all measures that would serve to reduce its extent."[141] But this was not really true, even of Lipset. He feared the costs of equality in terms of individualism and elite culture and education too much for that.[142] In the end he saw no need for socialism in the United States. The basic problems of economic need had been met by the welfare state. He accepted the compromise.

THE DEFENSE

The fundamental tenets of postwar liberalism, then, were rather clear and reasonably coherent. They included belief in a pluralistic, tolerant society, which represented the individual (especially his intellectual and political freedom), and which incorporated a considerable degree of state welfare while acknowledging the legitimacy of capitalism. Of these elements, only the attitude toward the state represented a revision of classic liberalism, and it was not generally seen as a basic change, only one of degree. We may say that skepticism about absolutes and utopias did not transform postwar liberalism in any way except its version of democratic theory. The old values emerged intact.

But they did not seem secure to postwar intellectuals. They did not seem secure not merely because of the problems of justification, which sometimes vexed postwar intellectuals, as we have seen, but more because intellectuals perceived they were under scrutiny and attack above all by the forces of international Communism. It would indeed be impossible to understand the process by which intellectuals after 1945 defined the old liberal values if one did not realize how central a role in that definition was taken by the counterattack on Communism. Few doubted Sidney Hook's essential, if somewhat hyperbolic, accuracy when he asserted long after 1945 that "We face grim years ahead. The democratic West will require the critical support, the dedicated energy and above all, the intelligence of its intellectuals if it is to survive as a free culture."[143]

One needs to be careful when one looks back on political thought from 1945 to 1964, since in some circles today anti-Communism has a bad name. It had no bad reputation then. Liberal values were self-consciously understood as the alternative to Communism and a good deal of their definition came in specific dialectic with Communism. This was especially true of the 1940s and the 1950s when the Cold War was most intense. An early expression came in a 1948 issue of the *Partisan Review*, once a Communist-controlled publication, which had a symposium on the state of writing in America. The responses of these literary intellectuals manifested great concern with Communism and the necessity of its defeat. It was not a collection of jingoistic rantings, but essay after essay somehow progressed from the initial discussion to articulating an anti-Communist concern. Lionel Trilling weighed in with a sharp criticism of Soviet materialism.[144] Leslie Fiedler remarked that one had to face the fact that intellectuals' commitment to freedom always faced enemies and they were represented "most spectacularly these days by the Soviet Communist world-view."[145] Clement Greenberg thought that a writer had to make a choice if he believed in liberty, that as "a person the writer ought indeed to involve himself in the struggle against Stalinism to the point of commitment."[146]

The fighting mentality of American intellectuals was well illustrated by Arthur Schlesinger's *The Vital Center* (1949). Schlesinger was active in the creation of Americans for Democratic Action, an organization of liberals set up after the war both to promote liberalism and to defend it against Communism. His book showed he did not doubt there was a contest in the world between American liberalism and Soviet Russia. There could be no illusion about the enemy. There was no sense in fooling oneself that Communists could possibly be allies or that one could cooperate with them at home or in the realm of international affairs. There the first and supreme goal must be halting the imperialist Communist march that Schlesinger saw on every hand. He advocated no pointless sabre rattling, but neither did he tolerate any wishful thinking, such as the hope that appeasement would somehow create a revolution in Communist consciousness.[147]

Another famous manifestation of the mood of anti-Communism and the active defense of liberalism was the American Committee for Cultural Freedom, a participant in the larger Western Congress for Cultural Freedom. Many American intellectuals belonged to and were active in this organization in the late 1940s and early 1950s and they published in the British magazine *Encounter*. The general topic of many of their contributions was international Communism's threat to liberalism. Freedom and the reality of pluralism were the issues. Postwar liberals felt confronted by a movement they believed did not honor these values and indeed sought their destruction. Christopher Lasch has claimed that in "effect . . . the intellectuals of the ACCF defined cultural freedom as whatever best served the interest of the United States government,"[148] but this was not quite the case. It is a latter-day analysis that ignores the fact that so many postwar intellectuals saw the issue in terms of competing values. That they linked their values time and again with their America is certainly true enough, but they did so, in their own minds, because they thought America exemplified the proper norms, not because they were mere nationalists or uncritical supporters of the United States government. To be sure, they were uncritical. There were few liberals who expressed much skepticism as they defended postwar liberalism. Writers in *Encounter* spoke of skepticism, but it is hard to find much evidence of it.[149]

The campaign continued unabated through the 1950s and beyond. Sidney Hook claimed that if American intellectuals wanted to preserve their right to free speech they would have to act and fight against Communism. Communism was clearly imperialistic and its "totalitarian obsession" formed a stark and shocking contrast to the ethos of freedom.[150] Irving Howe, in his work on the political novel, agreed. He wrote movingly of novels that spoke out against Soviet totalitarianism, making George Orwell in particular a hero in the struggle.[151] Reinhold Niebuhr was eloquent, as always, in the same cause. He insisted that American intellectuals and the United States were involved in a fight of enormous significance against "a monstrous evil" quite unparalleled in human history. He had no reservations about the nature of "the world struggle in which we are engaged. We are defending freedom against tyranny."[152] Walt Rostow had an equally powerful sense of the great stakes at issue. Much lay in the balance and Rostow frequently emphasized what he took to be the dangers of Communist totalitarianism. Indeed even then Rostow's animosity to Communism seemed to dominate all else. Two decades later he could still be found defending the disastrous Vietnam War in unaltered but now exhausted cliches of singleminded anti-Communism.[153]

Irving Kristol obviously thought the same way and in an article contrasted Western science, devoted to freedom and its maintenance, with the grim record of Soviet science. Here was a concrete illustration of what it meant to cherish liberty.[154] Leslie Fiedler, like Kristol, had little patience with European intellectuals who did not understand what was at stake. He was appalled at the support the Rosenbergs, longtime apologists for the Soviet Union, were able to attract from naive European intellectuals.[155] For him the Rosenbergs had not merely desecrated the most basic political values but they were people "who blasphemously deny their own humanity."[156] Fiedler saw no need to execute them, but he considered it frankly preposterous that anyone who knew the history of Communism and the record of the Rosenbergs could possibly go on believing in their innocence. Those who shouted that their fate was a result of McCarthyism were not only naive and unaware of what was at stake in the struggle against Communism, but also deluded into believing there was something wrong with "calling a Communist a Communist, or deciding by legal process that a spy is a spy."[157] They clearly did not understand the threat posed to liberty by Communism.

An issue of the *Partisan Review* in the 1950s returned to the same conclusions. There was criticism of "obsession" with nonexistent Communists on the domestic front, but there was militant opposition to the external Communist movement, "perhaps the gravest danger that the nation has had to cope with since the Civil War."[158] As one contributor said, there was now more and more a clear recognition that the American culture "we profoundly cherish is now disastrously threatened from without."[159] James Burnham, in those days no uncritical admirer of the United States, asserted that whatever reservations one had about America, no one should doubt for a moment that it was "incommensurably superior" to the dangerous Soviet Union.[160]

As time went on liberal values were less often defined principally in opposition to Communism, but this did not mean there was any less enthusiasm for those norms or any more sympathy for Communism. So many intellectuals found themselves engaged in a defense of liberalism in America against other threats we have treated elsewhere, first McCarthy and then the radical Right and the Birchers. There was also a lessening of the fear that Communism was about to overwhelm the old liberal values to which American political intellectuals remained steadfast after 1945. Yet the old antagonism remained well into the 1960s. It found a good many outlets, a good many moments for its expression. E.E. Schattschneider did not think it strange to remark, for example, in his study of American government, *The Semi-Sovereign People*, that more popular participation in government was needed because the United States was engaged in a "titanic struggle for survival" with the forces of Communism. Nor did his fellow social scientist Alan Westin hesitate to remind his readers in 1962 that the United States had to be understood as "a nation waging a global battle for peace, freedom, and security."[161] Arthur Schlesinger continued to invoke the same themes in his years of alliance with the Kennedys in the early 1960s. Nothing basic had altered. There was still a "world civil war" with Communism and it imposed on us a continuing recognition "that we need a new conviction of national purpose . . . as a matter of desperate necessity." In the 1960 campaign Kennedy repeatedly charged that the United States was underdefended vis-a-vis the Soviet Union, a position Schlesinger had advanced for fifteen years. To be sure, Schlesinger had usually not focused on the question of armaments, but he did not hesitate to repeat Kennedy's famous assertions about the so-called missle gap. He worried about a struggle with Russia on many fronts.[162]

Overall, there was always the paradox, which the dialectic with Communism made so clear, that skeptical liberalism was not particularly skeptical about the adequacy of the old liberal values. Most political intellectuals may not have had absolute justifications for liberalism, but they were convinced liberalism was the truth. Some, indeed, were much more convinced than they had been in the 1930s. The militant campaign against Communism, which had so many adherents, did not reveal much skepticism for the simple reason that American political thought was not skeptical about Communism or its liberal alternative.

GLIMMERS OF RECOGNITION

If the dominant theme of American political thought in the two decades after World War II was skepticism, skepticism about absolute answers, utopias, and the hopes of classical democratic theory, it certainly did not include skepticism about liberal values or the necessity of their defense. Does this permit us to conclude that American intellectuals were far more ideological than they thought they were?

We know the general belief was that ideology was illegitimate and we know much effort of first-class minds went into devising some substitute for it after 1945. But the question of the extent of American intellectuals' skepticism remains. One cannot make much headway in the study of American thought in this era by assuming it is obvious that one or another interpretation will do. It is not a simple matter. Nor can we answer the question with any finality here, and we will return in our next chapter to make an attempt. What may be said here is that many intellectuals perceived the consensus on the old liberal values. They recognized that pluralism and individualism legitimated a variety of political opinions and even life-styles, but few that strayed from the liberal paradigm. This is why Arthur Schlesinger thought it made sense to say that "all of America is liberalism" and Leslie Fiedler claimed "there is only *one* America."[163] As Clinton Rossiter saw it, the appeal of this American value consensus among intellectuals as among other Americans could hardly be underestimated. "The American consensus is unique in its virility and broad appeal . . . our principles, which are few, are remarkably uniform."[164] Moreover, Rossiter insisted in *Parties and Politics in America* that the truth was such general consensus was an unmistakably "blessed fact."[165]

Rossiter, like many others who acknowledged and welcomed the consensus on liberal values, rarely linked the old liberal norms with ideology, of course, for ideology was not the realm of skeptics. There were those, however, who thought ideology did not go away as easily as most American intellectuals seemed to believe. Those on the outside, like William F. Buckley, saw consensus on behalf of liberal values betraying unmistakable signs of certainty and ideology. Liberals were "tireless moralizers" in his view, not skeptics at all.[166] A few thinkers took it for granted that American liberals like all other self-conscious people could not escape an ideological perspective. For example, C.J. Friedrich and Z. Brzezinski made this assumption and carefully discussed the outlook of totalitarians not as ideology but as "totalitarian ideology."[167] But, in the end, there were few among the host of self-confident liberal intellectuals who saw much connection between the values they so vigorously endorsed and ideology. Few really agreed with David Riesman's measured remark that "Rejecting ideology . . . is more easily said than done. There is always a tacit ideology."[168]

NOTES*

1. Richard Hofstadter, *The Age of Reform* (New York: Vintage, 1962–1955), p. 15.

2. John Kenneth Galbraith, *The Affluent Society* (Boston: Houghton Mifflin, 1958), p. 9.

3. Chester Eisinger, *Fiction of the Forties* (Chicago: University of Chicago Press, 1963), p. 19.

4. Arthur Schlesinger, Jr., *The Vital Center* (London: Andre Deutsch, 1970–1949), p. 245.

5. Max Lerner, *America as a Civilization* (New York: Simon and Schuster, 1957), p. 730.

6. Sidney Hook, *Heresy Yes, Conspiracy No* (New York: John Day, 1953), p. 255.

7. Sidney Hook, *Political Power and Personal Freedom* (New York: Criterion, 1959), p. 16.

8. For example: Lionel Trilling, *The Liberal Imagination* (New York: Viking, 1950), p. xv.

9. Herbert Stember, "Anti-Intellectualism in the United States," *The Journal of Social Issues*, no. 3 (1955): 24.

10. Peter Gay, *The Enlightenment*, vol. 1 (New York: Vintage, 1968–1966), p. 171.

11. Arthur Schlesinger, Jr., "Liberalism in America: A Note for Europeans" (1956), in *The Politics of Hope* (Boston: Houghton Mifflin, 1962), p. 320.

12. James W. Smith, *Theme for Reason* (Princeton: Princeton University Press, 1957), p. 200.

13. Judith Shklar, *Legalism* (Cambridge: Harvard University Press, 1964), p. 5.

14. Henry Kariel, *The Decline of American Pluralism* (Stanford: Stanford University Press, 1961), ch. 13.

15. Trilling, *Imagination*, pp. x–xi.

16. Shklar, *Legalism*, p. 5.

17. Lerner, *Civilization*, p. 76, passim.

* Some books listed here have two dates: the first is the date of the edition referenced here; the second is the date the work was originally published.

18. Schlesinger, "Bernard De Voto and Public Affairs" (1960), in *Hope*, p. 396.

19. Clinton Rossiter, *Marxism: The View from America* (New York: Harcourt Brace and World, 1960), p. 239.

20. Ibid., p. 205.

21. For example, David Braybrooke and Charles Lindblom, *A Strategy of Decision* (New York: Free Press, 1970–1963), ch. 8 and pp. 150–67.

22. Peter Viereck, *Shame and Glory of the Intellectuals* (New York: Capricorn, 1965–1953), p. 190.

23. Edward Shils, *The Torment of Secrecy* (Glencoe, Ill.: Free Press, 1956), p. 158.

24. Smith, *Theme*, p. 131.

25. Peter Gay, *Voltaire's Politics* (New York: Vintage, 1965–1959), pp. 15–16, 31–32, passim.

26. Judith Shklar, *After Utopia* (Princeton: Princeton University Press, 1957), p. 292.

27. Louis Hartz, *The Liberal Tradition in America* (New York: Harcourt, Brace and World, 1955), p. 12, passim.

28. Richard Hofstadter, *Anti-Intellectualism in American Life* (New York: Knopf, 1963), pp. 62–63; David Spitz, *Democracy and the Challenge of Power* (New York: Columbia University Press, 1958), p. 28; Henry Mayo, *An Introduction to Democratic Theory* (New York: Oxford University Press, 1960), p. 304.

29. Theodore Adorno et al., *The Authoritarian Personality* (New York: Harper & Row, 1950).

30. Smith, *Theme*, p. 120.

31. Donald W. Hanson, *From Kingdom to Commonwealth* (Cambridge: Harvard University Press, 1970), pp. 357–358 and 372 represents a good if late example.

32. Hook, *Heresy Yes*; or, at least, this is one reading of Hook's book.

33. Lerner, *Civilization*, pp. 627–28.

34. Arthur Schlesinger, Jr., "Probing the American Experience" (1958), in *Hope*, pp. 197 and 205.

35. Shils, *Torment*, p. 227.

36. Hook, *Political Power*, p. xiii.

37. Smith, *Theme*, p. 313; Thomas Thorson, *The Logic of Democracy* (New York: Holt, Rinehart and Winston, 1962), p. 91.

38. Seymour Martin Lipset, "The Sources of the 'Radical Right'" (1955), in *The Radical Right*, ed. Daniel Bell (Garden City, N.Y.: Doubleday-Anchor, 1964–1963), p. 316.

39. Samuel Stouffer, *Communism, Conformity, and Civil Liberties* (Gloucester, Mass.: Peter Smith, 1963–1955), ch. 5 and p. 146, passim.

40. Hartz, *Liberal Tradition*, pp. 10–11.

41. Herbert Marcuse, *One-Dimensional Man* (Boston: Beacon, 1964), p. 12.

42. Ibid., p. xv.

43. Ibid.; see his long and rather fascinating chapter on the state of American philosophy.

44. Herbert Marcuse et al., *Critique of Pure Tolerance* (Boston: Beacon, 1965), p. 85.

45. Ibid.

46. William F. Buckley, Jr., *Up from Liberalism* (New York: Hillman, 1961), p. 105.

47. Ibid., pp. 41 and 48.

48. Ibid., p. 8.

49. William F. Buckley, Jr. and L. Brent Bozell, *McCarthy and His Enemies* (Chicago: Regnery, 1954), p. 326.

50. Ibid., p. 317.

51. William F. Buckley, Jr., *God and Man at Yale* (Chicago: Regnery, 1951), p. 180.

52. Ibid., pp. 170–71.

53. Viereck, *Shame*, pp. 286–87, 294, and 296.

54. Hook, *Heresy Yes*, passim.

55. Hook, *Political Power*, ch. 23.

56. Richard Hofstadter and Walter Metzger, *The Development of Academic Freedom in the United States* (New York: Columbia University Press, 1955); Hofstadter, *Anti-Intellectualism*.

57. Russell Kirk, *Academic Freedom* (Chicago: Henry Regnery, 1955), pp. 118–26; chs. 1, 2, and 4.

58. Milton Konvitz, "Sidney Hook: Philosopher of Freedom," in *Sidney Hook and the Contemporary World*, ed. Paul Kratz (New York: John Day, 1968), p. 23; Abraham Kaplan, "American Ethics and Public Philosophy," in *The American Style*, ed. Elting Morison (New York: Harper and Bros., 1958), p. 80.

59. Hook, *Political Power*, p. xiii.

60. Lerner, *Civilization*, p. 453; and Charles Frankel, *The Case for Modern Man* (New York: Harpers, 1956–1955), chs. 1 and 2.

61. Milton Friedman, *Capitalism and Freedom* (Chicago: University of Chicago Press, 1962).

62. Daniel Bell, *The End of Ideology* (New York: Collier's, 1962–1961), p. 406; Hook, *Heresy Yes*, p. 19.

63. Thorson, *Logic*; Schlesinger, *Vital Center*, for example, p. 208; Erich Fromm, *The Sane Society* (New York: Fawcett, 1967–1955), p. 311.

64. Bell, *Ideology*.

65. Shils, *Torment*, pp. 169 and 221.

66. Spitz, *Democracy*, pp. 30–42.

67. Schlesinger, "Bernard De Voto and Public Affairs" (1960), in *Hope*, pp. 174–77; Schlesinger, "The Highbrow in American Politics" (1953), in *Hope*, p. 227.

68. Viereck, *Shame*, p. 126.

69. Buckley, *Liberalism*, p. 219.

70. Friedman, *Capitalism*, pp. 1–2.

71. Marcuse et al., *Critique*, passim; "The Port Huron Statement" (1962), in *The New Radicals*, eds. Paul Jacobs and Saul Landau (New York: Random House, 1966).

72. Mayo, *An Introduction*, p. 143.

73. Fromm, *Sane Society*, and Marcuse, *One-Dimensional Man*, both make this argument throughout.

74. The burden of Hook, *Heresy Yes*; Schlesinger, *Vital Center*, pp. 210-18.

75. Eric Hoffer, *The True Believer* (New York: Harpers, 1951).

76. Glenn Tinder, *The Crisis of Political Imagination* (New York: Scribner's, (1964-1950), ch. 8.

77. Erich Fromm, *The Art of Loving* (New York: Harper, 1956).

78. David Riesman et al., *The Lonely Crowd* (New Haven: Yale University Press, 1961-1950), ch. 12.

79. Earl Latham, *The Group Basis of Politics* (Ithaca: Cornell University Press, 1952), p. 13.

80. Lon Fuller, *The Morality of Law* (New Haven: Yale University Press, 1965); Lerner, *Civilization*, p. 206.

81. Paul Tillich, *The Courage To Be* (New Haven: Yale University Press, 1952).

82. C. Wright Mills, *The Sociological Imagination* (New York: Oxford University Press, 1959), pp. 171-73; Tinder, *Imagination*, chs. 1 and 2.

83. Chester Eisinger, *Fiction of the Forties* (Chicago: University of Chicago Press, 1963), p. 19 and ch. 6.

84. Trilling, *Imagination*, p. x.

85. Philip Rahv, "Our Country and Our Culture: A Symposium," *Partisan Review* 19 (May-June 1952): 309.

86. Mark Schorer, "Our Country and our Culture: A Symposium," *Partisan Review* 19 (May-June 1952): 316-17, passim.

87. Lerner, *Civilization*, pp. 871-73.

88. Henry Commager, *The American Mind* (New Haven: Yale University Press, 1959-1950), p. 412.

89. Hofstadter, *Anti-Intellectualism*, pp. 343 and 355.

90. Erik Erikson, *Childhood and Society* (New York: Norton, 1950).

91. Sloan Wilson, *Man in the Gray Flannel Suit* (New York: Simon and Schuster, 1955); William H. Whyte, *The Organization Man* (New York: Simon and Schuster, 1956).

92. Solomon E. Asch, "Opinions and Social Pressure," *Scientific American* 193 (1955): 31-35; Stanley Milgram, "Some Conditions of Obedience and Disobedience to Authority," *Human Relations* 18 (1965).

93. Riesman, "Our Country and Our Culture," p. 311.

94. Riesman, *Lonely Crowd*, pp. 64-65, 82, and 234.

95. Ibid., pp. 194-95, chs. 1 and 2 passim.

96. David Riesman, *Individualism Reconsidered and Other Essays* (Glencoe, Ill.: Free Press, 1954), pp. 101-2.

97. Erich Fromm, "Love in America," in *The Search for America*, ed. Huston Smith (Englewood Cliffs, N.J.: Prentice-Hall, 1959), pp. 123 and 129.

98. C. Martin Jay, *The Dialectical Imagination* (London: Heineman, 1973).

99. C. Wright Mills, *White Collar* (New York: Oxford University Press, 1951).

100. Fromm, *Sane Society*, ch. 5; Marcuse, *One-Dimensional Man*, p. 1.

101. Marcuse, *One-Dimensional Man*, pp. 57-61.

102. Lerner, *Civilization*, pp. 650-57.

103. Seymour Martin Lipset, *Political Man* (Garden City, N.Y.: Doubleday-Anchor, 1963-1969), p. 453.

104. Richard Hofstadter, "Have There Been Discernable Shifts in American Values during the Past Generation?" in *The American Style*, ed. Elting Morison (New York: Harper and Bros., 1958), pp. 353–57.

105. Schlesinger, "Time and the Intellectuals," in *Hope*, p. 236.

106. Clyde Kluckhohn, "Have There Been Discernable Shifts in American Values during the Past Generation?" in *Style*, ed. Morison, pp. 185–187, 202, 203, and 206.

107. Schlesinger, *Vital Center*, pp. 33–34 and 312.

108. Ibid., pp. 16 and 176–83.

109. Ibid., p. 152.

110. Ibid., p. 150.

111. Lerner, *Civilization*, ch. 5 and pp. 33–34.

112. Ibid., p. 317.

113. Ibid.

114. Rossiter, *Marxism*, pp. 138 and 140.

115. Clinton Rossiter, *Parties and Politics in America* (Ithaca: Cornell University Press, 1960), p. 8.

116. John Hingham, ed., *The Reconstruction of American History* (London: Hutchinson, 1963–1962), p. 22.

117. David Potter, *People of Plenty* (Chicago: University of Chicago Press, 1954).

118. Seymour Martin Lipset and Richard Bendix, *Social Mobility in Industrial Society* (Berkeley: University of California Press, 1959), pp. 11–75; W. Lloyd Warner and James Abegglen, *Big Business Leaders in America* (New York: Harper and Bros., 1955); and Warner and Abegglen, *Occupational Mobility in American Business and Industry* (Minneapolis: University of Minnesota Press, 1955).

119. Michael Harrington, *The Other America* (New York: Macmillan, 1962).

120. Richard Hofstadter, *The Paranoid Style in American Politics and Other Essays* (New York: Knopf, 1965), pp. 212–37.

121. Adolph A. Berle, Jr., *The Twentieth Century Capitalist Revolution* (New York: Harvest, 1960–1954).

122. Schlesinger, "Whittaker Chambers and His Witness" (1952), in *Hope*, p. 192.

123. Schlesinger, "Liberalism in America," p. 69, and "The New Mood in Politics" (1960), p. 92, in *Hope*.

124. Viereck, *Shame*, pp. 262–63.

125. Ibid., p. 314.

126. Galbraith, *Affluent Society*, pp. 190 and 209.

127. Ibid., chs. 10, 11, and 18; pp. 322–23 and 352.

128. John Kenneth Galbraith, *American Capitalism—The Concept of Countervailing Power* (Boston: Houghton Mifflin, 1956–1952), pp. 8–9 and 151.

129. Robert Dahl, *A Preface to Democratic Theory* (Chicago: University of Chicago Press, 1956), p. 50; Giovanni Sartori, *Democratic Theory*, (New York: Praeger, 1967–1962), pp. 326, 336–337, 346, and 349.

130. Viereck, *Shame*, p. 204.

131. Rossiter, *Marxism*, pp. 91–92.

132. Irving Howe, *Politics and the Novel* (New York: Meridian, 1957), frontispiece.

133. For example, Sartori, *Democratic Theory*, pp. 365 and 367.

134. For example, Erich Fromm, *The Art of Loving* (New York: Harper, 1956).

135. Friedman, *Capitalism*, pp. 2 and 4.

136. Ibid., pp. 113, 115, 132–33, 176–77, and chs. 2 and 6.

137. Buckley, *God and Man*, p. 107.

138. Ibid., passim.

139. Russell Kirk, *The Conservative Mind* (Chicago: Regnery, 1953), ch. 10.

140. For example, Kariel, *Decline*, p. 274 and ch. 14.

141. Lipset, *Political Man*, p. xxii.

142. Ibid., pp. 449–51.

143. Hook, *Political Power*, p. 452.

144. Lionel Trilling, "The State of American Writing, 1948: A Symposium," *Partisan Review* 15 (August 1948): 829.

145. Leslie Feidler, "The State of American Writing 1948: A Symposium," *Partisan Review* 15 (August 1948): 875.

146. Clement Greenberg, "The State of American Writing, 1948: A Symposium," *Partisan Review* 15 (August 1948).

147. Schlesinger, *Vital Center*, pp. 9, 135, and ch. 10.

148. Christopher Lasch, *The Agony of the American Left* (New York: Vintage, 1969), p. 86.

149. Ibid., pp. 75–98. Lasch brought this interpretation to my eye, and my reading of the magazine makes his interpretation, in this case, convincing to me.

150. Hook, *Heresy Yes*, pp. 55, 83, and 255.

151. See Howe, *Politics*.

152. Reinhold Niebuhr, *The Irony of American History* (New York: Scribner's, 1952), pp. 1 and 22.

153. W.W. Rostow, "The National Style," in Morison, ed., *Style*, pp. 296–97.

154. Irving Kristol, "Men of Science and Conscience," *Encounter*, October 1953, pp. 57–58.

155. Leslie Fiedler, "A Postscript to the Rosenberg Case," *Encounter*, October 1953, pp. 13–15 and 20–21.

156. Ibid., p. 21.

157. Ibid., p. 17.

158. Leslie Fiedler, "Our Country and Our Culture: A Symposium," *Partisan Review* 19 (May–June 1952): 308.

159. Newton Arvin, "Our Country and Our Culture: A Symposium," *Partisan Review* 19 (May–June 1952): 287.

160. James Burnham, "Our Country and Our Culture: A Symposium," *Partisan Review* 19 (May–June 1952): 290.

161. E.E. Schatteschneider, *The Semi-Sovereign People* (New York: Holt, Rinehart and Winston, 1960), p. 112.

162. Schlesinger, "New Mood," in *Hope*, p. 86, passim.

163. Schlesinger, "Liberalism in America," in *Hope*, p. 63.

164. Rossiter, *Parties*, p. 53.

165. Ibid., p. 108.

166. Buckley, *Liberalism*, p. 62, passim.

167. Carl J. Friedrich and Z. Brzezinski, *Totalitarian Dictatorship and Autocracy* (Cambridge: Harvard University Press, 1965–1956), p. 88 and ch. 7.

168. David Riesman, "The Intellectuals and the Discontented Classes: Some Further Reflections," (1962), in Bell, ed. *Radical Right*, p. 156.

9 The Conservative Mood

American political thought in the twenty years after the conclusion of World War II produced no new systems or truths, and perhaps few new insights. Yet these years were not a time of inactivity in intellectual life. American political intellectuals learned to doubt final answers and the idealized citizen. They reformulated the traditional theory of democracy. They attempted to reconstruct a basis for liberal values. It was not a sterile era at all, however much it was to seem so from the perspective of the later 1960s and beyond.

Above all, American political intellectuals found they had become *conservatives*. They learned to acknowledge they were committed to the preservation of liberal values in the United States, which they believed came close to fulfilling those norms in practice. America was imperfect, but they did not doubt that it deserved their support. There is little question that most intellectuals accepted and often liked their newfound role. Certainly they were rarely the kind of conservatives who mindlessly applauded every part of the status quo. They were often critical of one feature or another of America and by the 1960s they were ready to join Kennedy to "get the country moving again." But only rarely were they in genuine opposition. Only rarely were they convinced it was the American fact that had to yield, rather than some overoptimistic theories. The story of intellectuals in this period, at least those who did much of the political thinking from 1945 to 1964, is in the end a story of the conservative mood.

In the 1940s and 1950s many of the most perceptive thinkers saw this trend. It was nothing they denied or tried to hide. Sometimes they were a bit bemused at how it had happened. At other times a few tried to assure themselves that they were still radicals while simultaneously being conservatives, which was no mean feat. In the 1940s Arthur Schlesinger proclaimed his devotion to the "vital center," assuring his readers he was a radical all the while. He announced the paradox that the "object of the new radicalism is to rest on the center."[1] Although this position amounted to little more than manipulation of words, his formulation of his view was a revealing one.

For the most part political intellectuals accepted their new view and their new role calmly and perceptively. They knew they were part of the conservative mood. They appreciated that the America they accepted was basically "a conservative nation." Or they followed Edward Shils's example and frankly declared they were now writers of conservative disposition.[2] Or they agreed with Eric Goldman, who sympathetically treated Truman's 1948 electoral victory as a moment of conservative transformation for modern American liberalism. In Goldman's eyes Truman's victory was no statement for change, no ringing endorsement of a new vision or a new program. It was, instead, a sign, a revelation, of the fact that liberalism "had turned into a form of conservatism." It occurred in an age when liberalism was no longer engaged in an exciting fight for what liberals thought were new ideas and dreams. Liberals now had responsibilities. They were in charge. They were the keepers of the American dream and the American power. Certainly there were fights that would have to be made, but they were really conservative fights in the main, fights against McCarthy, the radical Right, and enemies abroad.[3]

Goldman's beautifully written *Rendevous with Destiny* recalled with admiration past liberal campaigns undertaken for major changes in the United States. Goldman told a dramatic story of the rise of liberalism, of its long struggle, and of its present triumph. His book was charged with the spirit of battle and excitement, but his work was not meant so much as an inspiration as history. He was proud of the past record of liberalism but he was also proud of the new chapter, the chapter of responsibility that lay ahead for modern liberals. He had no regrets at the passing of the dramatic days of past contests.

Clinton Rossiter, on the other hand, thought the more appropriate history to examine was the record of American conservatism. During the 1950s Rossiter tried hard to find a place for his chastened liberalism within conservatism as it had unfolded in America. He did not entirely succeed no matter how many distinctions he made in *Conservatism in America* between "good" and "bad" conservatives, between American conservatives and those rooted in elitist and foreign European soil. Certainly he was not welcomed by the likes of Russell Kirk or William F. Buckley who did not see themselves as conservative liberals. But Rossiter had the correct perception about the opinion of most who thought seriously about the role of the political intellectual in America. He knew they were like him: "we are all more conservative than we were a generation ago."[4]

The Schlesingers, Goldmans, and Rossiters did not really try to formulate elaborate explanations for this fact. They were historically inclined and attuned to the events of the 1930s and 1940s. They knew the effects of depression, war, totalitarianism, and disillusionment. Others like Robert Dahl offered more deterministic, social scientific explanations, suggesting that a conservative reconciliation with the status quo was simply natural, given the modern-day evidence regarding political behavior. It is a fact, Dahl observed, that "everyone must take the boundaries of his political world as given by prior tradition."[5] There were a host of other, often quite complex, explanations for the drift toward conservatism.

Perhaps the most thoughtful commentator on the trend was Richard Hofstadter. He was far from uncritical of America in his own day and his histories were almost abrasively critical of many episodes in the American past. Yet Hofstadter recognized and welcomed the conservatizing of American political thought. There was no doubt in his mind that by the 1950s he and his fellow liberals found "themselves far more conscious of those things they would like to preserve than they are of those things they would like to change."[6] He perceived that the Rossiters of his era were no accident. It was only logical that "liberals are beginning to find it both natural and expedient to explore the merits and employ the rhetoric of conservatism."[7]

Hofstadter, too, was one of the first to appreciate the significance of the attraction of so many intellectuals and political theorists to Adlai Stevenson and his campaigns for the presidency in 1952,

1956, and, less unanimously, 1960. Hofstadter noted with approval Stevenson's realization that "liberals have become the true conservatives of our time."[8] To Hofstadter, Stevenson did not represent any new infusion of blood into the veins of liberalism. He stood for liberalism at its midcentury best: thoughtful, decent, responsible, and nonradical. His campaigns were not campaigns for change, but campaigns for improving the quality of what we had. His celebrated campaign speeches (especially in 1952) made so many liberals proud because they were, or seemed to be, elegant statements of the faith, eloquently delivered. Stevenson's campaign was liberalism in its best dress and impressive dress it was, too, but it was liberalism in the fashion of American political thought of the age, the dress of conservatism. Stevenson was a liberal hero because Stevenson was liberalism grown up, liberalism that was responsible, liberalism that accepted the basic contours of the status quo.

Hofstadter had no patience with anyone who in his opinion was inclined to foment or join one or another "revolt against modernity." He was especially critical of deviant intellectuals. Those who took the path of declaring their "alienation" from the contemporary world won no plaudits from him. Nor did political radicals. Their "strident" radicalism represented nothing of value.[9] Hofstadter assailed intellectual critics of America more and more sharply by the 1960s because they did not appreciate, especially after the troubled McCarthy era, how much intellectuals had gained in postwar America. Hofstadter thought the voice of intellectuals was now respected. He basked in the esteem so many political intellectuals somewhat mysteriously believed they received during the Kennedy administration. As a result, to him the early 1960s appeared to provide even more reason than ever for satisfaction with the United States.[10]

There was little reflection on the possible costs of the drift toward sometimes uncritical acceptance of a liberal United States. Although Sheldon Wolin's *Politics and Vision* was perhaps the most admired work by an American professional political philosopher in the postwar period, few were prepared to accept his conclusions. He complained that politics in America, and indeed the West as a whole, had for some time lost the guidance of general theory and the inspiring vision of a good society and had sunk to the level of quarrels among particular, selfish interests within an accepted status quo. As a consequence, the modern world had contributed little to the tradition of political philosophy or to the betterment of our human life together.[11] Wolin's complaints went largely unheeded not because other thinkers denied his analysis, but rather because they did not see it as a source of complaint. Wolin sounded too much like an ideologue and a utopian. Visions and new political philosophies are not the aspirations or the instruments of conservatives.

THE FOCUS ON STABILITY

The realization by intellectuals that there was much in America that deserved defense, and that indeed America as a whole merited defense, produced the concern with *stability* that is such a controversial feature of political thought in the postwar period. No aspect of liberal political thinking was more attacked in the New Left period and none remains more suspect today. In many cases latter-day denunciations of the interest in stability in the 1950s and early 1960s confuse a concern for stability, which was general, with a knee-jerk affirmation of the status quo, which was not quite as widespread. Such an analysis leads us away from the significance of the attention given to stability among postwar political intellectuals. Theirs was rarely a conservatism based on resignation to just any set of dominant values and institutions. For some thinkers stability may have been an end in itself, and certainly there was a fetish with stability among many social scientists that went beyond acknowledging it as one important value among many. More commonly political intellectuals had a sympathy for stability that was rooted in historical analysis that recoiled at the European alternatives the 1930s had proposed to the American liberal values (imperfectly) existing in the United States. Overall there is no doubt that the attention given to stability assumed agreement about the appropriate values and their proximate achievement in the United States. It assumed the United States was a manifestation in practice of liberal norms and therefore very much worth preserving.

This was not a universal opinion, but in general the conservative disposition of liberals derived from sentiments about the relation between their theory and American practice more than from a mindless apolitical stance. The stress on stability, then, did not substitute for political thought in the postwar years, contrary to what many critics later charged. It was rather an integral part of the political thought of the time, the practical program of people who had their values and interests largely realized and wanted them maintained. This may seem a doubtful assertion when one confronts the sheer mass of writing that celebrates stability in the period, which often makes no references to any values or institutions whose existence stability will serve. Yet the same literature is even more replete with the defense of America as a great liberal civilization. The linkage is not always made, but it is always assumed. Liberals favored stability not out of bourgeois timidity but because they believed America deserved to continue to exist.

The focus on stability was widely recognized as a fact of the postwar period. For example, no one denied, as one prominent social scientist said, that for some time "political research has confined itself largely to the study of given conditions to the neglect of political change."[12] Nor did the developments of the Kennedy years in the early 1960s reverse the pattern. The scent of change was certainly in the air in those now remote years, but the kind of changes sought were rarely conceived as a threat to or alternative to the ongoing, stable order. They were changes within the liberal paradigm.

The heyday of stability as a priority and unquestioned value among the broader intellectual community was in the 1940s and 1950s. Two of the most memorable examples were the analysis of Max Lerner in his sometimes restrained hymn to America (1957) and Arthur Schlesinger's earlier "radical" defense. Lerner suggested that because America was a middle-class country, it was therefore relatively free of destabilizing conflict. America was a land where most people had much to defend including their wealth and their tradition of civil liberties, and Lerner believed they knew it. He welcomed this fact. There would be no class conflict, which he did not think belonged in America. Stability was our reality and our blessing.[13]

Schlesinger's analysis was less penetrating but much more unreserved. He tended to talk in terms of governmental institutions rather than social structures since he located the success of American stability in our form of government. It had no peer and there is no reason to think he believed there was any conceivable peer. "The American government is the outstanding modern example of a governmental system whose stability is maintained by an equilibrium among its component parts."[14] Schlesinger was obsessed in the 1940s by his fear that stability might be destroyed by enemies abroad or people at home who might not agree with him that the "supreme political virtue is prudence."[15] Stability was needed to maintain what worked so well; indeed, stability was so vital, so central, that in politics "the goal is stability" first and "preservation of all the elements of the system" next.[16]

The most serious reflections concerning stability, how to maintain and advance it, came from social scientists. We have already encountered the work of Bernard Berelson and his colleagues on voting behavior, work produced by men whose taste for public apathy eventually provoked much controversy. They devoted a great deal of attention to stability. They took for granted that all reasonable Americans wanted stability and felt ignorant political masses could threaten it. They argued that for democracy (read the American form of government) to endure, "the intensity of conflict must be limited, the rate of change must be restrained, stability in the social and economic structure must be maintained."[17] Seymour Martin Lipset advanced the same position. He recognized full well, as few of his social science colleagues did, that class conflict was unlikely to go away, no matter how many times social scientists said it had already gone away or had never existed in the first place. He also realized the dangers of too much consensus, fearing it could produce a brittle system unable to deal with a changing world. Yet he returned again and again to the topic of stability. His greatest interest lay here. The reason was no secret. Like the rest, Lipset feared conflict that moved beyond "moderation" or "moderate tension." These are vague words, moderate and moderation, and yet they were not so vague at the time. Their meaning was well understood. They meant conflict that went beyond agitation for liberal reform was too dangerous. Lipset did not hide this position; on the contrary he ably defended it, drawing on his elaborate studies to show the consequences of immoderate politics at home and in Europe. His entire treatment of the radical Right in the 1950s and 1960s was based on this understanding. The Right was dangerous in America because it did not accept the liberal consensus and therefore it was likely to upset the system if it could gain the power to do so. It deserved to be called "radical."[18]

David Truman, another defender of pluralist democracy, on the other hand, did not think the radical Right was so much a danger to stability as class politics was. He argued in *The Governmental Process* (1950) that the supreme virtue of pluralism was its overlapping group memberships. Because so many people belonged to more than one interest group they necessarily had divided loyalties. These loyalties muted their passion and their energies, ensuring systemic security and stability. He was hopeful that class politics with its single loyalties would gain no foothold here.[19]

We must turn back to the very influential postwar political scientist Robert Dahl to see the stability theme developed most fully and most thoroughly. In his series of influential books written throughout our period, books that led the way to the creation of the new democratic theory of pluralism, Dahl repeatedly turned to the topic of stability and its virtues.[20] He did not endorse, nor should he be confused with the view that endorses, mere reification of the status quo. Yet Dahl strongly singled out stability as a, if not indeed the, prime political value. In fact, to Dahl the single greatest virtue of American pluralism was that it was a superb "system for reinforcing agreement, encouraging moderation, and maintaining social peace." Its best feature was its proven capacity to "settle conflicts peacefully."[21] Well into the late 1960s, until Dahl's opinion underwent some change, his devotion to stability remained high. He could remark with utter conviction that stable party opposition in political systems constituted "one of the greatest social discoveries that man has ever stumbled onto."[22] Altogether Dahl concluded that the political system of America he worked so hard to describe and support was successful at the great task of providing stability.

CHANGE

Whenever Dahl considered *change* it was always with a watchful eye. It could easily degenerate into disorder. "Peaceful adjustment" and "stability," not changes, were paramount objectives. His approach to change can basically be described as therapeutic. The problem was how to control change, how to "handle conflict."[23] To be sure, he did take part in the development of a liberal theory of change, or more properly adjustment, but that came second to the problems of controlling change and managing conflict. Dahl led the way to a conservative view of change.

Dahl's views of change in the context of stability should remind us that liberal thinkers insisted they were not mere defenders of the status quo. Stability may have ranked at the top of their values, but there was interest in change of sorts as well. Democratic theorists confidently asserted that the strength of the liberal position was that it incorporated change and was skillful at handling change as well as stability. Neither change nor stability needed to be sacrificed in postwar America.[24]

What had to be kept in mind was the kind of change that was possible. Peter Gay called for change, but only change that dealt with limited "attainable goals" rather than dramatic, sweeping ends.[25] Arthur Schlesinger made the same argument, defending change that was undogmatic, restricted, and deeply tinged with compromise, the very "strategy of Democracy."[26] Like many others, Schlesinger called proper change "muddling through." It was not neat, it was not perfectly planned, and it was not vast, but it did accomplish things. Schlesinger acknowledged that it offended those he considered the purists and the fanatics, but it was the American way and the only way if we also wanted a stable order.[27] Reinhold Niebuhr took it for granted that thoughtful people had learned the necessity of "proximate solutions for insoluble problems."[28] David Spitz used almost identical terms. He declared that all sensible people must understand "there are only approximate solutions," "only a never-ending quest for particular solutions," only a search for and reconciliation with "piecemeal solutions."[29] This attitude toward change matured into what came to be designated the *theory of incrementalism*. This development transformed liberal thinking about change and made it considerably more sophisticated, but it resulted in no transformation of the modest hopes and conservative inclinations of the original attitude. Perhaps the best single expression of the theory of liberal incrementalism was David Braybrooke and Charles Lindblom's *A Strategy of Decision*. There is no doubt of its authors' secure reputations, nor of the book's influence.

Incrementalism meant making change in small and gradual movements, and Braybrooke and Lindblom argued that there were a number of convincing reasons for acting in this way. Above all, they contended that only this approach could actually get problems solved. It was realistic as an approach to change, focusing on specific policy objectives and on identifiable—and remediable— evils. They insisted they did not necessarily ignore ideological factors, but they did not see any value in concentrating on ideologies when one turned to talking about change. Grand value schemes did not have anything specific to offer the practical liberal who wanted to move against one problem or another. All they could offer were ringing and hopelessly vague abstractions that never could resolve problems. Their most certain effect was likely to be negative, since they diverted people from the concrete changes that could be accomplished.[30]

The argument of the incrementalists included the belief that it is really impossible to make change without extensive information not only about policy objectives, but also about how to get there. Incrementalism depended on the general belief that knowledge is not easy to acquire and that change can quickly get out of hand and go in unexpected and dangerous directions. It built on crucial assumptions about the complexity of the world of social interaction and human incapacity to understand and control the social and political environment. Indeed, this was its keystone. As Braybrooke and Lindblom remarked, incrementalism assumed "man's limited intellectual capacities, limited information, and the costliness of analysis."[31] Robert Dahl agreed when he wrote later that making incremental change through regularized channels allowed more "rationality" and predictability.[32]

Too little was known about the processes of change to allow anyone much basis for being sanguine about the results of any sweeping changes. No less an authority than Talcott Parsons, the leading sociological theorist of the era, proclaimed that "a general theory of the processes of change in social systems is not possible in the present state of knowledge."[33] In this situation who would easily dismiss the wisdom of a less risky approach like incremental-ism? At least incrementalism would not prove to be the Pandora's Box of horrors as so many major efforts of radical change had. The memory of Fascist and Russian experiments in radical change lived on. They were not forgotten, nor were they likely to be. They in-duced a mood of caution that did not quickly diminish.

The critics of incrementalism might say, as they did, that all this was merely an elaborate apologia for the status quo. It certainly involved an apologia for the ongoing order in America, but it was not only that. The theory and the assumptions of incrementalism were part of the mood of conservatism and they did betray a con-siderable aversion to risk. Yet the gospel of "dealing prudently" derived in part from the most serious problems of predicting and controlling the forces of change. To note the tendency of American political intellectuals to adopt an incrementalist theory of change that was unmistakably conservative and say no more overlooks their development of the theory, their conviction that it was a theory of change rather than a mere defense of the status quo, and their conviction that there was no other way. It was a sincere as well as convenient conviction.

It could even be presented, with a bit of nerve, as Braybrooke and Lindblom did, as the most radical attitude toward change that could be imagined. After all, liberals did believe in change and they felt only the incrementalist theory was committed to a truly open-ended vision of change. Only incrementalism took change in politi-cal and social aspects of life for granted as part of the flow of the universe. Their opponents, they charged, were committed to change only in the most conditional of senses. They may have wanted revolutions, but only until they reached their abstract goals. Then they did not want change anymore. Then they wanted to rest in utopia, fixed forever in perfection. They were not really believers in change nor did they truly accept change. They wanted a static world after they made their leap to utopia.[34]

A BROADER CONGENIALITY TOWARD CHANGE

Many American intellectuals in the postwar period wanted to maintain a critical perspective. This determination to remain

critical of American life, including political life, is often forgotten
now and was certainly ignored in the late 1960s, but intellectuals
after World War II were not always apologists for the status quo.
There were two expressions of this disposition to criticize, but we
can take only one of them with any seriousness. One consisted of
little more than ritualistic statements such as Peter Viereck's
characteristic remark: "I am not saying: stop attacking America's
many faults." They did not seem to mean anything except that
many intellectuals did not wish to have their perspectives confused
with complete celebration of the status quo, but they rarely
resulted in any concrete criticism. They were more like a warning
to the self than a guide to behavior. A famous example was Daniel
Bell. He frequently announced that although he was "anti-ideological" he was by no means to be treated as a "conservative." He reminded intellectuals that although he could appreciate their "fears"
about the dangers of political action and their newfound tendency
to renounce ideologies, still it was necessary to keep up criticism of
the existing order. Bell did not make clear from what perspective,
or with what justification, he could any longer sally forth and make
such criticisms. Nor is there any particular indication that Bell in
fact did so. His concerns focused on the dangers and foolishness of
ideology more than anything else. When he did criticize America, it
was the other America that disturbed many liberals, the America of
McCarthy and the John Birch Society, not the America he believed
to be ascendent.[35]

Other prominent intellectuals did the same. Richard Hofstadter
protested that he did not wish to be linked with the "New Conservatives" (Buckley et al.). He was a liberal and wanted change.[36]
Yet his master work, *The Age of Reform*, was almost entirely devoted to showing the dangers of (irrational) movements for change,
especially the Populists. So with Lipset, who as much as any major
figure in American intellectual life repeatedly identified himself
with the European Left. He reiterated his themes that some conflict
was good and so was change, but he also told his readers that
America did not need radical change. It was not necessary here.[37]
Max Lerner, another older radical from the 1930s, summed up the
attitude. In *America as a Civilization* he observed that "I love my
country and my culture, but it is no service to them, nor to the

creed of democracy, to gloss over the rough facts of American life."
He did not want to be identified with "complacency."[38] Yet his
book may be fairly described as an extended, if also informative,
panegyric to America. Few books have been written that are as
long and few today seem so dated.

Newton Arvin stated in the *Partisan Review* (1953) that criticism
was important, but it must be "creative dissidence" rather than
"mere negative self-alienation."[39] Similarly, Lerner warned against
"self-hatred."[40] Both sentiments reflected the attitudes of many
intellectuals in America in the postwar years. They believed in
criticism, but America was now part of themselves. They could
help their country, but they must not go too far on the road to
criticism. In his defense of criticism Lionel Trilling observed that
American intellectuals in the postwar era were homeless if they
could not turn to the United States. The European world of Dada
or Marxism, which had attracted so many in previous decades, was
gone and Beat Poetry proved singularly unattractive as a weak
substitute. Many intellectuals did the logical thing: they accepted
America. Their affirmation of criticism was largely a remembrance
of things past.

Yet there was a second expression from intellectuals who also
were at home in America but were worried about the accepting
mood of many Americans including intellectuals. After his worst
fears of the 1940s and early 1950s quieted, Arthur Schlesinger
began to complain that stability had become too pervasive a gospel
in America. We needed to show more respect for intellectual
gadflies because we were too fond of "complacency" and "self-
righteousness," which, he correctly noted, were not the same thing
as "skepticism" and "self-doubt." He now believed the great
division in the United States lay between those who favored liberal
change within a stable order and those who were rigidly committed
to the status quo. By the early 1960s his criticism grew, although it
never approached a radical position, as did his defensive assertions
that he had never believed the United States was perfect or that "the
America of the 50's did . . . necessarily represent the triumphant
culmination of the American experiment."[41]

Reinhold Niebuhr raised more specific and more profound
questions far earlier than Schlesinger. As early as his *The Irony of*

American History (1952), Niebuhr expressed his characteristic ambivalence about America as it faced the larger world. The question to him was whether the United States was prepared to accept the world responsibility it now faced in the atomic age. He feared Americans did not understand that their longstanding pride in America as a special land of chosen people was not really appropriate for the new demands placed upon a world power. Historical destiny had given power into the hands of America, but it needed to learn that virtue did not exist without sin, lest the power become a world force for evil. He doubted America's claims to specialness and innocence and urged the wisdom of modesty and generosity.[42] His analysis was not only a call for continuing self-criticism within America, but also an example of such criticism, which involved far more than window dressing. His critique was serious, his worries extensive, his vision of the American record skeptical.

Niebuhr was certainly an exception, but an exception from within the liberal consensus. Niebuhr had serious reservations about America, but he did not really probe into the heart of liberalism or the American order. He accepted even as he criticized. Still, his analysis of American thought was perceptive. He saw (and exaggerated) the liberal consensus and he saw the self-confidence of the intellectuals of the liberal order. His uniqueness lay in his alarm at its self-satisfaction.

More characteristic was the work of Clinton Rossiter. He, too, was addicted to the postwar idea that America could be best understood as a unitary or consensual experience, one that constituted a tradition with which he was almost wholly satisfied. It was liberal in its pluralism, individualism, and openness. Indeed, the "American temper is, above all, a standing reproof to dogmatism" while at the same time the "outlook of a race of men for whom many of the ideals of Liberalism have been made reality."[43] There was much sense, consequently, in a disposition that welcomed a conservative mood, for much had been accomplished in America and only fools would brush aside the remarkable American achievements for something else. Rossiter's preoccupation was with Communism as the something else, but he had no enthusiasm for right-wing radical movements either. Both jeopardized a status quo he supported. Rossiter gave no indication that he possessed any reservations about his conclusions. He was typical in failing to penetrate to the level of Niebuhr. Only rarely did he unself-consciously slip and recognize that his conservative liberalism, which he so often contrasted with Marxism, had less to do with the contrast between skepticism and fanaticism than it did with the particular variations between "two faiths."[44]

RADICAL CRITICS

There were genuinely radical intellectuals in America in the years 1945–64. We may tend to forget them, but no picture of American political though could possibly be complete that did not acknowledge their existence. Three whom we have noticed a good deal were Erich Fromm, Russell Kirk, and Herbert Marcuse. What they had in common was their non-American intellectual origin. Fromm and Marcuse came from Europe, and an intellectual community, dominated by the thought of Freud and Marx, and Kirk, born an American, had his philosophical heart in eighteenth-century Burkean England. They were outsiders looking in, and what they saw they did not like. They were the real critics, who thought they were voices crying in the proverbial wilderness. Their assessment was true enough, even though neither Fromm nor Kirk was ignored in the 1950s. Fromm was particularly attractive to intellectuals who shared his concern that America was far too conformist for its own good and for the good of authentic individualism. We know already that many thinkers gave considerable attention to the problems of a mass society they thought existed or might exist for America. Fromm talked their language.[45] There was another Fromm, however, who did not. This was Fromm the radical communitarian who promoted socialism, participatory democracy, and "the art of loving." This Fromm was unquestionably radical. He did not have much respect for the United States, or much hope for it or for the world he predicted would soon enough end in atomic war.[46]

Russell Kirk's books had some vogue outside of strictly conservative circles, just because this was an age open to conservatism. Kirk was conservatism's best historian as he showed in *The Conservative Mind*, but his writings were topical as well. He was quite capable of attacking whatever disturbed him with frank words and angry phrases. He knew full well that Burke would not be happy in America of the 1950s and 1960s. Kirk rarely refused the opportunity to complain that there was too much materialism, boredom, and softmindedness in America.[47] Yet he also remembered that Burke taught the virtue of being content, and Kirk tried to be content. He was part of the American consensus, on the watch for those who were too critical. His thought was curious for this very fact. His instincts were those of a traditional conservative, loyal to hierarchy, gentility, and aristocracy, even though these values did not seem to him to be honored in the United States. Yet at the same time he tried to be a Burkean conservative and not reject the status quo. He missed the chance to present a genuinely Burkean critique of America because he could not forget Burke. Kirk made it clear that whatever the imperfections of the United States, and Kirk thought they were overwhelming, still he agreed that the American people had "more to conserve, probably, than have any other modern people."[48] He warned would-be critics that it was not healthy to be too critical of America. One should not "be discontented with this imperfect world of ours"[49] and fall into the "personal Hell" that comes from possessing a "gnawing grudge against one's own civilization."[50]

Kirk's genuine ambivalence could not be hidden amidst his earnest affirmations of the American system. But it was only rarely that he had the courage of his convictions and admitted to himself and his readers that his analysis led to the conclusions that the "thinking conservative, in truth, must take on some of the outward characteristics of the radical today."[51] Usually he shrank back, proving once again that radical thought of all sorts did not find much fruitful soil in the America of the 1940s and 1950s.

By the early 1960s radical ideas were again entering American intellectual life, emerging from the civil rights struggles. The intellectual fruits of this development were at first quite small, which is not surprising since as Michael Walzer put it, the first issue was "how is it possible in America in 1962 to grow up political?"[52] The early signs were interesting. There were not a few evidences of sympathy for John Kennedy and far more mentions of him and Castro than there were of Marx. Much of the emerging mood was directed at existing practices, policies, and institutions but there was no alternative ideology. Celebration of participatory democracy, self-development, and liberation were the fragments of an early program. Sympathy for the Old Marxist Left of the 1930s was slight. It was mechanical and hostile to life, as dead as its liberal refugees claimed it was.[53]

Moreover, from the beginning, criticism of radical stirrings came from the lonely remnant who believed they had carried the torch through the dark decades after 1945. Louis Coser, for example, denounced the as-yet weak, new current. Its proponents appeared to be "self-centered" and devoted to "self-absorption and vanity." They showed alarming indications that they were ahistorical, antidemocratic, and antiliberal, especially in their sympathy for Castro. Above all, Coser was bitter at their disinterest in or disrespect for others who had carried the banner before them and who had fought "The whole pack of right-turning intellectuals and attacked the American Celebration and the literary trumpeters of the Cold War."[54]

All the complaints that were so bitterly to divide the Old Left and the New Left in a few years emerged at the start, but it was not until Herbert Marcuse published *One-Dimensional Man* (1964) that the future was fully augured, the future of the turbulent late 1960s and early 1970s and those years of uncertainty and confusion. Marcuse found nothing redeeming in his critique of America and American liberalism. His attack was broad and it was merciless. The truth was, he proclaimed, that "this society is irrational as a whole."[55] It was in the control of forces that cared little or nothing about authentic human needs and everything about capitalism and order. What was required was critical analysis and eventually major revolution. Critical analysis was to serve the function of unmasking the deceptions of liberal capitalism, its greed, its elitism, its mass culture, and its imperialism. It was to tear away the "false consciousness" that constituted actual repression of human needs and was the major block before radical change that could allow genuine human fulfillment.[56]

Marcuse's perspective, of course, was yet another viewpoint that confirms the impression American intellectual life was both consensual and conservative. Everywhere Marcuse looked he saw intellectuals either escaping politics or repeating the same liberal dogmas. They faithfully agreed with the population at large that all was well in America. They refused to question whether the existent order might be a travesty of any proper vision of democracy and justice. He expressed disgust at what he termed the "Happy Consciousness"—the belief that the real is rational.[57] As a Marxist he believed this was nonsense. That few agreed with him did not change his mind. "The fact the vast majority of the population accepts, and is made to accept, this society does not render it less irrational and reprehensible."[58]

Page after page revealed the depths of Marcuse's critique of American liberals as uncritical conservatives. Marcuse refused to rest content with simply illustrating the tendency toward conservatism and consensus. He wanted to prove there was no complexity, no variation at all, only a greyness of unanimous agreement. In his excessive emphasis on consensus he exceeded even "consensus historians" such as Louis Hartz and Daniel Boorstin, men who were not fainthearted in their search for patterns of consensus. He made a mildly consensus-oriented intellectual such as Arthur Schlesinger look like the most thoroughgoing conflict historian, since Schlesinger saw some conflict in American thought even if we had to appreciate that it usually took place in a country and tradition that "is essentially based on a liberal consensus."[59] Marcuse's insight was marred in the end because he could not distinguish between kinds and degrees of criticism. Unless it fit his own radical Marxist position, whatever American intellectuals said or wrote always was just one more justification of the old order.

The stark pessimism of *One-Dimensional Man* is famous. There is little in this book of radical criticism that concedes anything to the chances of change in America. It faithfully reflects not the heady days of the New Left, but the mood of postwar political thinking. It could only have been pessimistic as a result, and it was. Faced with consensus, "false consciousness," and the technological means to keep consensus going, Marcuse concluded that there was no basis for thinking America would develop in what he judged to be a better direction—"Nothing indicates that it will have a good end." He did not give up all hope, but the dream of making America into a different nation was "nothing but a chance."[60]

Marcuse stands out, then, among serious radical intellectuals in America because he had so very little hope. His pessimism may appear extreme, but it was a view appreciated by others among the small band of radical intellectuals of the Left who also felt isolated. The "deep undercurrent of pessimism running through their work" was only natural given their analysis. It was, indeed, inevitable, since "Left intellectuals of every theoretical cast . . . shared a general awareness of the massive power and essential stability of the American social order."[61] Against these factors, who could have expected to make an impact? Who could have expected that in a few years radical hopes would soar (momentarily) once again?

Certainly there must have seemed to be slight basis for hope for radicals in an intellectual atmosphere more congenial to cooling radicals like Irving Howe. In 1952 Howe could still assail postwar intellectuals for their frequent paeans to America, but by 1961 he had come to respect "the heroism of tiredness," which in his time could "consist of nothing but stillness."[62] Howe continued to go through the motions of favoring substantial change, but his ardor cooled more and more. The gap between his position and Daniel Bell's was not so wide. Ex-radical Bell self-consciously summed up his personal journey by reporting the following tale:

> The Rabbi of Zans used to tell this story about himself. In my youth when I was fired with the love of God, I thought I would convert the whole world to God. But soon I discovered that it would be quite enough to convert the people who lived in my town, and I tried for a long time, but did not succeed. Then I realized that my program was too ambitious, and I concentrated on the persons in my household. But I could not convert them either. Finally it dawned upon me: I must work upon myself, so that I may give true service to God. But I did not accomplish even this.[63]

THE PRAISE OF AMERICA

Bell must be supplemented by Marcuse to provide an accurate account of those years. There was disagreement; there were doubts; there were alternative visions. Yet we know from this study that these were not the dominant themes. Indeed, nothing impresses one so much in reading political intellectuals of the period as the depth of their conviction that the attractions of America were without equal. Beyond, or beneath, their philosophical and political problems lay a profound conviction that America was the best civilization, with the most satisfactory political order, in the world. Sometimes this may have been a defensive posture, for we know in many cases the threat of Communism was on their minds. But mostly this judgment was not at all defensive; it was self-confident and joyous. Whatever its faults, America was worth celebrating, and intellectuals did indeed celebrate it from 1945 into the early 1960s.

Peter Viereck was easy to convince. He early claimed "the American way of life . . . is almost a miraculous achievement."[64] Leslie Fiedler admitted he was harder to convince. A visit to Italy led to his discovery that America was a most impressive nation, one that had much to offer even intellectuals like himself.[65] This judgment was popular as well among normally critical New York intellectuals in the 1950s. Columbia's Charles Frankel published *The Case for Modern Man* in 1955 and angrily assailed those who no longer had faith in liberal America. Our prospects were good, the reality was satisfactory, and who could not agree?[66] In a special section of a 1952 issue of the intensely intellectual *Partisan Review* the mood came through most directly. The magazine editors noted, with some apparent reservations, that intellectuals liked America now and wanted to be a part of the nation again. They knew that "many writers and intellectuals now feel closer to their country and its culture."[67] This feeling was not merely a general, and vague, sentiment, but it was also an explicitly political one, for "there is a recognition that the kind of democracy which exists in America has an intrinsic and positive value: it is not merely a capitalist myth but a reality which must be defended against Russian totalitarianism."[68] Lionel Trilling, too, made his way to awkward reconciliation. He did not believe one could call America a cultural garden, but he conceded there was no longer any sense in looking to Europe for answers or in ignoring the pleasant fact that the cultural curve in America was markedly on the upswing.[69] Murray Kempton was more enthusiastic, although he, too, had his reservations. But mainly the United States he saw was "an America made glorious.

. . . Its wealth, its resources, its almost universally exalted living standards."[70]

Social scientists joined the celebration with more abandon and they kept at it longer, right up to the end of the era. Examples were everywhere, expressed not just by the fact that they revised democratic theory to fit the American reality they so admired, but even more in explicit statements of support and confidence. Daniel Bell proclaimed America good because it was an open society, one that deserved enormous praise because it was doing so well in economic growth, in providing unparalleled living standards for the masses, in guaranteeing bountiful amounts of personal freedom, and in developing culture.[71] He also shared David Riesman's judgment that "Americans possess increasingly competent government, without having expended much energy to get it."[72] Nathan Glazer marveled at American wealth and democracy, forces that had decisively defeated Communism at home.[73] Seymour Martin Lipset joined the chorus as well. Although he still claimed to be a member of the socialist Left, he believed America was better than socialist dreams. It was the realization of those dreams in practice. Although this claim was scarcely plausible, he often assured his readers that the United States was "a nation in which *Leftist values* predominate," a truth that was only natural since *"the values of socialism and Americanism are similar."*[74]

Clinton Rossiter certainly did not think America had much to do with socialism, but he was equally as enthusiastic as Lipset was about the United States. His main interest was the American political system and his estimate was that it was a remarkable success. Our political parties were striking examples of those rare political institutions that prove to be both representative and unifying institutions. Their viability gave him confidence that "American politics in 1984 will look much like American politics in 1960" and reassured him that "Whatever America finds necessary to do in the years to come, the politics of American democracy will surely make possible."[75] Walt Rostow experienced an identical sense of optimism as he surveyed American postwar experience. We had demonstrated a capacity to respond to complex and sometimes challenging times: "American society has . . . responded to the innovational challenges it has faced at home and abroad; and it has begun to restructure its attitudes and institutions in the directions required to meet them."[76] Even Edward Shils saw grounds for optimism in the growing reconciliation of intellectuals and politicians in the years after World War II. The McCarthy episode was only an ugly interruption in a long-run trend that offered him much hope.[77]

No area of social science attracted more individuals who were more firmly attached to the American paradigm than did the study of the so-called Third World nations and in none did it lead to more unfortunate and erroneous analyses. Few American students of the less-developed world made any major criticisms of the United States or its foreign policy toward the Third World in the postwar period. On the contrary, there was strong support for American policies that undertook to speed the process of "modernization" in the Third World toward a Western and often American socioeconomic and political goal. Its greatness was never questioned. There was an unmistakable inclination "to identify modernity with virtue" and to classify modernity with "Western society writ abstractly and polysyllabically."[78] A mood of optimism surged through the ranks of many social scientists, since "development" appeared to be proceeding nicely toward expected results, often watched with an attitude of unmistakable benevolence by social scientists. Certainly it was true that American development "theories manifested, on the whole, a sanguine view of the patterns and prospects for political change and development in the Third World. . . . many of them fell prey to . . . the idea that political systems always develop and never decay." Many also assumed it was possible to achieve American political values of the era such as economic growth, constitutional government, and stability all at the same time, which turned out to be no more than "wishful thinking."[79]

In the postwar decades there were a number of differing kinds of modernization theories and they altered over time, but it is not clear how much any of them promoted an understanding of the actual situation of Third World states or promoted an understanding of the complex and often ambiguous patterns of change that actually occurred in the Third World. Few, if any, led to much reflection on the value of change in the United States. The hypothesized teleology of development toward the Western and American model was hardly likely to do so. As Samuel Huntington remarks, "the extraordinary acceptance of the modernization theory . . . in the 1950s derived in part from the fact that it justified complacency . . . the theory of modernization thus rationalized change abroad and the status quo at home."[80]

Yet explicit as many social scientists were, they never quite directed their energies to the American cause as much as the consensus historians. The latter today are recognized not only as first-class historians, but as the most self-conscious symbol of intellectual celebration of America from 1945 to the early 1960s.

There are many examples, and not least is S.E. Morison's ringing defense of the American tradition in his presidential address significantly entitled "Faith of an Historian" in 1951,[81] but there is no doubt that Daniel Boorstin was the most flamboyant and aggressive celebrant of them all. His *The Genius of American Politics* (1953) pictured America as a land of pragmatic citizens who did not need and did not want ideology. We were practical and sensible and we were better.[82] His histories that followed in the 1960s carried on this theme in fascinating and entertaining directions. Boorstin abjured political thought and intellectual history for social history and the pragmatic story of American inventions and social growth. America did not need justification nor did our pragmatic way of life. This, indeed, was our great benefit, our best feature among many. We were a great, experimental civilization free from the lure of intellectual self-justifications and our continuing success depended on our remaining free of this trap.[83] According to Boorstin, the prevalent belief in the United States of "the inevitability of the particular institutions, the particular society," was neither false nor at all harmful.[84] The fundamental reality of America as Boorstin saw it was in its stable institutions and society. Our triumph was based on "the marvelous success and vitality of our institutions."[85] Boorstin did not expect any change and therefore he counted himself an optimist about the American future.

Boorstin's sentiments were hardly unique. Consider Henry Steele Commager's able *The American Mind* (1950) where enthusiasm knew no bounds. To be sure, Commager conceded that the United States had not been without faults, but he contended that much turned on how one viewed those faults. Commager felt no personal hesitation: "only a perfectionist would not recognize our failures as venial."[86] Commager was especially pleased as was Boorstin at the enduring optimism of Americans, despite the reigning skeptical mood. How could anyone blame Americans for this optimism, he asked? "That Americans had been largely successful in what they undertook was undeniable. They had—at least in large measure—formed a more perfect union, established justice, insured domestic tranquility, provided for the common defense, promoted the general welfare."[87]

Or consider Max Lerner's judgment in *America as a Civilization*. Lerner insisted that America was "one of the memorable civilizations of history," one in which he had the utmost faith.[88] He argued that America was an unusually coherent civilization, one in which consensus was grounded in dynamic confidence.[89] Like Eric Goldman in *Rendevous with Destiny*, Lerner identified America with progress and hope, confident that the future looked good.[90] He knew there were critics, but Lerner had no qualms about taking them on. He defended the United States against the charge that it was a grossly materialistic civilization. He denied assertions that America was a closed civilization, where reality denied the rhetoric of access. He refused to accept an image of America as a racist society, arguing the blacks were succeeding in America.[91] The truth was far different from the complaints of critics. America fit "the image of Prometheus stealing fire from the gods in order to light a path of progress for men. The path is not yet clear, nor the meaning of progress, nor where it is leading but the bold intent, the irreverence, and the secular daring have all become a part of the American experience."[92]

Last, we may ponder the example of Arthur Schlesinger. He was rarely completely uncritical of America, but throughout the two postwar decades he painted a flattering picture of the United States. In his major work of the late 1940s, *The Vital Center*, he met directly the accusations of left-wing radicals that America was a failure, a mere hunting ground for capitalist spoilers. Democracy in America, he argued, was not at all the captive of big business. Nor did he agree with their implicit assumption that business values and liberal values were always antithetical. It was true enough that

earlier in *The Age of Jackson* (1945) and later in the New Deal
histories Schlesinger expressed some unmistakably negative
attitudes toward big business,[93] but it was not an unusual expression of his ambivalent but essentially capitalistic views that led
him to remind his readers that capitalism and liberalism were both
partisans of a "free society" and they stood together in vigorous
opposition to "the totalitarians."[94] In this spirit he participated as
well in the revision of the status of the Robber Barons in American
history that occurred after World War II. According to Schlesinger
it was time for a revision of their image. They had been unduly ma-
ligned and their contributions to the development of America
ignored.[95]

Later in his histories of the New Deal, which appeared in the
1950s and 1960s, Schlesinger extolled what he took to be the
successes of the American political experience. The Depression and
the New Deal were not for Schlesinger a story of total failure followed by tentative recovery, but a remarkable adventure in
complex political action and leadership that spoke well for American society and its political institutions.[96] His later book of essays,
The Politics of Hope (1962), represented new heights in his appreciation of the United States, perhaps because it was now under the
leadership of his patron John Kennedy. Never before had he felt
quite so enthusiastic. To be sure, Schlesinger inserted the usual
skeptical liberal caveat. People of his persuasion, the party of hope,
were determined to remain "humane, skeptical, and pragmatic."
They could have "no dogma, no sense of messianic mission, no
belief that mortal man can attain Utopia, no faith that fundamental
problems have final solutions." But although Schlesinger did not
forget his education in Niebuhrian restraints, his mood was still
exultant. He was delighted that his longtime desires were now being
fulfilled. He had long believed "that the impulses of Hope . . .
would soon break out and launch the United States into a new and
more entertaining [!] epoch." Under President Kennedy the dream
had come true. We now had "young, vigorous, intelligent, civilized,
and experimental" leadership whose "Mistakes these days tend to
be the mistakes of rationality, not the mistakes of complacency."[97]

Whether the Bay of Pigs and the beginning of our commitment to
the Vietnam War may be said to be "mistakes of rationality" is

doubtful, but Schlesinger was more concerned with other things, especially the new status of intellectuals in the Kennedy 1960s. He fairly gushed with enthusiasm at the progress he thought he observed. "The life of the mind enjoys a new freedom and a new status. There has never been such an official interest in and support of the arts. Wit has become respectable; it is even presidential now. Satire has burst out. . . ."[98]

Schlesinger's embarrassing celebration of the Kennedy years should not obscure the basic meaning of the conclusion of Schlesinger, Lerner, and all the rest. Many, even most, political intellectuals appeared convinced that the gap between liberal values and America was all but closed and it seems clear that this conviction was central to their affirmation of the United States. The old faiths, the old certainties, may have been undermined, but many political intellectuals clearly reified their image of American liberal pragmatic reality as a substitute.

THE LIBERAL TRADITION IN AMERICA

Amidst the books that poured forth the common praise of America appeared Louis Hartz's *The Liberal Tradition in America* (1955). From one perspective this was a brilliant essay that fit the spirit of the age almost exactly. It presented a picture of consensus many others saw and applauded. It painted the consensus as liberal, focusing on the familiar (if vague) values of individualism, consent of the governed, and capitalism. It artfully described the strength of the consensus within American history. It tried to explain the origins of the consensus.

There was much more to Hartz's analysis than all this, however, so much more that it stands out now as the most penetrating work by an American participant in the liberal postwar era of political thought. For one thing, Hartz flatly disagreed with those who claimed that American liberalism was not an ideology. On the contrary, he was convinced that American liberalism was an enormously powerful and constricting ideology. It might not seem so, but that was mostly because it was not challenged at home by other ideologies. Its lines could be softer, its claims weaker, because they were not confronted. Thus Hartz in effect took direct issue with the conviction of postwar liberalism that its values had little to do with ideology and were instead skeptical, pragmatic, and open-ended.

Hartz suggested the ideology was indeed firmly held, tremendously firmly held. It was so deeply treasured, in fact, that the United States was far from the condition of tolerance about which so many liberals congratulated themselves. Americans were true believers, and like all true believers quite prepared to crush those who saw differently. The fabled consensus was in part the result of intolerance rather than the obvious result of rational men and women. It was "an absolute moral ethos, 'Americanism.' "[99] All in all, Hartz thought he saw something contrasting sharply with what most liberal intellectuals in America saw: "America's absolutism: the sober faith that its norms are self-evident. It is one of the most powerful absolutisms in the world."[100]

Moreover, far from joining in the celebration of this America, Hartz worried a great deal about whether our tremendous self-assurance did not pose enormous threats to the whole world as well as to dissidents at home. America's power clearly frightened Hartz. Power at the behest of an absolutism could become an egregious cause of world suffering. America faced a world full of nonliberals, an obdurate world. Could it learn to tolerate in the world as it had not tolerated at home? Could it learn to be skeptical in the world arena as it had not been skeptical at home?

Only today can we appreciate, as his age did not, how significant Hartz's anxieties were. His own liberalism allowed his book to appear partly as another, if classic, statement of the general consensus and partly as a minor criticism of excesses. Perhaps that was all he meant. From our vantage point, though, the book reaches far into postwar political thought. It challenges the whole structure. It is a truly skeptical work and, as such, it seeks to expose the absence of skepticism among the skeptics. Hartz said that the skeptical liberals were actually ideological liberals; that skeptical opponents of utopia were really utopians, except that they saw utopia not in a far off age, but in present-day America; that skeptical new democratic theorists were actually proponents of a democratic faith: operating American democracy; that incrementalists were at best ambivalent about change not because they were skeptical but because they were unskeptical of America.

Hartz is faulted today on a number of grounds. Some say, correctly, that Hartz exaggerated the extent of consensus in American history. Others complain, correctly, that Hartz refused to take seriously political thought in all periods of American history, including the years after the war. But what people *said* did not impress him. What he *saw* was consensus, its brute force, its intolerance, and its potential dangers. He overstated, say his critics, and they are right. Yet perhaps that is not quite the point. Perhaps the point is that Hartz saw what the age did not see.

Our study hardly allows us to conclude with Hartz that skepticism was not present. In three specific areas there is no doubt that political thought from 1945 to 1964 was skeptical. It was skeptical of absolute justifications of political values. It was skeptical of radical and future utopias. It was skeptical of hopeful assessments of human behavior in politics. Yet Hartz is also right, as we have seen; it was not skeptical of America or of American liberalism. Political intellectuals' optimism regarding America, American political processes, and the American future allowed them to remain confident, sure of themselves, even as they were, in their way, skeptical.

From its start with the City on the Hill, American political thought had had one final refuge, the specialness of America; this was its faith even in the skeptical age of 1945–64. We may well wonder if that is to remain with us any longer. If it is not, then at last American political thought—for better or for worse—will become skeptical as it was not in the two decades after World War II. Then we will see a revolution—in directions we cannot predict—in our political thought.

NOTES*

1. Arthur Schlesinger, Jr., *The Vital Center* (London: Andre Deutsch, 1970–1949), ch. 8 and pp. 255–56.

*Some books listed here have two dates: the first is the date of the edition referenced here; the second is the date the work was originally published.

2. Abraham Kaplan, "American Ethics and Public Philosophy," in *The American Style,* ed. Elting Morison (New York: Harper and Bros., 1958), p. 47; Edward Shils, *The Torment of Secrecy* (Glencoe, Ill,: Free Press, 1956), p. 17.

3. Eric Goldman, *Rendezvous with Destiny* (New York: Vintage, 1962-1955).

4. Clinton Rossiter, *Conservatism in America* (New York: Vintage, 1962-1955), p. 163.

5. Robert Dahl, *A Preface to Democratic Theory* (Chicago: University of Chicago Press, 1956), p. 53.

6. Richard Hofstadter, *The Age of Reform* (New York: Vintage, 1962-1955), p. 14.

7. Ibid.

8. Ibid.

9. Richard Hofstadter, *Anti-Intellectualism in American Life* (New York: Knopf, 1963), pp. 419 and 420.

10. Ibid., pp. 4-5 and 432.

11. Sheldon Wolin, *Politics and Vision* (Boston: Little, Brown, 1960), ch. 10.

12. David Easton, *The Political System* (New York: Knopf, 1953), p. 42.

13. Max Lerner, *America as a Civilization* (New York: Simon and Schuster, 1957), pp. 494-95.

14. Schlesinger, *Vital Center,* p. 171.

15. Ibid., p. 10.

16. Ibid., p. 169.

17. See Bernard Berlson et al., *Voting* (Chicago: University of Chicago Press, 1954), pp. 311-23.

18. Seymour Martin Lipset, *Political Man* (Garden City, N.Y.: Doubleday-Anchor, 1963-1960), passim, but especially ch. 7 and pp. 1, 78, and 79.

19. David Truman, *The Governmental Process* (New York: Knopf, 1960-1951), ch. 16.

20. Dahl, *Preface,* pp. 31 and 125; Robert Dahl, *Political Opposition in Western Democracies* (New Haven: Yale University Press, 1969), pp. 35-48, 386, 392, and 456.

21. Dahl, *Preface,* pp. 150-51; Robert Dahl, *Pluralist Democracy in the United States* (Chicago: Rand McNally, 1969), p. 24.

22. Dahl, *Opposition,* pp. xvii-xviii and 68-69.

23. Dahl, *Preface,* pp. 137-38, 145, and 150; Robert Dahl, *Who Governs?* (New Haven: Yale University Press, 1961), pp. 5-7, 265-66, and chs. 27-28; Dahl, *Modern Political Analysis* (Englewood Cliffs, N.J.: Prentice-Hall, 1963), ch. 7 and pp. 84 and 89.

24. Giovanni Sartori, *Democratic Theory* (New York: Praeger, 1965-1957), p. 169; Henry Mayo, *An Introduction to Democratic Theory* (New York: Oxford University Press, 1960), pp. 218-25.

25. Peter Gay, *Voltaire's Politics* (New York: Vintage, 1965-1959), p. 25 and ch. 3.

26. Schlesinger, *Vital Center,* p. 174.

27. Ibid., p. 186.

28. Reinhold Niebuhr, *The Children of Light and the Children of Darkness*

(New York: Scribner's, 1944), p. 118.

29. David Spitz, *Democracy and the Challenge of Power* (New York: Columbia University Press, 1958), p. 171.

30. David Braybrooke and Charles Lindblom, *A Strategy of Decision* (New York: Free Press, 1970-1963), ch. 5 and pp. 102 and 103.

31. Ibid., p. 113.

32. Dahl, *Opposition*, pp. 391-92.

33. Talcott Parsons, *The Social System* (Glencoe, Ill.: Free Press, 1951), p. 486.

34. Ibid., pp. 107-9, and 232.

35. Daniel Bell, *The End of Ideology* (New York: Collier's, 1962-1961), p. 16; Peter Viereck, *Shame and Glory of the Intellectuals* (New York: Capricorn, 1965-1953), p. 117.

36. Hofstadter, *Reform*, p. 14-15.

37. Lipset, *Political Man*, p. 371.

38. Lerner, *Civilization*, p. xii.

39. Newton Arvin, "Our Country and Our Culture: A Symposium," *Partisan Review* 19 (May-June 1952): 288.

40. Lerner, *Civilization*, p. xii.

41. Arthur Schlesinger, Jr., "Time and the Intellectuals" (1956), p. 235, and "Liberalism in America: A Note for Europeans" (1956), p. 67, in *The Politics of Hope* (Boston: Houghton Mifflin, 1962); also pp. ix-x.

42. Reinhold Niebuhr, *The Irony of American History* (New York: Scribner's, 1952), p. 54.

43. Clinton Rossiter, *Marxism: The View from America* (New York: Harcourt, Brace and World, 1960), pp. 15, 206, and 243.

44. Ibid., p. 2791.

45. Erich Fromm, *The Sane Society* (New York: Fawcett, 1967-1955), p. 315, passim.

46. Ibid., ch. 8 and pp. 37 and 312.

47. Russell Kirk, *A Program for Conservatives* (Chicago: Regnery, 1962-1954), pp. 193-208; Kirk, *The Intemperate Professor and Other Cultural Splenetics* (Baton Rouge: Louisiana State University Press, 1965), pp. 112-13; Kirk, *The Intelligent Woman's Guide to Conservatism* (New York: Devin-Adair, 1957), pp. 62-64; Kirk, *Confessions of a Bohemian Tory* (New York: Fleet, 1963), p. 89; Kirk, *The American Cause* (Chicago: Regnery, 1957), ch. 6 and pp. 96 and 106-8.

48. Kirk, *Program*, pp. 2-3 and 40.

49. Kirk, *Women's Guide*, p. 26.

50. Kirk, *Splenetics*, p. 19.

51. Kirk, *Program*, pp. 8 and 311.

52. Michael Walzer, "The Young Radicals: A Symposium," *Dissent* 9 (Spring 1962): 129.

53. See, for example, "The Port Huron Statement," in Paul Jacobs and Saul Landau, *The New Radicals* (New York: Random House, 1966).

54. Louis Coser, "The Young Radicals: A Symposium," *Dissent* 9 (Spring 1962): 159-62.

55. Herbert Marcuse, *One-Dimensional Man* (Boston: Beacon, 1964), p. ix.

56. Ibid., p. xiii.

57. Ibid., p. 84.

58. Ibid., p. xiii.

59. Schlesinger, "Liberalism in America: A Note for Europeans" (1956), in *Hope*, pp. 64–65.

60. Marcuse, *One-Dimensional Man*, p. 257.

61. Peter Clecak, *Radical Paradoxes: Dilemmas of American Left: 1945–1970* (New York: Harper & Row, 1973), p. 15.

62. Irving Howe, *Partisan Review*, January–February 1954, pp. 7–33; Howe, *Politics and the Novel* (New York: Meridian, 1957), p. 226.

63. Daniel Bell, *Marxism Socialism in the United States* (Princeton: Princeton University Press, 1967–1952), p. 193.

64. Viereck, *Shame*.

65. Leslie Feidler, *An End to Innocence* (Boston: Little, Brown, 1952), ch. 4.

66. Charles Frankel, *The Case for Modern Man* (New York: Harper, 1961–1955).

67. Editors, "Our Country and Our Culture," *Partisan Review*, May–June 1952, p. 282.

68. Ibid., p. 284.

69. Lionel Trilling, "Our Country and Our Culture: A Symposium," *Partisan Review* 19 (May–June 1952): 319 and 323.

70. Murray Kempton, *Part of Our Time* (New York: Simon and Schuster, 1955), p. 3.

71. Daniel Bell, "Interpretations of American Politics" (1955), in *The Radical Right*, ed. Daniel Bell (Garden City, N.Y.: Doubleday-Anchor, 1964–1963), p. 73; Bell, *Ideology*, p. 38.

72. David Riesman, "Our Country and Our Culture: A Symposium," *Partisan Review* 19 (May–June 1952): 310-311.

73. Nathan Glazer, *The Social Basis of American Communism* (New York: Harcourt, Brace and World, 1961), conclusion.

74. Lipset, *Political Man*, pp. xxi and xxv.

75. Clinton Rossiter, *Parties and Politics in America* (Ithaca: Cornell University Press, 1960), pp. 54–58, 163, and 188.

76. W.W. Rostow, "The National Style," in Morison, ed., *American Style*, pp. 303 and 307-10.

77. Shils, *Torment*, pp. 13–14.

78. Robert A. Packenham, *Liberal America and the Third World* (Princeton: Princeton University Press, 1973), pp. 307-9; Samuel P. Huntington, "The Change to Change: Modernization, Development, and Politics," *Comparative Politics* 3 (April 1973): 294-95.

79. Packenham, *Liberal America*, pp. 225 and 287-89; Huntington, "Change to Change," p. 290.

80. Packenham, *Liberal America*, p. 197 and ch. 5; Huntington, "Change to Change," pp. 292 and 300.

81. Samuel Eliot Morison, "Faith of an Historian," *American Historical Review* 56 (January 1951).

82. Daniel Boorstin, *The Genius of American Politics* (Chicago: University of Chicago Press, 1953).

83. The argument of Daniel Boorstin, *The Americans: The National Experience* (New York 1965).

84. Boorstin, *Genius*, p. 33.

85. Ibid., p. 8.

86. Henry Steele Commager, *The American Mind* (New York: Yale University Press, 1959-1950).

87. Ibid., pp. 409 and 439.

88. Lerner, *Civilization*, pp. 55–61 and 950.

89. Ibid., p. 407.

90. Goldman, *Destiny*, p. 347; Lerner, *Civilization*, p. 47.

91. Lerner, *Civilization*, pp. 524, 250–262, and ch. 7.

92. Ibid., p. 263.

93. Arthur Schlesinger, Jr., *The Age of Jackson* (Boston: Little, Brown, 1945), which is particularly unsympathetic to banking interests.

94. Schlesinger, *Vital Center*, pp. xxiv and 153.

95. Ibid., p. 44.

96. Arthur Schlesinger, Jr., *A Thousand Days* (New York: Fawcett, 1967–1965); Schlesinger, *The Crisis of the Old Order* (Boston: Houghton Mifflin, 1957); Schlesinger, *The Coming of the New Deal* (Boston: Houghton Mifflin, 1959); Schlesinger, *The Politics of Upheaval* (Boston: Houghton Mifflin, 1960).

97. Schlesinger, *Hope*, pp. x and xi.

98. Ibid., p. xi.

99. Louis Hartz, *The Liberal Tradition in America* (New York: Harcourt, Brace and World, 1955), p. 286.

100. Ibid., p. 58.

10 Postscript: The 1964 Presidential Election

This book properly ends with the 1964 presidential election, before the turbulent years of unrest and conflict that broke out over the Vietnam War. In the years after 1964 there was no longer to be so great a consensus or so much confidence among American political intellectuals. Even by 1964 there were unmistakable signs that there was serious trouble ahead. This was most apparent in the outbreak of widespread and bitter racial turmoil and the emergence of a number of black American intellectuals who demanded major changes. By 1964 Martin Luther King had published his statement *Why We Can't Wait* (1964), which included his famous "Letter from a Birmingham Jail," and James Baldwin had angrily warned of *The Fire Next Time* (1963).[1] Other voices were heard, too, and in ever increasing loudness. White intellectuals began to discover that racial inequality and racial conflict posed serious issues for consensual America.[2] The breakup of consensus or the belief in the existence of a consensus seemed foreshadowed.

Yet 1964 was another, if perhaps final, moment of consensus for postwar intellectuals. The 1964 election united them as never before in public defense of their conservative marriage of liberal values and postwar America. Never were the issues clearer and never was their position more explicit. Although there are those who may challenge the notion that Barry Goldwater's candidacy for presidential office represented a radical threat. to the liberal order dominant in America, there were few intellectuals of prominence who expressed any such doubts then. No words drew the battle line more sharply than those pointed ones that Barry Goldwater delivered in his speech accepting the Republican Party's nomination: "I would remind you that extremism in the defense of liberty is no vice. And let me remind you also that moderation in pursuit of justice is no virtue." Here were words that raised every fear of an enemy that postwar liberals had fought abroad and at home for two decades. They were apparently the words of an ideologue, a fanatic, a utopian, a radical.

Perhaps the most detailed and most characteristic analysis of what the Goldwater effort meant came from Richard Hofstadter. During the campaign he was extremely upset about Goldwater, who he interpreted as an unquestioned threat to (Hofstadter's) America.[3] Later he remained disturbed. He attacked Goldwater's addiction to arguments that depended on "eternal truths."[4] They were as foolish as they were dangerous. Not surprisingly, Hofstadter contended that this habit was linked with an approach to politics that was disastrously radical and that had proved at the polls that many people still could be roused by its fanatic appeals.[5] Hofstadter's Goldwater, rather like Hofstadter's Populists and his Joseph McCarthy, was trapped by ideology and "nostalgic reveries." His speeches teemed "with the Fundamentalist revolt against the conditions of modernity" and he peddled economic ideas that were hopeless relics of a bygone era.[6] He was, indeed, another example of the fanatical ideologue in politics trying to destroy what liberal America had built so slowly and so well. Goldwater was another "pseudoconservative" because in fact the true conservatives in America in 1964 were liberal intellectuals. As Hofstadter saw it, the Goldwater campaign truly threatened "the legitimacy of the political order itself." Goldwater represented "a repudiation of our traditional political ways" by a man "whose public reputation was marked not with standpattism or excessive caution but with wayward impulse and recklessness." His advisors "brought him as close as any presidential candidate has ever come to subverting the whole pattern of our politics of coalition and consensus."[7]

Murray Kempton made many of the same points in a series of articles for *The New Republic* in 1964. Two in particular are especialy revealing. In the August 8 issue he explored the mind and past of Karl Hess, author of many of Goldwater's most controversial speeches. Before Kempton was through with him, Hess emerged as a dangerous ideological zealot, a rank authoritarian, a violent

anti-Democrat, and even an anti-Zionist.[8] In another issue Kempton compared Goldwater's convention victory to Chekov's play
The Cherry Orchard. Goldwater's supporters like Chekhov's peas-
ants were foolish enthusiasts, alarming in their naivete and ama-
teurism.[9] Kempton's distaste and unease were as obvious as Hofstadter's.

One after another the intellectual spokesmen of their age sounded
the alarm. A symposium in *The Partisan Review* was filled with
intellectuals denouncing Goldwater's effort as a crusade for "fanaticism" attractive only to the "tax nut, Roosevelt-haters, T.V.A.—
haters . . . flouridophobes . . . old maids afraid of rape by a Negro,"
all in all "one of the most morally disgusting events in American
history."[10] Hans Morgenthau announced his displeasure, character-
izing Goldwater's nomination as "a portentious and ominous event"
that he blamed on the old enemy "romantic activism."[11] Daniel Bell
treated Goldwaterism as "intellectual farce" that promoted "sinister
politics." Goldwaterites were victims of what Bell considered to be
the old fallacies most intellectuals had discarded after 1945. They
were especially dangerous because they could not resist the trap of
moralism and insisted upon thinking about politics in terms of
"'good guys' and 'bad guys,' the righteous (and self-righteous) and
the sinners." Like other radicals they were consumed with social
discontent and were really no more than "the angry cry of a social
stratum with its back to the world."[12]

Bell's analysis meant to him that the Goldwater movement had
genuinely totalitarian potentiality, a perfectly consistent argument
that many political intellectuals made in 1964, although usually
only implicitly. Some intellectuals, though, took off their gloves
and frankly charged that Goldwater represented incipient Fascism.
Certainly Philip Rahv predicted the triumph of Fascism if Goldwater won.[13] Michael Harrington insisted that American democracy was at stake. "The defeat of Barry Goldwater is a precondi-
tion for the future of democracy in the United States."[14] Others
were uncertain. Was Goldwater a largely harmless if "contemptible
political buffoon" or did he represent "Armageddon"?[15] Some
voices sought to muffle hysteria about apocalyptic visions" of an
America that is about to show its fascist colors under the charismatic leadership of a Goldwater."[16] One rare observer even under-

stood the significance of the intellectual agitation in our terms, re-
marking that "the experience of fascism shell-shocked my generation . . . which probably leads us to exaggerate the political meaning
of things that are just stupid."[17]

What political intellectuals such as Bell, Hofstadter, and Kempton
argued in print, even when it did not go to the lengths of comparing
Goldwater to Hitler, was seconded by long lists of intellectuals in
political advertisements in the fall of 1964. *The New York Times*
reported the names of leading political intellectuals who believed
the choice was clear for "the intelligent voter . . . between mature
responsibility and blind reaction." Hans Morgenthau agreed, as
did Max Lerner, as did Reinhold Niebuhr, and so many more.[18]
Perhaps they were right in their judgment of the meaning of Barry
Goldwater's candidacy, but their passionate opposition to it in the
name of liberalism and liberal America was no testimony to their
self-image as nonideological and broadly skeptical intellectuals.
Never more than at the end of the postwar era was it more obvious
that American political intellectuals in the two decades after World
War II were as much believers as they were skeptics.

NOTES*

1. Martin Luther King, Jr., *Why We Can't Wait* (New York: Signet, 1964);
James Baldwin, *The Fire Next Time* (New York: Dial, 1963).

2. For an early recognition, cf. the discussion in Huston Smith, ed., *The Search
for America* (Englewood Cliffs, N.J.: Prentice-Hall, 1958), Part II.

3. Richard Hofstadter in "Some Comments on Senator Goldwater," *Partisan
Review*, Fall 1964, pp. 590–92.

4. Richard Hofstader, *The Paranoid Style in American Politics and Other
Essays* (New York: Knopf, 1965), pp. 94–95.

5. Ibid., pp. 102 and 137.

6. Ibid., pp. 94, 98, and 118.

7. Ibid., pp. 94, 100, and 103.

8. Murray Kempton, "Karl Hess: Goldwater Finds His Sorenson," *The New
Republic*, August 8, 1964.

* Some books listed here have two dates: the first is the date of the edition referenced
here; the second is the date the work was originally published.

9. Murray Kempton, "They Got Him," *The New Republic*, July 25, 1964.

10. "Some Comments on Senator Goldwater," *Partisan Review*, Fall 1964, p. 593.

11. Hans J. Morgenthau, "Some Comments on Senator Goldwater," *Partisan Review*, Fall 1964, pp. 595–96.

12. Daniel J. Bell, "Some Comments on Senator Goldwater," *Partisan Review*, Fall 1964, pp. 584–86.

13. Philip Rahv, "Some Comments on Senator Goldwater," *Partisan Review*, Fall 1964, p. 603.

14. Michael Harrington, "Should the Left Support Johnson?" *New Politics* 3 (Summer 1964): 6.

15. "Comments," p. 592.

16. Ibid., p. 607.

17. William Phillips, "Some Comments on Senator Goldwater," *Partisan Review*, Fall 1964, p. 597.

18. *The New York Times*, October 30, 1964, pp. 12 and 30.

Bibliography *

Aaron, Daniel. "Conservatism, Old and New." *American Quarterly* 6 (Summer 1954).

_____. *Writers on the Left*. New York: Avon, 1961.

Adorno, Theodore, et al. *The Authoritarian Personality*. New York: Harper & Row, 1950.

Aiken, Henry David. "The Revolt Against Ideology" (1964). In *Ideology, Politics and Political Theory*, edited by Richard Cox. Belmont, Calif.: Wadsworth, 1969.

Almond, Gabriel. *The American People and Foreign Policy*. New York: Harcourt, Brace and World, 1950.

_____. *The Appeals of Communism*. Princeton: Princeton University Press, 1954.

_____. "Politics and Ethics: A Symposium." *American Political Science Review* 40 (April 1946).

_____, and Coleman, James. *The Politics of Developing Areas*. Princeton: Princeton University Press, 1960.

_____, and Verba, Sidney. *The Civic Culture*. Princeton: Princeton University Press, 1963.

American Political Science Association, Committee on Political Parties. *Toward a More Responsible Two-Party System*. New York: Holt, Reinhart and Winston, 1950.

Arendt, Hannah. *The Origins of Totalitarianism*. New York: Meridian, 1958–1951.

Arnold, Thurman. *The Folklore of Capitalism*. New Haven: Yale University Press, 1937.

_____. *The Symbols of Government*. New Haven: Yale University Press, 1935.

Arvin, Newton. "Our Country and Our Culture: A Symposium." *Partisan Review* 19 (May-June 1952).

Asch, Solomon E. "Opinions and Social Pressure." *Scientific American* 193 (1955).

Ayer, A.J. *Language, Truth and Logic*. New York: Dover, 1952–1936.

Bachrach, Peter, and Baratz, Morton. "Two Faces of Power." *American Political Science Review* 56 (1962).

Baldwin, James. *The Fire Next Time*. New York: Dial, 1963.

Banfield, Edward. *Political Influence* Glencoe, Ill.: Free Press, 1961.

Barber, Bernard. "Anti-Intellectualism in the United States." *The Journal of Social Issues*, no. 3 (1955).

* Some books listed here have two dates: the first is the date of the edition referenced in this volume; the second is the date the work was originally published.

Barrett, William. *Irrational Man*. Garden City, N.Y.: Doubleday-Anchor, 1962–1958.

Bay, Christian. "Politics and Pseudopolitics." *American Political Science Review* 59 (1965).

Bell, Daniel. "The Dispossessed." In *The Radical Right*, edited by Daniel Bell, pp. 1–38. Garden City, N.Y.: Doubleday-Anchor, 1964–1963.

_____. *The End of Ideology*. New York: Collier's, 1962–1961.

_____. "Ideology: A Debate." *Commentary* 38 (October 1964).

_____. "Interpretations of American Politics," In *The Radical Right*, edited by Daniel Bell, Garden City, N.Y.: Doubleday-Anchor, 1964–1963, pp. 39–62.

_____. *Marxian Socialism in the United States*. Princeton: Princeton University Press, 1967–1952.

_____. ed. *The New American Right*. New York: Criterion, 1955.

_____, ed. *The Radical Right*. Garden City, N.Y.: Doubleday-Anchor, 1964–1963.

_____. "Some Comments on Senator Goldwater." *Partisan Review*, Fall 1964.

Benedict, Ruth. *Patterns of Culture*. New York: New American Library, 1960–1934.

Bennett, Lenore, Jr. *What Manner of Man*. New York: Pocket Books. 1968–1965.

Berelson, Bernard, et al. *Voting*. Chicago: University of Chicago Press, 1954.

Berle, Adolph A. Jr. *The Twentieth Century Capitalist Revolution*. New York: Harvest, 1960–1954.

Berman, Ronald. *America in the Sixties: An Intellectual History*. New York: Free Press, 1968.

Berryman, John. "The State of American Writing, 1948: A Symposium." *Partisan Review* 15 (1948).

Bickel, Alexander. *The Least Dangerous Branch*. Indianapolis: Bobbs-Merrill, 1962.

Boorstin, Daniel. *The Americans: The Colonial Experience*. New York: Random House, 1958.

_____. *The Americans: The National Experience*. New York: Random House, 1965.

_____. *The Genius of American Politics*. Chicago: University of Chicago Press, 1953.

Braybrooke, David, and Lindblom, Charles. *A Strategy of Decision*. New York: Free Press, 1970–1963.

Brecht, Arnold. *Political Theory*. Princeton: Princeton University Press, 1959.

Buckley, William F., Jr. *God and Man at Yale*. Chicago: Regnery, 1951.

_____. *Up From Liberalism*. New York: Hillman, 1961.

_____, and Bozell, L. Brent. *McCarthy and His Enemies*. Chicago: Regnery, 1954.

Burnham, James. "Our Country and Our Culture: A Symposium." *Partisan Review* 19 (May-June 1952).

Burns, James MacGregor. *The Deadlock of Democracy*. Englewood Cliffs, N.J.: Prentice-Hall, 1967–1963.

_____. *John Kennedy: A Political Profile*. New York: Harcourt, Brace and World, 1960.

_____. *Roosevelt: The Lion and the Fox*. New York: Harcourt, Brace and World, 1956.

Bury, Chris. "The Liberal Misinterpretation of McCarthyism." Unpublished paper, University of Wisconsin-Madison, 1977.

Campbell, Angus, et al. *The American Voter*. New York: Wiley, 1964–1960.

Cassinelli, C.W. *The Politics of Freedom*. Seattle: University of Washington Press, 1961.

Cassirer, Ernst. *The Myth of the State*. Garden City, N.Y.: Doubleday, 1955).

Clecak, Peter. *Radical Paradoxes: Dilemmas of the American Left: 1945–1970*. New York: Harper & Row, 1973.

Cnudde, Charles, and Neubauer, Deane. *Empirical Democratic Theory*. Chicago: Markham, 1969.

Cohn, Norman. *The Pursuit of the Millennium*. London: Temple Smith, 1970–1957.

Commager, Henry Steele. *The American Mind*. New York: Yale University Press, 1959–1950.

Converse, Philip. "The Nature of Belief Systems in Mass Publics." *Ideology and Discontent*, edited by David Apter. New York: Free Press, 1964.

Coser, Louis. "The Young Radicals: A Symposium." *Dissent* 9 (Spring 1962): 158–63.

_____, and Howe, Irving. *The American Communist Party*. Boston: Beacon, 1957.

Cox, Richard, ed. *Ideology, Politics and Political Theory*. Belmont, Calif.: Wadsworth, 1969.

Crick, Bernard. *In Defense of Politics*. Chicago: University of Chicago Press, 1962.

Dahl, Robert. *Modern Political Analysis*. Englewood Cliffs, N.J.: Prentice-Hall, 1963.

_____. *Pluralist Democracy in the United States*. Chicago: Rand McNally, 1969.

_____. *Political Opposition in Western Democracies*. New Haven: Yale University Press, 1969.

_____. *A Preface to Democratic Theory*. Chicago: University of Chicago Press, 1956.

_____. *Who Governs?* New Haven: Yale University Press, 1961.

_____, and Lindblom, Charles. *Politics, Economics, and Welfare*. New York: Harper & Row, 1963–1953.

Davis, Robert Gorham. "The State of American Writing, 1948: A Symposium." *Partisan Review* 15 (1948).

Deane, Herbert. *The Political and Social Ideas of St. Augustine*. New York: Columbia University Press, 1966–1963.

Dexter, Lewis. "Politics and Ethics." *American Political Science Review* 40 (April 1946).

Diggins, John. "The Perils of Nationalism: Some Reflections on Dan Boorstin's Approach to American History." *American Quarterly* 23 (May 1971).

_____. *Up From Communism: Conservative Odysseys in American Intellectual History*. New York: Harper & Row, 1975.

Downs, Anthony. *An Economic Theory of Democracy*. New York: Harper & Row, 1957.

Draper, Theodore. *The Roots of American Communism*. New York: Viking, 1963–1957.

Easton, David. *The Political System*. New York: Knopf, 1953.

Edelman, Murray. *The Symbolic Uses of Politics*. Urbana: University of Illinois

Press, 1964.

Editors. "After the Apocalypse." *Encounter*, October 1953.

———. "Some Comments on Senator Goldwater." *Partisan Review*, Fall 1964.

Eisinger, Chester. *Fiction of the Forties*. Chicago: University of Chicago Press, 1963.

Elliot, William Yandell. *The Pragmatic Revolt in Politics*. New York: Fertig, 1968–1928.

Erikson, Erik. *Childhood and Society*. New York: Norton, 1950.

Eulau, Heinz. "The Politics of Happiness." *Antioch Review* 16 (1956).

Fiedler, Leslie. *An End to Innocence*. Boston: Beacon Press, 1950.

———. "Our Country and Our Culture: A Symposium." *Partisan Review* 19 (May–June 1952).

———. "Postscript to the Rosenberg Case." *Encounter*, October 1953.

———. "The State of American Writing, 1948: A Symposium." *Partisan Review* 15 (August 1948).

Frankel, Charles. *The Case for Modern Man*. New York: Harper & Row, 1956.

Friedman, Milton. *Capitalism and Freedom*. Chicago: University of Chicago Press, 1962.

Friedrich, Carl J. *The New Image of the Common Man*. Boston: Beacon, 1950.

———, and Brzezinski, Z. *Totalitarian Dictatorship and Autocracy*. Cambridge: Harvard University Press, 1965–1956.

Fromm, Erich. *The Art of Loving*. New York: Harper, 1956.

———. *Escape From Freedom*. New York: Holt, Rinehart and Winston, 1941.

———. *The Sane Society*. New York: Fawcett, 1967–1955.

Fuller, Lon. *The Morality of Law*. New Haven: Yale University Press, 1965.

Galbraith, John Kenneth. *The Affluent Society*. Boston: Houghton Mifflin, 1958.

———. *American Capitalism—The Concept of Countervailing Power*. Boston: Houghton Mifflin, 1956–1952.

Gay, Peter. *The Enlightenment*. Vol. I. New York: Vintage, 1968–1966.

———. *The Enlightenment*. Vol. II. New York: Knopf, 1969.

———. *Loss of Mastery*. Berkeley: University of California Press, 1966.

———. *Voltaire's Politics*. New York: Vintage, 1965–1959.

———. *Weimar Culture*. New York: Harper & Row, 1968.

Germino, Dante. "The Revival of Political Theory." *Journal of Politics* 25 (1963).

Gilbert, G.M. "Anti-Intellectualism in the United States." *The Journal of Social Issues*, no. 3 (1955).

Glazer, Nathan. *The Social Basis of American Communism*. New York: Harcourt, Brace and World, 1961.

Goldman, Eric. *Rendezvous with Destiny*. New York: Vintage, 1962–1955.

Gouldner, A.W. "Metaphysical Pathos and the Theory of Bureaucracy." *American Political Science Review* 49 (June 1955).

Greenberg, Clement. "The State of American Writing, 1948: A Symposium." *Partisan Review* 15 (August 1948).

Greenstein, Fred. *The American Party System and the American People*. Englewood Cliffs: Prentice-Hall, 1963.

Halberstam, David. *The Best and the Brightest*. New York: Random House, 1972.

Hallowell, John. *Main Currents in Modern Political Thought*. New York: Holt, 1950.

_____. "Politics and Ethics: A Symposium." *American Political Science Review* 40 (April 1946).

Hanson, Donald W. *From Kingdom to Commonwealth*. Cambridge: Harvard University Press, 1970.

Hartshorne, Thomas. *The Distorted Image*. Cleveland: Case Western Reserve, 1968.

Hartz, Louis. *The Liberal Tradition in America*. New York: Harcourt, Brace and World, 1955.

Hicks, Granville. *Where We Came Out*. New York: Viking, 1954.

Hingham, John, ed. *The Reconstruction of American History*. London: Hutchinson, 1963–1962.

Hoffer, Eric. *The True Believer*. New York: Harpers, 1951.

Hofstadter, Richard. *The Age of Reform*. New York: Vintage, 1962–1955.

_____, *The American Political Tradition*. New York: Vintage, 1959–1948.

_____. *Anti-Intellectualism in American Life*. New York: Knopf, 1963.

_____. "Have There Been Discernable Shifts in American Values during the Past Generation?" *The American Style*, edited by Elting Morison. New York: Harper and Bros., 1958.

_____. *The Paranoid Style in American Politics and Other Essays*. New York: Knopf, 1965.

_____. "Pseudo-Conservatism Revisited: A Postscript." In *The Radical Right*, edited by Daniel Bell. Garden City, N.Y.: Doubleday-Anchor, 1964–1963.

_____. "The Pseudo-Conservative Revolt." In *The Radical Right*, edited by Daniel Bell. Garden City, N.Y.: Doubleday-Anchor, 1964–1963.

_____. "Some Comments on Senator Goldwater." *Partisan Review*, Fall 1964.

_____, and Metzger, Walter. *The Development of Academic Freedom in the United States*. New York: Columbia University Press, 1955.

Hook, Sidney. *Heresy Yes, Conspiracy No*. New York: John Day, 1953.

_____. *Political Power and Personal Freedom*. New York: Criterion, 1959.

Howe, Irving. *Politics and the Novel*. New York: Meridian, 1957.

_____. *World of Our Fathers*. New York: Harcourt Brace Jovanovitch, 1976.

Huntington, Samuel. "The Change to Change: Modernization, Development and Politics." *Comparative Politics* 3 (April 1973).

Hyman, Herbert H. "England and America: Climates of Tolerance and Intolerance." In *The Radical Right*, edited by Daniel Bell. Garden City, N.Y.: Doubleday-Anchor, 1964–1963.

Jacobs, Paul, and Landau, Saul, eds. *The New Radicals*. New York: Random House 1966.

Jay, C. Martin. *The Dialectical Imagination*. London: Heinemann, 1973.

Kaplan, Abraham. "American Ethics and Public Philosophy." In *The American Style*, edited by Elting Morison. New York: Harper and Bros., 1958.

Kariel, Henry. *The Decline of American Pluralism*. Stanford: Stanford University Press, 1961.

Kempton, Murray. "Karl Hess: Goldwater Finds His Sorenson." *The New Republic*, 8 August 1964.

_____. *Part of Our Time*. New York: Simon and Schuster, 1955.

_____. "They Got Him." *The New Republic*, 25 July 1964.

Kennan, George. *American Diplomacy 1900-1950*. New York: Mentor, 1951.

Key, V.O., Jr. *The Responsible Electorate*. Cambridge: Harvard University Press, 1966.

_____. *Public Opinion and American Democracy*. New York: Knopf, 1961.

King, Martin Luther, Jr. *Why We Can't Wait*. New York: Signet, 1964.

Kirk, Russell. *Academic Freedom*. Chicago: Regnery, 1955.

_____. *The American Cause*. Chicago: Regnery, 1957.

_____. *Beyond the Dreams of Avarice*. Chicago: Regnery, 1956.

_____. *Confessions of a Bohemian Tory*. New York: Fleet, 1963.

_____. *The Conservative Mind*. Chicago: Regnery, 1953.

_____. *The Intelligent Woman's Guide to Conservatism*. New York: Devin-Adair, 1957.

_____. *The Intemperate Professor and Other Cultural Splenetics*. Baton Rouge: Louisiana State University Press, 1965.

_____. *A Program for Conservatives*. Chicago: Regnery, 1962-1954.

Kuckhohn, Clyde. "Have There Been Discernable Shifts in American Values during the Past Generation." In *The American Style*, edited by Elting Morison, New York: Harper and Bros., 1958.

Konvitz, Milton. "Sidney Hook: Philosopher of Freedom." In *Sidney Hook and the Contemporary World*, edited by Paul Kautz. New York: John Day, 1968.

Kornhauser, William. *The Politics of Mass Society*. Glencoe, Ill.: Free Press, 1959.

Kristol, Irving. "How Basic Is Basic Judaism?" *Commentary*, January 1948.

_____. "Men of Science and Conscience." *Encounter*, October 1953.

Lane, Robert. *Political Life*. New York: Free Press, 1959.

_____, and Sears, David. *Public Opinion*. Englewood Cliffs, N.J.: Prentice-Hall, 1964.

Lasch, Christopher. *The Agony of the American Left*. New York: Vintage, 1969.

Lasswell, Harold. *The Political Writings of Harold Lasswell*. New York: Free Press, 1951.

_____. *Politics: Who Gets What, When, How*. New York: Peter Smith, 1950-1936.

_____, and Kaplan, H. *Power and Society: A Framework for Political Inquiry*. New Haven: Yale University Press, 1961-1950.

Latham, Earl. *The Group Basis of Politics*. Ithaca: Cornell University Press, 1952.

Lerner, Max. *American as a Civilization*. New York: Simon and Schuster, 1957.

Leuchtenberg, William E. "Anti-Intellectualism in the United States." *The Journal of Social Issues*, no. 3 (1955).

Levy, Leonard. *Jefferson and Civil Liberties*. Cambridge: Harvard University Press, 1963.

Lindblom, Charles E. *The Intelligence of Democracy*. New York: Free Press, 1965.

Lippmann, Walter. *Essays in the Public Philosophy*. Boston: Little, Brown, 1955.

Lipset, Seymour Martin. *Political Man*. Garden City, N.Y.: Doubleday-Anchor,

1963–1960.

_____. "Some Social Requisites of Democracy: Economic Development and Political Legitimacy." *American Political Science Review* 53 (March 1959).

_____. "The Sources of the 'Radical Right.'" In *The Radical Right*, edited by Daniel Bell. Garden City, N.Y.: Doubleday-Anchor, 1964–1963.

_____. "Three Decades of the Radical Right: Coughlinites, McCarthyites, and Birchers," In *The Radical Right*, edited by Daniel Bell. Garden City, N.Y.: Doubleday-Anchor 1964–1963.

_____, and Bendix, Richard. *Social Mobility in Industrial Society*. Berkeley: University of California Press, 1959.

MacCallum, Gerald. "Negative and Positive Freedom." *Philosophical Review* 76 (1967).

Mailer, Norman. "Our Country and Our Culture: A Symposium." *Partisan Review* 19 (May-June 1952): 282–326.

Mannheim, Karl. *Ideology and Utopia*. New York: Harcourt, Brace and World, 1959.

Marcuse, Herbert. *One-Dimensional Man*. Boston: Beacon, 1964.

_____, et. al. *Critique of Pure Tolerance*. Boston: Beacon, 1965.

Maritain, Jacques. *Man and the State*. Chicago: University of Chicago Press, 1961–1951.

Matson, Floyd. *The Broken Image*. New York: Braziller, 1964.

Mayo, Henry. *An Introduction to Democratic Theory*. New York: Oxford University Press, 1960.

McCloskey, Herbert. "Consensus and Ideology in American Politics." *American Political Science Review* 58 (June 1964).

_____, et al. "Issue Conflict and Consensus Among Party Leaders and Followers." *American Political Science Review* 54 (1960).

Milbraith, Lester. *Political Participation*. Chicago: Rand McNally, 1965.

Milgram, Stanley. "Some Conditions of Obedience and Disobedience to Authority." *Human Relations* 18 (1965).

Miller, Perry. *Jonathan Edwards*. New York: Meridian, 1959–1949.

Miller, Warren, and Stokes, Donald. "Constituency Influence in Congress." *American Political Science Review* 57 (1963).

Mills, C. Wright. *The Power Elite*. New York: Oxford University Press, 1961–1956.

_____. *The Sociological Imagination*. New York: Oxford University Press, 1959.

_____. *White Collar*. New York: Oxford University Press, 1951.

Morgenthau, Hans J. *Politics Among Nations*. New York: Knopf, 1960–1948.

_____. "Some Comments on Senator Goldwater." *Partisan Review*, Fall 1964.

Morison, Samuel Eliot. "Faith of an Historian." *American Historical Review* 56 (January 1951).

_____. *The Intellectual Life of Colonial New England*. Ithaca: Cornell University Press Reprint, 1960–1956.

Morrison, Elting, ed. *The American Style*. New York: Harper and Bros., 1958.

Morton, Marian J. *The Terrors of Ideological Politics: Liberal Historians in a Conservative Mood*. Cleveland: Case Western Reserve, 1972.

Nash, George. *The Conservative Intellectual Movement in America Since 1945.* New York: Basic Books, 1976.

Neumann, Franz, et al. *The Cultural Migration.* Philadelphia: University of Pennsylvania Press, 1953.

Neustadt, Richard. *Presidential Power.* New York: Wiley, 1964-1960.

Newman, William. *The Futilitarian Society.* New York: Braziller, 1960.

Niebuhr, Reinhold. *The Children of Light and the Children of Darkness.* New York: Scribner's, 1944.

_____. *The Irony of American History.* New York: Scribner's, 1952.

_____. "Our Country and Our Culture: A Symposium." *Partisan Review* 19 (May-June 1952).

Nuechterlein, James A. "Arthur M. Schlesinger, Jr., and Postwar Liberalism." *The Review of Politics* 39, no. 1 (January 1977): 3-40.

Oakeshott, Michael. *Rationalism in Politics.* New York: Basic Books, 1962.

Oppenheim, Felix. *Dimensions of Freedom, An Analysis.* New York: St. Martin's, 1961.

Packenham, Robert A. *Liberal America and the Third World.* Princeton: Princeton University Press, 1973.

Parsons, Talcott. "Social Strains in America." In *The Radical Right,* edited by Daniel Bell. Garden City, N.Y.: Doubleday-Anchor 1964-1963.

_____. "Social Strains in America: A Postscript." In *The Radical Right,* edited by Daniel Bell. Garden City, N.Y.: Doubleday-Anchor, 1964-1963.

_____. *The Social System.* Glencoe, Ill.: Free Press, 1951.

_____. *The Structure of Social Actions.* 2nd ed. Glencoe, ILL.: Free Press, 1949.

Phillips, William. "Some Comments on Senator Goldwater." *Partisan Review,* Fall 1964.

Polsby, Nelson. *Community Power and Political Theory.* New Haven: Yale University Press, 1963.

_____. "Towards an Explanation of McCarthyism." *Political Studies* 8 (1960).

Potter, David. *People of Plenty.* Chicago: University of Chicago Press, 1954.

Prothro, James, and Grigg, C.M. "Fundamental Principles of Democracy: Bases of Agreement and Disagreement." *Journal of Politics* 22 (1960).

Purcell, Edward. *The Crisis of Democratic Theory.* Lexington: University of Kentuckey Press, 1973.

Rahv, Philip. "Our Country and Our Culture: A Symposium." *Partisan Review* 19 (May-June 1952): 282-326.

_____. "Some Comments on Senator Goldwater." *Partisan Review,* Fall 1964.

Riesman, David. *Individualism Reconsidered and Other Essays.* Glencoe, Ill.: Free Press, 1954.

_____. "The Intellectuals and the Discontented Classes: Some Further Reflections." In *The Radical Right,* edited by Daniel Bell. Garden City, N.Y.: Doubleday-Anchor, 1964-1963.

_____. "The National Style." In *The American Style,* edited by Elting Morison. New York: Harper and Bros., 1958.

_____. "Our Country and Our Culture: A Symposium." *Partisan Review* 19 (May-

June 1952): 282–326.

———, et al. *The Lonely Crowd*. New Haven: Yale University Press, 1961–1950.

———, and Glazer, Nathan. "The Intellectuals and the Discontented Classes: Some Further Reflections." In *The Radical Right*, edited by Daniel Bell. Garden City, N.Y.: Doubleday-Anchor, 1964–1963.

Ransom, John Crowe. "The State of American Writing, 1948: A Symposium." *Partisan Review* 15 (1948).

Rogin, Michael. *The Intellectuals and McCarthy*. Cambridge: M.I.T. Press, 1967.

Rossiter, Clinton. *Conservatism in America*. New York: Vintage, 1962–1955.

———. *Marxism: The View from America*. New York: Harcourt, Brace and World, 1960.

———. *Parties and Politics in America*. Ithaca: Cornell University Press, 1960.

Rostow, W.W. "The National Style." In *The American Style*, edited by Elting Morison. New York: Harper and Bros., 1958.

Rovere, Richard. *The American Establishment*. New York: Harcourt, Brace and World, 1962.

———. *Senator Joseph McCarthy*. Cleveland: Meridian Books, 1961–1959.

Sartori, Giovanni. *Democratic Theory*. New York: Praeger, 1967–1962.

Schattschneider, E.E. *The Semi-Sovereign People*. New York: Holt, Rinehart and Winston, 1960.

Schlesinger, Arthur, Jr. *The Age of Jackson*. Boston: Little, Brown, 1945.

———. "The Case for Kennedy." *New York Times Magazine* 6 (November 1960).

———. *The Coming of the New Deal*. Boston: Houghton Mifflin, 1959.

———. *The Crisis of the Old Order*. Boston: Houghton Mifflin, 1957.

———. "A Eulogy: John Fitzgerald Kennedy." *Saturday Evening Post*, 14 December 1963.

———. Introductions, In *The faces of Five Decades*, edited by Robert Luce, pp. 25–26, 99–100, 229–330, and 339–40. New York: Simon and Schuster, 1964.

———. *The Politics of Hope*. Boston: Houghton Mifflin, 1962.

———. *The Politics of Upheaval*. Boston: Houghton Mifflin, 1960.

———. "Reinhold Niebuhr's Place in American Thought and Life." *Reinhold Niebuhr: His Religious, Social, and Political Thought*, edited by Charles Kegley and Robert Bretall. New York: Macmillan, 1961.

———. "The Right to Loathsome Ideas." *Saturday Review* 32 (14 May 1949).

———. "Stevenson and the American Liberal Dilemma." *Twentieth Century* 153 (January 1953).

———. *A Thousand Days*. New York: Fawcett, 1967–1965.

———. *The Vital Center*. London: Andre Deutsch, 1970–1949.

Schorer, Mark. "Our Country and Our Culture: A Symposium." *Partisan Review* 19 (1952).

Schumpeter, Joseph. *Capitalism, Socialism, Democracy*. 3rd ed. New York: Harper, 1950.

Shils, Edward. "Ideology and Civility: On the Politics of the Intellectual" (1958). In *Ideology, Politics, and Political Theory*, edited by Richard Cox. Belmont, Calif.: Wadsworth, 1969.

_____. *The Torment of Secrecy*. Glencoe, Ill.: Free Press, 1956.

Shklar, Judith. *After Utopia*. Princeton: Princeton University Press, 1957.

_____. "Facing Up to Intellectual Pluralism." *Political Theory and Social Change*, edited by David Spitz. New York: Atherton, 1967.

_____. *Legalism*. Cambridge: Harvard University Press, 1964.

Singer, Marcus. "Moral Skepticism." In *Skepticism and Moral Principles*, edited by C. Carter. Evanston, Ill.: New University Press, 1973.

Skotheim, Robert. *Intellectual History and Historians*. Princeton: Princeton University Press, 1969.

Smith, David. "A Symposium," *American Political Science Review* (September 1957).

Smith, Huston, ed. *The Search for America*. Englewood Cliffs, N.J.: Prentice-Hall, 1959.

Smith, James W. *Theme For Reason*. Princeton: Princeton University Press, 1957.

Spitz, David. *Democracy and the Challenge of Power*. New York: Columbia University Press, 1958.

Stember, Herbert. "Anti-Intellectualism in the United States." *The Journal of Social Issues*, no. 3 (1955).

Stouffer, Samuel. *Communism, Conformity, and Civil Liberties*. Gloucester, Mass.: Peter Smith, 1963–1955.

Straus., Leo. *Natural Right and History*. Chicago: University of Chicago Press, 1953.

Thompson, Kenneth. *Political Realism and the Crisis of World Politics*. Princeton: Princeton University Press, 1960.

Thorson, Thomas, ed., *The Logic of Democracy*. New York: Holt, Rinehart and Winston, 1962.

_____. *Plato: Totalitarian or Democrat*. Englewood Cliffs, N.J.: Prentice-Hall, 1963.

Tillich, Paul. "The Conquest of Theological Provincialism." *The Cultural Migration*. Philadelphia: University of Pennsylvania Press, 1953.

_____. *The Courage to Be*. New Haven: Yale University Press, 1952.

Tinder, Glenn. *The Crisis of Political Imagination*. New York: Scribner's, 1964–1950.

Toulmin, Stephen. *Reason in Ethics*. Cambridge: Cambridge University Press, 1968–1950.

_____, and Janik, Allan. *Wittgenstein's Vienna*. London: Weidenfield and Nicolson, 1973.

Trilling, Lionel. "Our Country and Our Culture: A Symposium." *Partisan Review* 19 (1952).

_____. *The Liberal Imagination*. New York: Viking, 1950.

_____. "The State of American Writing, 1948: A Symposium." *Partisan Review* 15 (August 1948).

Trow, Martin. "Small Business, Political Tolerance, and Support for McCarthy." *American Journal of Sociology* 44 (November 1958).

Truman, David. *The Governmental Process*. New York: Knopf, 1960–1951.

_____. "On the Invention of Systems." *American Political Science Review*, June 1960.

Viereck, Peter. "The Philosophical New Conservatism." In *The Radical Right*, edited by Daniel Bell. Garden City, N.Y.: Doubleday-Anchor, 1964–1963.

_____. "The Revolt Against the Elite." In *The Radical Right*, edited by Daniel Bell. Garden City, N.Y.: Doubleday-Anchor, 1964–1963.

_____. *Shame and Glory of the Intellectuals*. New York: Capricorn, 1965–1953.

Voegelin, Eric. *The New Science of Politics*. Chicago: University of Chicago Press, 1952.

Waltz, Kenneth. *Man, the State and War*. New York: Columbia University Press, 1965–1954.

Walzer, Michael. "The Young Radicals: A Symposium." *Dissent* 9 (Spring 1962): 129–31.

Warner, W. Lloyd, and Abegglen, James. *Big Business Leaders in America*. New York: Harper and Bros., 1955.

_____. *Occupational Mobility in American Business*. Minneapolis: University of Minnesota Press, 1955.

Wechsler, Herbert. "Toward Neutral Principles of Constitutional Law." *Principles, Politics, and Fundamental Law*. Cambridge: Harvard University Press, 1961.

Weldon, T.D. *The Vocabulary of Politics*. Baltimore: Penguin, 1953.

Westin, Alan F. "The John Birch Society." In *The Radical Right*, edited by Daniel Bell. Garden City, N.Y.: Doubleday-Anchor, 1964–1963.

White, G. Edward. "The Rise and Fall of Justice Holmes." *University of California Law Review* 39 no. 51 (1971).

White, Morton. *Social Thought in America*. Boston: Beacon, 1957–1947.

Whyte, William H. *The Organization Man*. New York: Simon and Schuster, 1956.

_____. "Politics and Ethics: A Symposium." *American Political Science Review* 40 (April 1946).

Wildavsky, Aaron. *Leadership in a Small Town*. Totawa, N.J.: Bedminster, 1964.

Wills, Gary. *Nixon Agonistes*. New York: Mentor, 1969.

Wilson, Sloan. *Man in the Gray Flannel Suit*. New York: Simon and Schuster, 1955.

Wise, Gene. *American Historical Explanation*. Homewood: Illinois Dorsey Press, 1973.

Wolin, Sheldon. *Politics and Vision*. Boston: Little, Brown, 1960.

Young, James P. *The Politics of Affluence*. San Francisco: Chandler, 1968.

Index

ABOUT THE AUTHOR

Robert Booth Fowler is Associate Professor of Political Science at the University of Wisconsin at Madison. His writings include *Contemporary Issues in Political Theory* and *Obligation and Dissent: A Reader,* as well as contributions to scholarly journals.